THE COMISSION

THE COMISSION

The amazing story of eighty ministry groups working together
to take the message of Christ's love to the Russian people

CONTRIBUTORS

Bruce Wilkinson
Paul Eshleman
Paul Kienel
Paul Johnson
Terry Taylor
Anita Deyneka
Margaret Bridges
Mary Lance Sisk
J.B. Crouse
John Kyle
Ralph Plumb

PREFACE BY

Joseph Stowell

MOODY PUBLISHERS
CHICAGO

ISBN 0-8024-3537-8

Contributors:
Donna Bahler
Mick Haupt
Mark Rais
Connie Veldkamp

Cover photograph: Joel DeSalla
Cover design: Mick Haupt

1 3 5 7 9 10 8 6 4 2
Printed in the United States of America

Dedication

*This book is dedicated with fondness
and deep respect to the memory of
Peter Deyneka (1931-2000),
without whose wisdom and networking
the CoMission would not have been successful.*

*This book is also dedicated to
Alexei Brudnov (1948–1999), Director of Alternative Education
for the Ministry of Education in the former Soviet Union.
His support, commitment and dedication were
primarily responsible for our opportunity to minister
to 42,000 teachers in 142 cities of the USSR.*

Gratis

114179

CONTENTS

PRINCIPLE ONE

.

REALIZE THAT WORKING TOGETHER PLEASES GOD.

There are at least two reasons for this. No organization or denomination is gifted to do everything that needs to be done for the Lord in an area. The Scriptures say "One can chase a thousand, two can put 10,000 to flight." In areas where there are open doors for the gospel, the message will go out more quickly and with greater power when we cooperate.

Secondly, it is with the heart of God to work together. In John 17:20–23, the unity of believers is not an option in evangelism. It is the sign that God left to validate and show the deity of Jesus and is present-day evidence of God's love for mankind. Our love for one another is the evidence that we are followers of Jesus. Is it any wonder that our unity as believers is continually attacked? Could loving one another be our greatest God-given secret weapon for worldwide evangelism?

DR. JOSEPH M. STOWELL, president of Moody Bible Institute, Chicago, is a frequent speaker at churches and conferences throughout the United States and overseas. He is a widely read author of books and magazine articles. He is heard daily on the radio program "Proclaim!" and weekly on "Moody Presents." Dr. Stowell served seventeen years as a pastor before taking the helm of Moody. Joe and his wife, Mary, live in Chicago and have three grown children and eight grandchildren. Dr. Stowell served the CoMission as chairman of the C.I.S. Church Relations Committee.

PARTNERING ON PURPOSE

Church Relations Committee

Joseph M. Stowell, Chairman

THERE ARE ONLY a few experiences that, upon reflection, stand out as strategically important in the course of a lifetime. And when these experiences have an exponential impact on the work of Christ, they are even more enviable. For thousands of followers of Jesus, in more than eighty organizations, the CoMission and its ministry behind the former Iron Curtain at the close of the 20th century ranks as one of these historical opportunities.

The CoMission was born in the midst of a great cauldron of turmoil—politically, economically, culturally, and spiritually. The dissolution of the Soviet Union is now a fact of history, but in the years of 1990 to 1992 its surprising collapse created a vacuum that left its citizens grasping for something to hold on to amidst the staggering changes. It was, without a doubt, the most dramatic period of change in the last 100 years.

The Communist Party disintegrated. One by one, the fifteen members of the Union of Soviet Socialist Republics became independent countries as the great communist monolith crumbled. Throughout Eastern Europe, countries began to throw out their communist leaders and embrace democracy.

For the average person, the rate of change was break neck and mind-numbing. The ruble, once more valuable than the dollar, collapsed. People carried bags full of bills—so worthless was the currency. Corruption was everywhere. It was customary for everyone to be employed by the government—and for everyone to steal from the government. In back alleys, government fuel trucks, stolen by some enterprising person, pumped gas to waiting lines of cars at a cheaper price. Drunks wandered the streets at night, products of cheap vodka and no meaningful work. Doctors and street sweepers alike sometimes earned the same salary.

The nation of "reluctant slaves," ruled by either the tsars or the Communist Party, now had no direction. The long lines in the stores continued. The military had no money to pay the troops or repair its equipment. Factories shut down and food was scarce.

The CoMission Executive Committee meets with Russian pastors in Moscow.

On the spiritual side, there was great curiosity. Since very few Bibles and almost no Christian literature had been allowed for seventy years, people had studied ESP and the books of Uri Gellar, investigating the paranormal in some attempt to get at the supernatural. And, of course, because Bibles were banned along with Christian films, they became in great demand when the doors started to open.

In the midst of this vacuum of faith, God raised up a unique confederation of eighty-two organizations who decided to work together in this newly opened harvest field. It is an amazing story! And it produced some principles of partnership which will be both a challenge and an encouragement to the Church in the decades to come.

This is a unique book—and I don't want you to miss its uniqueness as you read. You are going to encounter this faith-building story from six different perspectives:

1. You are going to see the wonderful power there is for the Kingdom when organizations work together. As great as the reports are about what happened in Russia, I believe the greatest contribution of the CoMission may be in its example of how Christian ministries can work together if they are willing to humble themselves and submit to one another.

2. Secondly, you will hear portions of the story from the perspectives of the twelve members of the Executive Committee. Someone once described God's work as the weaving of a divine tapestry. Certainly each organization contributed a unique thread to the work of the CoMission, which produced a masterpiece of cooperative ministry. At times, it appeared to those involved like the underside of a tapestry – a bunch of knots threatening to become unraveled. But God is always gracious to repentant people who don't seek their own gain.

3. Thirdly, you will see that God has moved deeply in the hearts of those involved. Everyone who was a part of the effort felt both the touch of God and the difficulty of responding to the great spiritual and organizational challenges. People did not become part of the CoMission by accident or slick recruiting. This was a divine call.

4. Fourthly, I think you will enjoy the summary of the principles of working together that we uncovered as we progressed through the five-year partnership. They might serve as a roadmap for your own cooperative efforts in the future. The summary of the principles may be found in the appendix.

5. Fifthly, for those of you who are interested in organization, you will see how the work was pulled together so that we could function effectively. In the five years of its operation there was no paid CoMission staff. Everything was done by people who volunteered their time, raised their support, or were loaned to the cause by a partnering organization. Because of this, you will find a great number of people mentioned in the appendix. This was truly a team effort!

6. Finally, sprinkled throughout the book you'll find stories of individuals whose lives were changed as they came into contact with CoMission volunteers.

We didn't do everything right. We learned a lot of lessons along the way. All of us, without exception, were awed by what we saw God do. We will never be the same. For the rest of our lives, we will forever be drawn toward working together with other members of the Body of Christ. It seems to be so much more fun that way. Maybe that's just how God intended it!

It is our prayer that, though the CoMission and its work are finished, this account will provide a stimulus and a model for others to strike partnerships that share resources and mobilize even greater movements for Christ. Today there are teachers, students and their families who are faithful followers of Jesus because of the unselfish partnering of key individuals and organizations. And, perhaps as significant, hundreds of those who gave a year of their lives never came home. Today they continue to minister to the people of Russia and Ukraine.

PRINCIPLE
TWO

MAKE REPENTANCE CENTRAL TO ALL
ORGANIZATIONAL PLANNING.

The sins of pride, territorialism, credit taking and individualism are endemic in Christian leaders and we did not hold a meeting during the five years of the CoMission in which we did not repent of our sins. When new people joined the group who had not repented, problems and conflicts arose immediately. And, among some of us who had already repented, we found that some of the old habit patterns of wanting our *own* way, and *our* strategy, and *our* material came back and we had to repent again to keep the CoMission moving forward.

DR. BRUCE WILKINSON is the author of the #1 New York Times bestsellers *The Prayer of Jabez* and *A Life God Rewards,* as well as *Secrets of the Vine, The Dream Giver, Experiencing Spiritual Breakthroughs,* and numerous other books. He is the chairman of Global Vision Resources, Turn the Tide for Children, and Ovation Productions. Bruce and his wife, Darlene Marie, have three children and five grandsons. They divide their time between Georgia and South Africa.

CHAPTER ONE

SHARING THE VISION OF THE COMISSION

The Executive Committee

Bruce Wilkinson, Chairman
the CoMission Executive Committee, and
Chairman of the Publicity and Public Relations Committee

DURING THE PAST twenty centuries, there have been defining moments when nations unexpectedly opened their doors to Christianity, but perhaps never on the scale of the massive open door to Russia in 1991. After seventy years in which atheistic communism had persecuted Christianity, murdered millions of people, closed thousands of churches, and made it a risk to even own a Bible, the people were desperate to learn about God and His Word.

When the Iron Curtain fell, the Church responded on an unprecedented level, mobilizing what some have reported to be the largest movement of missions in the shortest amount of time since the birth of Christ. Never had more people responded to a spiritual need so quickly and so effectively. The largest and most expansive of these movements to the former Soviet Union was known as the CoMission. This book is a brief overview of the highlights, strategies, innovations and uniqueness of that movement.

Since many Christian leaders feared that this remarkable door might not remain open very long, the leadership rapidly developed faith goals, innovative strategies and unique structures. So bold were many of these initiatives, that initially many thought the CoMission could never work. But, through the repeated intervention of God and the remarkable sacrifices of thousands of individuals and dozens of organizations, the Lord used the CoMission to reintroduce Christianity to millions of Soviet children and adults. The achievements of the CoMission stand as a high watermark of what God can do when His people come together with a common burden and genuine unity to do God's work in God's way.

Although the name the "CoMission" was suggested by Pat McMillan to describe the joining together of diverse organizations to accomplish a common mission, many of us came to understand the CoMission as something far deeper. It came to mean the miraculous unity of God and man working in tandem to accomplish a common mission—His Great Commission.

The founding meeting of the CoMission at the Walk Thru the Bible headquarters in Atlanta, Georgia, the fall of 1991.

I. THE BIRTH OF THE COMISSION

The CoMission had many organizational roots across the Body of Christ, but the most seminal proved to be The *JESUS* Film Project and the four-day meetings with public school teachers, known as convocations. Had Paul Eshleman and his team not broken through this closed door and provided the entryway, the CoMission could not have been launched.

The convocation platform provided the foundation for the launch of the CoMission. As you'll read in the following chapters, everyone experienced a unique and meaningful connecting point with the movement. But, for me, the CoMission had its starting point at the Pushkin Convocation in November 1991.

Never will I be able to forget those hundreds of Russian educators who crowded into the auditorium at Pushkin's Pioneer Palace. They gathered for a week so that the American team could teach them about the Bible and a new course on Christian ethics and morals that they in turn could teach to their students.

To all of us, such a meeting could be nothing less than historic. The opening sentence of my first address acknowledged this: "When I attended high school in the United States, I thought you, the Russian empire, would attack us with the atomic bomb. Now here we are together, not as enemies, but as newfound friends. At the request of the Ministry of Education of Russia, our team is here to share with you the values of Christianity."

Only a few times in my life have I been so unsettled speaking in public. I thought that at any moment the KGB might rush into the room and send us to be imprisoned in Siberia for life. But instead, we enjoyed remarkable freedom.

The afternoons were devoted to training small groups of professional teachers. When I met my small group for the first time, they were skeptical and semi-hostile. Later they told me that they were sizing us up. "What is your real motive? Why are you here? What do you want from us? What is your hidden agenda?" In our first meeting, each ended his introductory comments with nearly the same words, spoken in bold italics, "I'm an atheist" or "I'm a communist."

What a beginning!

On the first day, my group was non-responsive; on the second, they hesitantly participated; the third, they openly enjoyed the process; and by the fourth day, all of them had placed their full trust in Jesus Christ, except one, my favorite. If you ever wanted to witness the transforming power of the gospel in the lives of people, that week would have been it. From morose to joyful, from despair to hope, from crushing oppression to freedom in Christ.

My favorite was a teacher in her mid-sixties, a typical grandmotherly "babushka." But, much to my dismay, my prayers for her were not answered. On the last afternoon, many tears were shed amidst the embraces of new friends who had grown to love each other in such a short time. But my babushka was nowhere to be found. I felt so very disappointed, and sought God to intervene in the life of this woman who didn't even speak one word of English.

But then someone tapped me on the shoulder and pointed over to the far wall where she stood, looking down at the floor. I walked over to her and without even a hint of what was going to occur, she spoke to me in perfect English! All week she had been secretly listening to our private conversations as she feigned not understanding a word of English.

"When you Americans came, I wanted no part of it. You were our enemy and I didn't trust you. But you came with something in your eyes that we hadn't seen before—light and peace. You taught the Bible—and then gave us one—and you spoke to us about this Jesus that you knew and loved. The walls of our defenses soon fell crashing down because each of us discovered something most precious: your whole team truly loved us. No one had ever loved us like that, especially with no ulterior motive. When you and your team loved us like that, I wanted the Jesus you loved. You opened my heart for Him." Slowly she reached into her pocket to give me a small gift wrapped in a cloth, "Here is my communist pin. I won't need it ever again. I gave my heart to Jesus."

Not only did the week prove to be a dramatic turning point for the teachers, but it became a defining moment for the forty convocation team members from America. We were faced with the reality of the amazing opportunity that God had presented to us. For me, that week planted a love and burden for the people of the former Soviet Union that was so deep, so visceral, so emotional, that I eventually committed myself and my family to whatever God had in mind for Russia and the surrounding communist republics.

At the time of this convocation, the CoMission didn't exist, nor was there an organized plan for a massive Christian movement with scores of Christian organizations joining together to send thousands of people to serve on teams in the CIS for a year or more.

In my life, the breakthrough that eventually launched the CoMission occurred on the fourth morning, in our early morning devotions, when the American ministry team met before heading over to the conference. That morning, I had been invited to lead the session, and, as you might anticipate, had prepared to share the Prayer of Jabez since it is a remarkable "missionary prayer."

But that morning, my heart was in such spiritual turmoil that I asked the group to share what they were feeling at this point in our week. How were they coping with this remarkable movement of the Spirit and the fact that we were soon leaving for the States? Could anyone share a word, a picture, a visual summary of what they were experiencing?

Softly, a woman began, "I can barely cope with the thought of flying home in two days. All I can think about now is looking down through the airplane windows at the hundreds of newborn spiritual babies crying, "Please, please don't leave us. We'll die if you leave us." She paused, wiped away a tear, and continued, "Everywhere, people are flooding to Christ, but when we leave, there's no one to help them grow. We are abandoning them."

Then a man on my left from Philadelphia shared a picture that for me became the defining moment of the launch of the CoMission vision. He described a vast peach orchard stretching as far as the eye could see in every direction. "All of us," he said, "were standing in a neat row, shoulder to shoulder, silently looking across this vast panorama. Every branch bent low, laden with the largest and most ripe peaches ever seen.

"We were speechless at the massive size of this harvest, when suddenly a wind blew down from the heavens and ripe peaches began falling to the ground everywhere. Dozens, hundreds, thousands, millions of peaches fell on the ground until we found ourselves standing knee-high in ripe peaches."

No one spoke as we tried to cope with the reality of this picture. Someone commented, "Oh, look—look at all that ripe fruit—someone had better do something quick before it rots on the ground!"

Heart-wrenching emotion burst through the room. "That's right!" I responded. "This may be the largest ripe harvest in modern history, just lying on the ground. We must do something. We must go back home and send hundreds—no, thousands—back to pick the ripe fruit before it rots."

Out of desperation, I turned to J.B. Crouse, newly-appointed president of OMS International. "This is a significant moment in history, pregnant with the hearts of these nations who have just been liberated from communism, desperately longing for God. Can you redeploy OMS missionaries from other nations to serve here?"

Then, to my good friend of many years, Dr. Paul Kienel, President of the Association of Christian Schools International (ACSI), "Paul, you have the largest faculty of Christian teachers in the world. Can you mobilize an army of Christian educators to come serve in Russia?"

The sense of responsibility overwhelmed all of us as wave after wave of deep desire to help swept over us. We all knew we had to do something. In the weeks that followed, tears flowed time after time. God was supernaturally planting His burden in many of our hearts.

The vision of the CoMission clarified rapidly during the first three pivotal organizational meetings conducted from December 1991 through March 1992. Each meeting enabled the movement to gain speed and formulate its goals, strategies, values, structures, and leadership. This book presents the stories of the other members of the Executive Committee, and, as you'll see, each one led an historic and heroic effort for the cause of Christ.

**The first meeting of ministry leaders held at the ACSI
headquarters in La Habra, California, early 1992.**

II. The Vision of the CoMission

One thing is certain about the vision of the CoMission: none of us had any plans or desire to launch another Christian organization. In fact, had someone invited us to start such a large and demanding movement in addition to everything we were already doing in our own organizations and ministries, I doubt if any of us would have responded.

Perhaps that's why God first broke our hearts, bonded us to the Russian people, burdened us with their desperate needs, and finally instilled in us the belief that we could, and must, rise up and respond immediately.

As is true in nearly all God-given visions, the burden pulled us forward. We did not proceed forward on our own, but by the compelling vision. After that trip to Russia, I wrote thirty key presidents of organizations in America that I felt could be interested in joining with us to serve the people of Russia. God sovereignly broke down the wall; God sovereignly launched the CoMission; and God sovereignly revealed the strategy, structure, and operating methodology of the movement.

God had sent His chariot from heaven, and we who were on the road of life got our cloaks caught in its spokes—and were carried along by His chariot to accomplish the vision in His heart. His vision became our vision. We came to know this part of His vision as the CoMission.

The vision was clear: to respond immediately to the open door in the former Soviet Union and through the means of the convocations, the new Morals and Ethics Curriculum, and the Video Bible Courses to bring the good news of Jesus Christ to all people. We sought to not limit our efforts to the main cities where it appeared that nearly everyone focused, but divided the entire area into sub-regions that we sought to send teams to achieve the CoMission goals and objectives.

III. THE STRATEGY OF THE COMISSION

Due to the massive scope of the CoMission movement, the leadership elected to develop a unified approach in the foundational issues of strategy, materials, and training. Although everyone thought that this idea would allow maximum effectiveness and efficiency, initially, very few felt it was possible. None of us had experienced a partnership at this depth before. The differences of theology, ministry approach, and realities of "turfism" were substantial.

When the CoMission began, the norm, the "corporate culture" of ministries, included distrust, competition, and organizational selfish ambition. Cooperation among ministries meant that we wouldn't compete, at least not openly. At the beginning of the CoMission, turfism reigned, carefully hidden beneath a Christian veneer. Although Christian organizations were open to each other, most protected themselves even when it had a negative impact on another. Organizations subtly used other organizations to further their own agendas.

The CoMission sought to break new ground by developing deep commitment and unity to each other and seeking each other's good above our own. In the first few months, this value was severely test-ed. On a plane trip early in the launch of the CoMission, I asked one of the key Campus Crusade leaders what he felt the best training group would be to serve all of the CoMission. (Crusade was already identified as the leader in evangelism and the convocations.) After a few moments, he said "The Navigators."

How then, I asked, would he feel about the Navigators training the scores of CCC staff and volunteers that would eventually serve in the CoMission? The reality of that statement hit hard. Then I asked, "If that were to happen, what distinctions of CCC would you feel were crucial for the Navigators to use in their training?" It didn't take but a moment, "The Four Spiritual Laws."

I broke into laughter. Although I agreed with both observa-tions, I couldn't get over the situation we faced at that very moment: The Navigators would train CCC personnel. The Navigators would use the CCC model of evangelism (instead of their own unique method which is also highly valued among the organization). What a shock to the existing system! We both laughed, since up to that point in history, such partnership could never be imagined. It would take a true miracle to move forward at such a deep level of trust.

At the March 1992 strategic CoMission meeting in Chicago, I stated that one of the goals I personally had for the CoMission was that the "norm" for ministry would become partnership and coop-eration rather than competition and isolation. Thankfully, the CoMission achieved that goal, and since then the Christian culture has changed substantially to embrace this biblical value.

There was considerable potential for division due to the wide doctrinal differences in CoMission members. We agreed that we would never focus on any doctrine as the basis of fellowship ex-cept the fundamentals of the faith, such as the deity of Christ, sal-vation by grace through faith alone, etc.

Freedom was afforded and secondary differences honored in the issues of church government, spiritual gifts, organizational methodo-logies, etc. In five years of intense effort across numerous nations, I'm not aware of one division caused by differing doctrinal viewpoints.

The core strategy of the CoMission developed out of the unique situation in the former Soviet Union and the invitation by the Ministry of Education of Russia. A five-year strategy was established (1992–1997) in which the CIS was divided into 150 sub regions that were then distributed by organizational selection to the different sending organizations and other agencies. A unified approach was established and followed which included a common strategy, unified set of materials, agency-wide training program, and unified leadership approach. Together, we formulated a standard approach to ministry in the former Soviet Union and then every member pledged to support it. The CoMission strategy was relatively simple, transferable, yet locally adaptable and culturally appropriate.

A Seven-Fold Strategy was developed and implemented:

Step One: *The Convocation and Morals and Ethics Training:*

The first stage of the CoMission focused on the convocation, the four-day intensive training conference using the Morals and Ethics Curriculum. The relationships established during the convocations provided the basis for efforts in each

Russian teachers attend a four-day convocation.

community. In a number of cases, a later follow-up training conference re-established the contacts when the CoMission teams arrived.

Step Two: *The* JESUS *Film*

The *JESUS* film provided the crucial tool to share the story of Jesus Christ and share the gift of salvation that He offers. On three different occasions, the film was used to present the gospel: First, the film opened the minds and hearts of the teachers at the convocation; second, the film opened the minds and hearts of the students at the teachers' schools; third, the film initiated the small-group outreaches with those in the community. In each situation, the *JESUS* film stirred the audience with the truth of the sacrificial death and resurrection of Jesus with an appropriate invitation to trust in Him personally.

Step Three: *The Teacher-Training Courses*

The CoMission reached a unique market niche from all the other Christian movements that operated in the former Soviet Union. When the wall toppled down, we discovered that the church was primarily filled with older women who had developed a strong value system of legalism to help protect against the secret infiltration of the KGB.

Most of the professionals and educators were not interested in participating in local churches, nor were they accepted since they came out of an atheistic background. Another new "wine skin" had to be developed. The CoMission focused specifically on the strategic educational community and provided the much-needed entryway into the community of faith.

When a CoMission team arrived in its location of service for a year, all the professional teachers were invited to a weekly teacher-training class featuring the innovative instructional philosophy in the fourteen-part teacher-training video series entitled *The Seven Laws of the Learner*. These courses were very well received, and ultimately tens of thousands of professional teachers participated.

Upon completion, the second six-part teacher-training series, *Teaching with Style,* equipped the educators with new methodologies that increased teacher effectiveness. These courses were offered at the invitation of the Ministry of Education of Russia, Ukraine, etc. During these classes, relationships between the CoMissioners and the professional teachers were developed and solidified. Since both courses were based upon the Bible, the teachers were introduced to the Book that had been outlawed for seventy years.

Step Four: *The Video Bible Classes*

On the basis of relationships developed during the Teacher-Training Conferences, the educators were invited to participate in a weekly Bible study using the Video Bible Curriculum. The teachers also invited parents of their students to attend with them. Thousands of these Bible studies were conducted during the five years of the CoMission. The video Bible classes provided the strategic link between professional educators and the general community.

Since the majority of the CoMissioners didn't speak Russian and most weren't comfortable (at the beginning of their year of service) to lead Bible studies, a standard series of video courses with a voiceover in the various languages (100 different sessions) were available, including *The Biblical Portrait of Marriage; The Foundations of Faith I: The Bible, Sin, and Salvation; The Foundations of Faith II: Satan, Angels, and Demons; The Prayer of Jabez; The Testing of Your Faith; The Supernatural Spiritual Life;* etc.

These courses served as the initial teaching tool. At the completion of each weekly session, the CoMissioners, through trained translators, led a stimulating and life-changing discussion.

At first, some wondered if the Video Bible Curriculum could work with all the distinct cultures that the CoMission worked with across the ten time zones. But, since the Video

Bible Curriculum focused specifically on biblical principles rather than cultural issues, it proved very successful. God only wrote one book, with one message—for all cultures, for all times and for all situations. As long as the timeless, universal principles of Scripture were presented, they always worked. The CoMissioners led the discussions that applied the truths to the culture and specific groups that they led.

Unless you participated in these discussions, it is difficult to grasp the power of God's Word when personally applied in the Russian culture, particularly during those tumultuous times. Since the Bible had been almost unavailable for two generations (seventy years), the biblical truths, for the most part, had been lost to society. Indoctrination in the government schools established a godless and "Bible-less" mindset.

I'll never forget teaching *The Biblical Portrait of Marriage* to 1,000 couples in Moscow in an all-day conference. Never had I witnessed such a silent and non-expressive group of people, their faces projecting shock and alarm. As the day went on, I noticed that the vast majority of the couples wouldn't even look into their spouse's eyes when I asked them to verbalize their commitment to the various biblical principles, such as, "I commit to love you unconditionally and remain loyal to you."

When the conference ended, I felt that the day had been a dismal failure. Over dinner that night with five Russian couples, I asked them through an interpreter why the audience was so silent and rigid. The oldest man immediately responded, "Our marriages in Russia are in shambles, with widespread alcoholism and practical divorce upwards of eighty percent. When we listened to you teach all day what the Bible taught as the answer to a happy marriage, we were in shock. Everything you taught was the exact opposite of what we believed and lived. In every single session, our hearts were pierced with the truth from the Bible. We knew that we had disobeyed God in every part of our marriage. We cannot thank you enough; many of our marriages were transformed today. But I must admit that it was among the most painful days in all of our lives."

Not only were these Video Bible Courses taught in the small groups led by the CoMissioners, but they also were loaned (along with a TV and video player) to thousands of families who took them home and led small group Bible studies with them in their own homes. The Word of God spread like wildfire in this dry and hungry land.

I experienced this firsthand while swimming in the Black Sea after an all-day training conference with about 450 professional teachers and principals. Four of the teachers from the conference made their way over to me in the water with a great deal of excitement. A woman who turned out to be a principal of a large school spoke in halting English.

"We all have watched your video courses, and they have changed our lives and our families. We cannot thank God enough for sending the CoMission into our lives. We have made lifelong friends with them! But, I must tell you something that my father made me promise before he died. I had brought the series *Foundations of Faith I: The Bible, Sin, and Salvation* home to show my children. To my shock, my ninety-three-year-old Jewish father sat in the room and watched spellbound the session on the Bible.

"When he watched the session on sin, he began to weep nearly uncontrollably, fell to his knees and began confessing his sins out loud—right in front of all of us. But, when he watched the next session on salvation, he once again fell to his knees and embraced Jesus Christ as his personal Savior." She began to weep, "He died shortly thereafter, and I know that he is in heaven. But, before he died, he made me promise that if I ever saw you, I would thank you for him. You brought the Bible to us, and he found Jesus!"

Then, as the four of them departed, another smiled and said, "Each of us became a Christian when we studied one of those courses. Thank God for the CoMission."

Step Five: *The Small-Group Discipleship Groups*

The next step was the most strategic, since it was a difficult transition from watching someone else teach the Bible to studying it oneself in the small-group format. It was not only difficult for the Russians, but it was equally difficult for the CoMissioners, as the majority had never led such a challenging Bible study.

Individuals who showed growing interest in the video Bible classes were invited to a more in-depth and intensive study of God's Word using the inductive Bible study method. During these weeks and months, individuals were taught how to study God's Word, and shared together in meaningful accountability. This became the foundation and launching pad for the next stage of development.

Step Six: *The Leadership Training*

As the months went by, the CoMission teams began to identify key individuals whom they felt should be invited to advanced leadership training. Numerous leadership conferences were conducted by the various Sending Organizations to equip these individuals for the next step of maturity and leadership.

One of the keys to the advanced leadership training was the Walk Thru the Bible initiative under the leadership of the late John Hoover. At the initial CoMission meeting, WTB committed to serve the whole movement by training 2,500 nationals to teach the Walk Thru Old and New Testament seminars in small-group studies, schools, and churches. This approach worked wonderfully, as it provided this unique methodology to Bible teaching which thrust hundreds of new Christians into leadership roles across the republics.

As leaders proved faithful, they were given more and more leadership in the CoMission movement, greatly accelerating the transition of the national Christians to full ownership of the ministry. Interestingly, many of these key leaders proved to be the translators who had served with the CoMission for the entire year. What a remarkable discipling tool the translation of hundreds of classes of the Bible proved to be!

Before our beloved Peter Deyneka died, he often addressed

CoMission teams during the annual Executive Committee trip to Russia. None of us can ever forget his strong encouragement, repeated over and over again, to all the CoMission Teams: "You have no idea what you are doing here. As a result of the CoMission, hundreds of new young leaders have arisen, hundreds of new churches and ministries are starting, Bible colleges and seminaries are launching; indeed, we can see the nation being transformed by God right before our eyes."

Stage Seven: *The Handoff to Local Leadership*

Ultimately, the goal of all biblical missions is to quickly transition leadership to those who prove faithful in each local community. During this seventh stage, the Sending Organizations transitioned the movement to the national leaders that they found most faithful and qualified.

As this crucial transition occurred, hundreds of ministries in local churches, schools, etc., were successfully launched and led by local believers. In this stage, the ultimate goal of the CoMission was achieved beyond our expectations. As you will read in later chapters, the lasting fruit of the CoMission was extensive in scope.

The CoMission sought to use the most effective methodology possible while granting maximum freedom to the various Sending Organizations to modify as the local situation required. By selecting and approving effective and proven ministry tools that were translated into various languages, the quality and doctrinal standards were relatively assured. By limiting the number of materials that were used, the CoMission more easily trained laymen to minister effectively.

IV. THE STRUCTURE OF THE CoMISSION

Structure follows strategy. As the CoMission strategy called for a high level of decentralization and organizational ownership, the structure developed to ensure that those values were implemented. Once again, the CoMission plowed new ground in seeking to maximize the effectiveness and efficiency of organizational structure.

Someone has said, "There is nothing more permanent than a temporary chairman." Upon reflection, it is truly amazing that the CoMission was a nonentity with a pre-determined life span of five years. The CoMission had no central bank account, nor assets of any kind. We never officially incorporated the CoMission as the centralized authority.

In 1997, when the CoMission officially ended, there were no assets to distribute. The sixty-plus million dollars that was raised and invested through the scores of established ministry organizations that comprised its membership nearly all found its way to ministry right on the field—not in corporate overhead.

Four hallmarks of the CoMission structure were as follows:

First, the CoMission structure relentlessly fought the normal drift toward organizational centralization. As the CoMission started gaining momentum, the natural inclination of nearly everyone was to start a new mission organization with a paid staff, national headquarters, centralized authority, etc. While nearly all of the CEOs of the Executive Committee were entrepreneurial, we felt that such a structure would seriously impede the accelerating movement. Therefore, the CoMission never incorporated, and every agency remained independent and grew to be widely interdependent. We worked through trust and enjoyed the wide benefits.

Second, the CoMission structure delegated authority and responsibility according to organizational and individual core competencies. The various responsibilities and their accompanying results were delegated to the most effective organization within the CoMission movement. The Executive Committee would discuss and unanimously select the best organization for each major task, invite that organization to take full responsibility and then submit to that organization. By accepting that responsibility, it meant that the organization took full responsibility and authority to fund, lead, administrate, and ensure that the quality standards were upheld, and the goals for that area achieved.

Key to this approach was the fact that when an organization accepted the responsibility for a given area, they also embraced the responsibility for all related costs in that area. For instance, Campus Crusade covered the costs for the *JESUS* film and school curriculum, the Navigators covered the costs for the CoMission's Training committee, Walk Thru the Bible assumed the costs for developing and translating the Video Bible Curriculum and recruiting and training the 2,500 WTB Bible instructors, etc.

Third, the CoMission structure was held together by relationships, trust, and submission. As widely discussed, the style by which CoMission ministry was conducted broke new ground. One of the primary goals of the movement was that by the third year, the various ministry labels (such as "I'm with xxx organization") would fall by the wayside. People would be identified as members of the CoMission Team, regardless of organizational affiliations. This was achieved and became a strong and widely held value.

Additionally, the movement worked hard to build and increase the foundation of trust and respect. Since the CoMission didn't have one official person in authority, and every organization was viewed as an equal partner, the task of making decisions and the working out of difficult issues was undertaken through community. I do not believe that the Executive Committee ever was divided on one single major decision. We worked together until unity was established or the matter was tabled for further study and discussion.

Fourth, the CoMission structure provided for policy and direction through the Executive Committee and implementation and procedures through the Executive Directors. The practical structure of the CoMission included the following areas:

1. **The CoMission Executive Committee** led in matters of policy, finances, direction, and unity. Due to the fact that the Executive Committee Chairpersons also served as Presidents/CEOs of leading member organizations, they selected Executive Directors who reported directly to them

and managed their committees on a daily basis.

2. **The CoMission Executive Directors** were the individuals who served as the managers for each of the committees and reported to their respective Executive Committee members. They were the backbone of the movement, and were the implementers of the vision and strategy. In order to coordinate and interrelate all the ongoing functions, the Executive Directors also formed their own committee, which was coordinated by King Crow, who also served as my Executive Director. They would implement the major policies and oversee the activities in the USA, as well as overseas. If a problem arose, they would present it to their Executive Committee leader who would then present it to the entire Executive Committee for any necessary actions.

3. **The CoMission Committees** led in all the matters relating to their respective areas such as Training, Sending Organizations, Publicity, Church Relations, Arrangements, etc. Each of the Executive Committee members served as a chairman of one of those committees. At the quarterly meetings, each committee chairman reviewed the achievements of the past quarter, overviewed the plans for the upcoming quarter, and recommended for action any major policy issues from his area.

V. THE FINANCES OF THE COMISSION

Since the CoMission did not have a centralized office responsible to generate and oversee all finances, each CoMission Committee was responsible for all the finances of its activities, even when the other members of the movement were affected. In order to raise funds for centralized tools such as CoMission recruitment tools and ministry videos, each participating organization contributed its fair share.

I remember inviting the CoMission organizations in the early days of the movement to pool the names of our donors and let them come to regional meetings and hear the challenge of the CoMission. One leader quipped, "If we succeed with that idea, it will be a greater miracle than the fall of the Berlin Wall."

In spite of those skeptical words, we held numerous fund raising events around the country. The first one in Dallas had a dismal turnout, but the results were astonishing. Hundreds of invitations went out, but just a handful of people showed up. Paul Eshleman and I were so discouraged because we had reserved the entire hotel ballroom, and less than thirty people showed up.

In the question and answer session after the presentation, one of the few attendees whom none of us knew remarked, "Don't tell me you guys are truly going to do things together, because Christian organizations never have and never will." The meeting ended. We had just a few pledges; I don't even know if it paid for our flights.

As we were walking down the hallway, Paul and I were bemoaning the dismal results. As we turned the corner in the hallway, that same man was waiting and proclaimed, "I believe in you men—and I'm going to be a major part of the launch of the CoMission." What he pledged was far beyond what we had hoped would come in from all the planned fund raising meetings across the nation!

He wasn't a donor to Walk Thru. He wasn't a part of Crusade. He just had heard about the CoMission and came to the meeting. What a great supporter he turned out to be! It was at that meeting—through this one individual—that God demonstrated that He would provide the funds.

VI. The Publicity and Public Relations Committee

One of the committees instrumental to the success of the CoMission was the Publicity and Public Relations Committee that was located in the WTB South Carolina Headquarters. This team of highly talented and very committed individuals was led by Ivy Harrington, Mary Anthony, Kevin Johnson, and Lisa Borden.

Every year, for five years, with the expertise of the Puckett Group in Atlanta, this team developed the best ministry video available in the marketplace. The videos were so effective that all of the participating

organizations used them by adding their own organizational introductions and conclusions. Their efforts enabled the movement to
ramp up so very quickly and recruit hundreds of individuals to serve
the movement.

VII. THE EXECUTIVE DIRECTORS

The most strategic of all the various committees, in addition to
the Executive Committee, was the Executive Directors. These individuals managed the day-to-day operations of the CoMission in the
United States and across the former Soviet Union. Before the committees were officially established, my executive assistant was Mary
Lee Griffith, who served with excellence in those overwhelming start-
up days that preceded the formal organization of the CoMission.

The leader of the Executive Directors was the person who served
alongside of me for the Executive Committee, King Crow, and his
assistant, Sabra Romeo. King and Anne Crow felt the call of God to
the CoMission, and moved from Dallas to Charlotte to serve in this
strategic capacity. Their sacrificial contribution cannot be overstat-
ed, as they provided much needed coordination between the managers of the operating committees. King served the movement well,
and all of us who worked in the CoMission are forever thankful to
God for sending him to us.

VIII. THE TRUE HEROES OF THE MOVEMENT: THE CoMISSIONERS

Without a doubt, the true heroes of the CoMission were those men
and women who responded to the call of God to join with us and
serve for a year or more in the former Soviet Union, in teams that num-
bered between six and twelve. As you'll read later in the book, many
overcame insurmountable odds and served in very difficult situations
and circumstances. The CoMissioners demonstrated the grave error
of believing that only "seminary-trained" or "full-time professional missionaries" or "speakers of the language" could serve with effectiveness.

Many quit their jobs, others took a year out of school, and some
actually sold their homes and everything that they owned. The fruit

of the CoMission that has multiplied throughout the entire Soviet empire stands as undeniable proof that the strategy of Jesus—of selecting laymen to do His service—is still a strategy that produces eternal fruit to the glory of God.

IX. THE EXECUTIVE COMMITTEE

Those who served on the Executive Committee together forged friendships so deep and so treasured that even after a dozen years since our first meeting, we regather each year just to spend time together and reminisce about those most remarkable years we served God in the vision of the CoMission. Many have shared that the CoMission was the high water mark of their lives and ministries— because it grew into a true movement of God.

When I reflect about how the vision began, and how God led us step by step, I remain in awe. We did not set out to form such a massive cooperative effort—we only responded to the call of God in our hearts.

My life and ministry has been so enriched by these great men and women of God who battled for our Great King together. The grace and mercy demonstrated to me time after time in my many weaknesses and failings surfaced many a tear of gratitude. Who among us is deserving of another's unconditional love?

It is with great love and affection that I remember our years of service together—of each one's heart and intense dedication to the Lord and His kingdom. I can only praise God for the rare privilege of serving Him in a movement that felt like Acts 29.

CLOSING COMMENTS:

Nostalgia floods my heart, and memories continue to inundate my mind as I write this chapter. It is impossible to overestimate the profound and lasting impact that the CoMission had on Russia, the CoMissioners, the donors and prayer warriors, the Executive Committee members, and on my own life.

Before concluding, may I share a short testimony of what this movement and its people did for just one person and his family—

my own? When the CoMission started, I didn't have a deep burden for the world. The Great Commission was something I believed in and taught, and then delegated to others in the organization that I led for twenty-five years. But, by the time the five years of the CoMission had run its course, my life had been radically transformed. I found myself a different man who now lives committed to the fulfillment of the Great Commission in my generation.

Great movements, like great truths, have the inbred power to transform a person, a family, a church, and even a nation. The CoMission proved to be a remarkable seedbed of such transformation. As a single seed can produce a massive orchard with ever-increasing size, so also can one movement spawn a never-ending movement of God. Is not that what happened 2,000 years ago?

After the CoMission completed its mission, its seeds bore fruit in my life as I launched a dynamic new ministry known as World-Teach in 1998 (the year after the completion of the CoMission). In its first five years, WorldTeach grew at an exponential rate, and now ministers in eighty-two nations with 33,374 trained nationals, who have conducted 47,811 Bible courses—averaging more than 130 Bible courses each day, every day of the year.

Then, in 2002, the Lord called our family to resign from Walk Thru the Bible and eventually to move to South Africa to serve Him alongside the African people. The ministry here in Africa has grown exponentially as the principles and practices that were innovated in the CoMission and were improved in WorldTeach are now implemented at even deeper levels.

I'm convinced that had the Lord not birthed the CoMission, not only would the global movement of WorldTeach not have been birthed, but neither would we have moved to Africa. There is much that could be shared at this point, but I believe the seminal point has been made. If the CoMission revolutionized one person to such a depth —with resulting global impact—then just imagine what the CoMission has truly done in the lives of the other thousands of Americans whose lives have been forever changed—and for the hundreds of thousands of people of the former Soviet Union who now are leading the transformation of their society back to God and His Word, which once was outlawed.

To God be the glory, great things He has done.

SERVANT
OF THE
LORD

Testimony of Helen Machekhina
JESUS Film Project Briefing, 2000:

We watched the JESUS film with our students, but I didn't look at the screen. I just looked after the pupils, to make certain they behaved themselves. I didn't understand or care because it was just a fairy tale to me.

Although I didn't pay a lot of attention to it at the time, I struggled with depression. One day I just lay down in the snow and I looked up at the sky and said, "Okay, here I am, depressed. I can't sleep. I don't want to live. I don't know what to do. I've heard that there is some power which can help me. So, I beg you, help me or take my life."

It was my very first prayer, and God helped me. However, I didn't realize it at the time. Then, in 1994, a convocation took place in our city in Yozanya. I went there, not because I wanted to hear about God, but mainly out of curiosity. I wanted to meet Americans.

At this first convocation, we received our Bibles and the JESUS film. When it was over and they left, I realized there was something about these people that I never saw in my own friends.

As I wept, I said, "Now I'm ready to talk to you; come back please," but they were gone. I opened the Bible and I started reading from Genesis. I did this in secret, sometimes in the kitchen or the bath. I was afraid people would notice and think I was crazy.

Some months later, a CoMission team came to our school, and I watched the JESUS film for the third time. When I saw the scene of the crucifixion of Christ, I realized that here on the cross I see God's Son, and God let His Son Jesus be crucified at the cross for my sins to save me personally.

I thought, "Am I ready to give my life for my sons' lives? Yes! I love them greatly. They're my sons."

I realized how dear I was to God, and that He loved me. My father had left me when I was four years old, so I didn't have a father. At this moment, I found my Father, the greatest Father in the world, who took care of me, who loved me all my life.

So, here I am. Now I love God with all of my heart, and I want to be His servant, His slave, His everything.

PRINCIPLES
THREE AND
FOUR

EXPECT OPPOSITION FROM YOUR OWN ORGANIZATION.

We were not prepared for this, but it happened—almost without exception. The leaders, board members, etc. from our own organizations thought that their CoMission participants were being taken advantage of or "used" for someone else's plan. How does the president of Navigators explain that the CoMission participants will be trained to share the Four Spiritual Laws published by Campus Crusade for Christ? And how do the Crusade workers explain that all CoMissioners will be using Navigator materials for follow-up?

GIVE THE CREDIT TO GOD.

Though this is the desire of all of us in ministry, we sometimes are guilty of stealing some of the glory for our organization or ourselves. Since none of us did the CoMission work alone, we all had trouble writing reports for our magazines and newsletters. If we took too much credit for ourselves, it would be a slap at the effort of the other members of the CoMission. So we just rejoiced in what God was doing—through so many different churches, backgrounds and confessions. And that is how the Lord has always intended that ministry should be reported. To God be the Glory! Great things *He* has done!!

PAUL A. ESHLEMAN has held numerous leadership positions within Campus Crusade for Christ International since 1966. Many consider him one of the foremost strategists in the Christian world today. Under his leadership as director of The JESUS Film Project, international viewership of the film *JESUS* has surpassed five billion. God used the *JESUS* film in a remarkable way to open the doors for the CoMission. Currently, this film version of the life of Christ, drawn from the Gospel of Luke, is available in more than 865 languages and has been used by 1,500 denominations and mission agencies. It has been shown in every country of the world and has been used to plant more than 750,000 churches. Paul is one of three founders of the CoMission. He served as vice-chairman of its Executive Committee and chairman of the Sending Organizations Committee. Paul and his wife, Kathy, who reside in Laguna Niguel, California, have two adult children and three grandchildren.

THE *JESUS* FILM OPENS THE DOOR

Sending Organizations Committee

Dr. Paul A. Eshleman, chairman

DURING THE LAST MONTHS before the collapse of the Soviet Union, nationwide premieres of the *JESUS* film took place across Russia and Eastern Europe. At a reception after the Moscow premiere, the government's education officials said, "You should show this film to our students." From that simple statement came a vision that eventually resulted in showings in thousands of schools—but not by The JESUS Film Project, or Western missionaries, or even the few pastors the nation had at that time. Instead, those who took the *JESUS* film to the classrooms of the Soviet Union, and nine other countries, were the teachers.

Beginning in May 1991 in Moscow, then in city after city, many educators, steeped in atheism and communism, arrived at four-day "convocations," curious to meet these visitors. They listened intently to lectures about how to build character and a moral foundation for society, as taught by Jesus. In convocation after convocation, the Spirit of God used exposure to the truth of the gospel and the life of Jesus, coupled with the loving witness of the small-group leaders, to melt hearts.

One of the high points of these convocations was the showing of the *JESUS* film. This straightforward account from Luke's Gospel proved to be a turning point in the lives of many who attended. For the first time, hardened teachers of atheism saw and understood God's unending love for them, and prayed to receive Jesus as their personal Savior and Lord.

From the beginning of our mission to Russia, we envisioned the convocation strategy as taking advantage of "a window of opportunity," one that we thought might not last more than five years. From May 1991 (the first convocation) to December 1996 (the last), 136 convocations were completed in 116 different cities. They drew a total of 41,618 educators.

So great was the educators' interest in knowing more about this God who loved them and died for them, that our short-term, volunteer teams were overwhelmed. The need was evident—but even had we mobilized a good portion of Campus Crusade's staff, the task would still have been beyond our abilities.

God, of course, was not taken by surprise—either by the spiritual hunger or our inadequate resources. None could have foreseen His plan: not to call just one or two organizations to minister, but to mobilize a cross-section of organizations, denominations and individuals who would work together to accomplish what none of them could do alone. Acknowledging the primary vision of the Great Commission of our Lord, which was behind all we were seeking to do, and the cooperative nature of this multi-organizational effort, we called this mobilization the CoMission.

"THE GREATEST FATHER"

In 1992, the CoMission began sending in one-year teams to continue the spiritual nurturing of the educators and to reach out to still others. There are now hundreds of stories of God's grace in the lives of Russian educators, including that of Helen Machekhina.

Growing up as a Young Pioneer, she became firmly grounded

in atheism. She learned to see Lenin and Stalin as her great-grand-parents.

In 1994, she attended a convocation in her city of Ryazan in order to speak to the visiting Americans, not to learn about God. Yet as she met with them, she later recalled, "I realized there was a light in them that I never saw in my people."

In October of that year, a CoMission team from America came to her school. Helen asked about a Bible study, but candidly told them, "I don't care about Jesus. I know there is no God. I just want to know the Bible."

Repeatedly, those times with team members brought her face to face with the love of God, through both the witness of Christians' lives and the *JESUS* film. The third time Helen watched it, she recalls, "When I saw the scene of the crucifixion of Christ, I realized that here on the cross, I see God's Son. God let His Son be crucified for my sins, to save me personally.

"I realized how dear I was to God; that He loves me. He sent His own Son to be crucified for my sins. My father had left me when I was four years old. At that moment, I found my real father. The greatest father in the world took care of me, who loved me all my life. I cried a lot."

From that moment on, Helen turned from teaching her pupils that there was no God to telling them of the living God who loves them. She used the curriculum with a fourth grade class, showing the *JESUS* film multiple times to both students and adults, and started a Bible study. So often does she talk about Jesus that she is often affectionately called "Helen the evangelist."

"I am so thankful," she said recently, "to all of you who have prayed for our country, who brought the truth to our country. You opened God to us."

THE FORMATION DAYS

In the early days of the CoMission, we had many questions: Could we show the film in every school in the Soviet Union? How should we begin? Who would set it up? How could it be paid for?

From the point of view of The JESUS Film Project there were lots of questions, few answers—and no time to think about it. The incredible success of the initial premieres of the *JESUS* film in various parts of the Soviet Union had resulted in great plans to do the same thing in every country that had once been deemed behind the "Iron Curtain." Every available person on our staff was involved in the theatrical release of the film. With contracts signed with fifteen studios, we were in a flat-out sprint to get the film translated and checked to meet the premieres scheduled to occur in fifteen areas of the Soviet Union and Eastern Europe during the last four months of 1990. We were showing in theaters in fifteen areas of the Soviet Union and Eastern Europe.

However, a stipulation included in all of the contracts proved far more successful than we had ever hoped. We asked that each studio invite the political, cultural, religious, and Communist Party officials in the area to the premiere showing. We reasoned first that if all the high government officials were seen publicly watching this film about God, it would be difficult for them to crack down on other people watching it. By their presence, they would be giving tacit approval for its showing anywhere. We knew that after the theater showings were completed, Christians would show it in other locations, and we didn't want them to get in trouble or be persecuted for it.

Second, we hoped that we would reach the leadership when they viewed the film, and that perhaps they would help open up other opportunities in the future.

And the Leaders Came

And the leaders came. In Bulgaria, the president, vice president, prime minister, and half of the ccabinet attended. In Russia, seven out of the nine ministers in the cabinet, and the chief advisors to Boris Yeltsin all turned out. Invariably, the ministers or deputy ministers of education of every country and language came to the premieres held in their areas. And, without exception, every one of them asked our representatives if we would show the *JESUS* film in their school system to their students.

This all began in Tbilisi, Georgia, site of our first *JESUS* film premiere. God had begun to move in answer to our prayers for the children! In the flickering blue-white light given off by the film projector, I studied the faces of the children watching *JESUS*. They sat mesmerized, totally captivated by the story. And more. Because this was not just any movie. This was not just another story. This was about God. These were the words of Jesus. To watch this film was to learn about how to live forever.

Awestruck, I remembered where we were: in the Soviet Union! In schools controlled by the Communist Party! Now, just six months after the first public showings in theaters, we were doing the first showing in a Soviet public school!

I was in Tbilisi on a Saturday, when schools were closed. Yet, when I made it known that we could have a special showing for a school, local officials opened the doors wide. The teachers and students welcomed us with much ceremony.

As we entered the large foyer of the school, students and teachers, dressed for a very special occasion, met us. One by one, ten-year-old girls with freshly braided hair and colorful ribbons came forward carrying bouquets of flowers for us. Smiles shy and cheeks blushing, they welcomed us with well-practiced English greetings: "Good afternoon, honored guests from America. We are happy to welcome you to our school." A slight curtsy, and it was the next one's turn.

Each of the best speakers in their English classes delivered a short greeting. Then, in our honor, they quoted for us Edgar Allen Poe's "The Raven." We toured their school, talked with the teachers, and moved to one of the larger classrooms to show the film.

At the scenes of the crucifixion, some covered their eyes. Others shed silent tears. This was the story of the Son of the God of the universe who came to die for their sins. This was personal, and oh, so deeply meaningful. When the invitation to receive Christ was given by the narrator at the end of the film, all the students and teachers began to pray the prayer out loud, with no embarrassment. Who wouldn't want to receive Christ?

Afterwards, I presented a copy of the film and the 16mm projector to the Georgia school system to be used in different schools each week. I was elated! What an incredible breakthrough!

Paul Eshleman presents *JESUS* film print to Rezo Chkeidze, director of the Georgian Film Studio, His Holiness Ilia II of the Georgian Orthodox Church, and the actor who dubbed the voice of Jesus, prior to the premiere showing in Tbilisi, Georgia.

INCREDIBLE HUNGER

While I was rejoicing in Soviet Georgia, Dr. Bill Bright, founder and president of Campus Crusade for Christ International, was in a Ukrainian school a thousand miles away, for a similar showing. As I watched the film report a few days later, I was struck again with the incredible hunger of the Soviet people to know God.

The showing of the film in that Ukrainian school was a landmark event. Six hundred students and teachers crowded the auditorium. Again, rapt attention. Excitement at the miracles. Audible gasps at the crucifixion. Tears at the burial. Radiant smiles at the resurrection.

And then Dr. Bright spoke: "The greatest day of my life was the day I received Christ as my own personal Savior." He asked how many had prayed the prayer of invitation to receive Christ at the close of the *JESUS* film, and more then half raised their hands in response.

The Young Pioneers, wearing their traditional red bandanas, passed out a copy of the evangelistic booklet *Have You Heard of the Four Spiritual Laws?* to each student. For decades, the Young Pioneers had been the first organization in the communist youth system for children from eight to fifteen years old. From the Young Pioneers they advanced to Comsomol, the Young Communist League. After Comsomol, a few would get invitations to join the Communist Party.

Yet, incredibly, here in this Soviet high school, the Young Pioneers were distributing *The Four Spiritual Laws*. Bill explained briefly the content of the booklet and showed them the prayer in the back that they could pray if they had not yet placed their faith in Jesus.

It was an awesome day. The teachers were then asked to come forward if they would like to receive a Bible. With shy smiles, wiping the wrinkles from their dresses, they stepped forward to receive what to them was an incredible gift. Worth a month's salary, and nearly impossible to obtain for decades, it was now a free gift to them. I could only compare what I was seeing with my own country. And in America? None of what was taking place here could happen in America. At that moment, Soviet schools had more freedom to preach the gospel than did our own schools.

Within six months of our first school showings in Georgia and Ukraine, the highest school officials in fifteen countries had asked us to come and show the film *JESUS*.

But by December 17, 1990, our *JESUS* film staff was nearing the point of total exhaustion. So much had been happening for the cause of the kingdom. Three days before that, we had finished the fourteenth and fifteenth premieres—in Budapest, Hungary, and in Bucharest, Romania. More invitations to show the film in the schools had been offered, but someone else would have to do it. We were just too spent. At a Christmas celebration with our staff, I realized that everyone was as exhausted as I was. It was a good kind of tired, though. We had given ourselves for the cause of the kingdom.

I gave them a few words of thanks before they left for the holidays to be with their families and friends and to rest: "I will never be able to repay you for the sacrifices you have made during these last months, but because of you and those who have provided the funds, many thousands of people in the former Soviet Union will celebrate their first real Christmas this year as members of God's family."

For Every Russian Child

Through the next several weeks, as strength gradually returned, I began to think about the children again. What if every school child in Russia could see the film? If they could now hear the gospel, how better to ensure a positive first impression of Jesus than to show them the true and accurate account contained in the *JESUS* film?

It was a question that wouldn't go away. Finally, one evening after watching the film footage from our first school showings in Ukraine and Georgia, I decided that reaching the schools in the USSR was something we had to at least attempt. The Lord had never let the thoughts leave my mind. He had given me a burden and a vision I could not put aside. So we plunged in, trusting Him, with great enthusiasm.

On January 23, 1991, we arrived in Moscow, and at ten the next morning, at the office of Eugene Kurkin, Deputy Minister of Education for the Russian Republic. We sat around a conference table under a large framed picture of Lenin and began the meeting. I told the deputy minister about the good reception we'd had at the theatrical premieres, and explained my vision for the course on Christian ethics and morality as a foundation for society.

He leaned back in his chair, folded his hands, and spoke pensively: "We don't know how many caverns there are in the foundation of our society after seventy years without God. You are making a very generous offer to give a film for every school. Do you know how many schools there are in the Russian Republic?

"I think so," I replied.

He answered, "65,000," as though he was sure I couldn't know that.

"Are you prepared to give a copy of the *JESUS* video to all those schools?" he continued, a little incredulous at the thought.

In my head, I quickly multiplied the 65,000 times the cost per video and realized it could be as much as $1.3 million, and then said, "Yes, we are." I didn't know where we would get the money, but this was not the time to think of that. This was the time to open the door for the gospel.

He then said, "It's interesting that you should come on this day. We have eighty-nine school districts in the Republic of Russia. We will have two or three representatives from each one in Moscow tomorrow for a special meeting of the Ministry of Education. We are going to discuss the whole issue of the separation of church and state. We will present your proposal and then let you know."

"Would you like to see the *JESUS* film at your meeting?" volunteered Juli Gusman, our Moscow distributor who had arranged our session. "We will bring a 35mm copy over from Dom Kino."

The deputy minister thought it would be great.

"We will also bring copies of the script for everyone," Juli added. The script was the Gospel of Luke.

The meeting concluded with warm handshakes and some discussion of what we might do in 278 teacher colleges. We left with their promise to consider a pilot project for leaders from 1,000 schools in three cities.

As we walked from the meeting, our hearts rejoiced. Later that day, one of the business leaders traveling with us asked how much the test project would cost.

About $100,000," I estimated.

"Let me know how much you need. I don't think I can do it all, but don't let finances stop the test," he said.

Incredible! I thought. What a joy to see the body of Christ pull together for the cause of the kingdom. That cooperation on the project was only the beginning.

Five days later I called Moscow from Hong Kong. "Did you see the film?" I asked the minister's interpreter.

"Yes, we did. And we all got copies of the booklet about Jesus. All 400 of us."

"Did you make a decision about the school project?"

"Yes, we want to go ahead."

One of many theater showings throughout Russia and Ukraine.

A HUNDRED DAYS

We were off! We set out to do the seemingly impossible. How would we write, translate, print, and ship all the materials needed in less than 100 days? We weren't sure, but we laid out a plan, and we went to work.

Through the next several weeks, the willingness of people to help with the project was like nothing I have ever seen. I called Blair Cook, a long-term veteran of the Campus Crusade ministry overseas who was between assignments.

"I want to tell you about an idea I have."

"Tell me what you're thinking," he said, a smile in voice. "I'm always interested in a good challenge."

"People in the Soviet Union write on their response cards at the theaters that they no longer have any basis for belief," I told him. "They don't respect the government or the Communist Party. They say they no longer know what is right and what is wrong."

I paused for a breath, and then continued, "I have approached the Ministry of Education in Russia to see if they would be willing to bring together one principal or one teacher from each school for a three- or four-day convocation. We would give each teacher a video copy of the *JESUS* film for his or her school and demonstrate how to teach a course called 'Christian Ethics and Morality: A Foundation for Society.' We have a chance to impact the whole Soviet Union school system.

"So, here is my idea: How would you feel about heading the process of putting the course together and conducting the first test if we can get a number of educators to agree?"

"It sounds fantastic," Blair responded. "Why don't you let my wife and me pray about it? I'll call you in a day or so."

He called me back the next day with, "We're on! How do we start?"

We finished the phone call with a few clarifications. I would handle the overall strategy, get the first convocation set up, and raise the funds. Blair would develop the curriculum, recruit the instructors and administer the convocations.

The Lord had already brought to us several years before a woman who would be instrumental in the curriculum and training that we would offer to elementary educators. A veteran of children's ministry, Vernie Schorr, began consulting with us at The JESUS Film Project when she heard about the large crowds that came and the follow-up efforts made afterwards, especially with adults. "What about the children?" she asked.

She spearheaded the development of an evangelistic booklet called *The Greatest Promise,* accompanied by four colorful booklets that helped solidify a child's decision to trust in Jesus. These materials would be foundational in the elementary track, along with a Character Development curriculum appropriate for grade-school children. The interactive approach Vernie helped develop there also quickly influenced our approach to the secondary educators. After decades of extremely formal education, the Russian educators, for the most part, responded eagerly to the role playing and small-group interaction.

A Move to Moscow

As preparations advanced, I soon realized someone would have to live in Moscow to take care of the details of these conferences. But I knew of no one available, so I prayed fervently that the Lord would provide someone to meet this essential need.

A few days later, Jerry Franks, a businessman and personal friend, called me. He and his wife, Karen, came to California from time to time to oversee a hotel they were building. On their last trip, he had mentioned some major financial problems.

I was glad to hear from him. "How is everything going?" I asked.

"Not that well," he sighed. "In fact, Karen and I have decided to make a change. We'll be in California next week on business. Can we have dinner?"

A week later, my wife, Kathy, and I met them in a lovely restaurant overlooking the ocean. It was March 16, 1990, only eight weeks until the first conference was scheduled to open in Moscow. I told him about the remarkable invitation that we had just received from Moscow—and the need for on-site personnel that had resulted. Jerry was interested, but not ready to jump into anything immediately.

After dinner we drove by to look at The *JESUS* Film Project's offices. When we finished the tour, I showed them a five-minute report on the showings of the *JESUS* film in Russia. As the pictures of the Soviet children came on the screen, the God who orchestrates the universe touched the Franks' hearts.

"What kind of help do you need?" Jerry asked.

"We need someone to move to Moscow and set up all of the convocations for the next year," I answered. "Right now we don't have anyone to send. If we don't find someone, we may not be able to hold these conferences."

"Karen and I will pray about it, and we'll let you know on Monday."

"Wouldn't it be great if the Lord sent them to work with us?" Kathy commented on the drive home. "They are perfect for the job." I agreed. Jerry had the educational background; he had once been the superintendent of a large Christian school in Ohio.

On Monday, Jerry called and said, "We're ready to go. This is not what we had planned, but we feel God wants us to do it for at least the next year. What's the next step?"

"Get your passport," I said. "We need to go to Moscow."

On April 2, we left for Moscow. On April 3, we rented Jerry and Karen an apartment. On April 4, we met with the Ministry of Education to begin work on contractual arrangements. And on May 15, Jerry and Karen moved into their apartment in Moscow—eight weeks after our dinner in California.

The April 4 meeting at the Ministry of Education was extremely difficult. New people had been assigned to work on the project. Some had not the slightest bit of spiritual interest. Others were hard-core communists. Gorbachev was still in power; the Communist Party's dominance had not yet collapsed. There was much opposition internally within the department to spiritual things, but we pressed on.

Mere months before, in early January 1991, the plan had begun to take shape. I had written down all of my ideas and begun to recruit help. The "to-do" list seemed endless when we began to divide up the responsibilities. On May 14, we arrived in Moscow for the first convocation, slated to begin the next day. But everything was in chaos.

RUSSIAN TEACHERS WELCOME THE GOSPEL.

May 15 dawned with a bright sun and warm weather. After the long, cold winter in Moscow, spirits were lighter, trees boasted leaves, and the last of the ugly brown slush along the streets had melted. Two hundred and fifty teachers and principals would be attending this first convocation for teachers. It was an historic event, a day for praising the Lord.

But we were in deep trouble.

Customs authorities had impounded two truckloads of materials shipped in from Germany. The authorities would not release them until the proper paperwork had been completed. Some inside sources told us that conservative religious officials, informed by border guards of the incoming materials, had gone to Yeltsin's office and obtained an order to confiscate them. It was not especially surprising—just one more hurdle to try to overcome. That was how things worked under the communists.

It meant, however, that we had no Bibles, no New Testaments, no Gospels of Luke or any other follow-up materials, no curriculum, no notebooks, no student notes, and none of the gifts we had brought for the teachers.

We did have *JESUS* videos, some books by Josh McDowell, and a few materials we had brought with us on the plane. Those would have to do. We would begin anyway.

During the next three days, I worked eighteen to twenty hours a day trying to get the materials released, or to secure replacements. We immediately sent telexes to the US to reprint all materials and air ship them to Russia as soon as possible. We had conferences scheduled in two more cities, and we needed the materials for them, even if we missed receiving the materials in Moscow.

I worked at creating new documents and getting them signed by different officials. Hour after hour, I sat in the Cosmos Hotel business center, cutting and pasting, getting new forms translated into Russian, and hoping that they now said the right things. We desperately needed high-ranking members of the Ministry of Education to sign for the importation of the materials. Many were afraid to take this step, and even after the papers were signed, other officials still blocked us.

On the first day, Jerry Franks and I spent ten hours driving a bus from one warehouse to the next to pick up some Bibles we had secured from other groups working in the city. The International Bible Society and others provided the New Testaments needed. We also went to the theater distributors and gathered up Gospels of Luke for the teachers.

On the third day, the truck drivers informed us that if we didn't clear up the paperwork in the next twelve hours, they were heading back to Germany. Ten hours later we had made only slight progress. I sent runners out on the streets in the neighborhood where the trucks had last been spotted to offer the drivers another hundred dollars each day if they would stay until the problem was resolved. They agreed to wait at least one more day.

BREAKING NEW GROUND

Meanwhile, the first convocation was about to get underway. With or without materials, we had to begin. We were breaking new ground. No one had ever tried before to do what we were doing. We could not stop now.

Our first convocation in Moscow was to be held in a suburb of Perova in a Pioneer Palace, local center of the Communist Youth Movement. The Communist Party had built these "palaces" in every community. They housed all the extracurricular activities of school children from ages eight to fifteen.

They looked a great deal like a well-equipped YMCA in the US. The buildings contained a gymnasium, classrooms, and an auditorium. The children would come every day after school for classes in music, dance, art, crafts, gymnastics, drama, and much more. When I met with the Ministry of Education officials, I learned that there were thousands of these "palaces" and hundreds of summer camps.

As we entered that Pioneer Palace on the first morning, we were greeted by a big, imposing, communist educational official. He was not smiling. "Welcome to Moscow," he said, knitting his forehead into a frown. "I am Gernady Fyodorov. We want to welcome you here, but I want to give you a word of warning. If these sessions are boring, no one will come back this afternoon."

His intimidating welcome had not come as a surprise. We had been told several times that Russian teachers would walk out if they were bored. We had brought the best instructors, but had decided that we would give a book or piece of material away every six hours or so during the conference. Now, with so many of the materials held in customs, we were concerned about keeping the participants attending. We need not have worried. The materials we had vanished quickly, and attendance increased every day.

The content of the conference teaching was built around four major themes:

The first introduced the listeners to the Christian worldview, as contrasted with a Marxist worldview. Dr. Udo Middelmann, Dr. Ronald Nash, and other Christian apologists provided a solid intellectual atmosphere. Their strategic overview reached teachers who had no idea what kind of a god we were talking about, much less one they could know personally.

The second major theme each morning centered on the foundational truths of Christianity. If the teachers were to understand the ethical and moral foundations that came from Christianity, they needed to know the basic tenets of the faith. During these sessions, we showed the *JESUS* film—because almost everything we know about God, we explained, we have learned through Jesus. After the showing was over, we gave them their own opportunity to receive Jesus as their personal Savior if they had never done so.

The third emphasis was on helping them to become better teachers. We taught them how to use storytelling, role-playing, and other interactive learning methods—quite a contrast for teachers who had always used the lecture method. But, they were extremely interested in how teaching is done in the West. During this time, the teachers actually practiced teaching certain stories from the Bible using these methods. It was thrilling to watch teachers who had never held a Bible before, go into a small group and prepare, then present a lesson on the Prodigal Son.

The final part of the convocation involved dividing the teachers attending into groups of eight to ten people. Each small group had its own interpreter to assist with the communication.

Small-group leaders, who came primarily from North America, helped to answer questions and make the conference personal for each one who attended.

"You should teach your courses and show the *JESUS* film in all the Pioneer Palaces and all the summer camps," the officials had suggested. There were more than 300,000 teachers who could use the Christian Ethics and Morality course.

THE RUSSIANS RESPOND

During the final session, we invited the Russian teachers to share what they had received from the convocation. Their responses were extremely moving. One teacher stood to say that, as a fourth grade teacher, she would ordinarily teach the subject of atheism. "We know now," she continued seriously, "that atheism is not the way for our country. But we have no money to print new textbooks. Thank you for bringing us this new material. I will begin teaching my students about God." Another teacher stood. "For the last year and a half, I have been trying to teach ethics to my class using fairy tales," she said. "Now I can teach them the truths of God's Word."

Despite all of the problems, the conference had been a great success. During every break, educators who had heard we were in the city surrounded us. One university instructor asked if we could help them rewrite all of their textbooks. "We don't know which parts of our history books are true and which are not," he explained. "Will you help us rewrite them so that they tell the truth? Could you help us take out the Marxist orientation and replace it with a Christian focus? After all, we have a Christian heritage."

During coffee breaks, officials who wanted to sell us Pioneer Palaces and camps approached us. Others had ideas for us to go on nationwide educational television. It was an open door for the gospel beyond any I have ever seen in my life. The teachers themselves were overcome with gratefulness as they received the materials we distributed.

I walked into the office of one of the administrators at the Pioneer Palace and caught her wrapping another two Bibles in some newspaper and hiding them behind a plant. We had forgotten one of the rules of communism: No worker was to have anything that the leaders did not have. We learned that we would have to bring at least 100 extra sets of materials to each conference just to give away to the officials who somehow were involved on every level.

We Keep Learning

The hunger for materials and learning was insatiable. As the convocations multiplied, we kept learning too. In many convocation settings, only half of the material could be presented, because the speaker had to wait for the interpreter to finish repeating the same phrase in the new language.

So, in order to have more teaching time, we brought earphones for each teacher and set up simultaneous translation booths. We decided to hire the professor who trained the top simultaneous translators for all political negotiations. Dr. Eugene Breus and his wife, Zlata, had translated for a number of years for the Soviet delegation at the United Nations. They were very, very good. Still, at this first convocation, we believed we had to have our own Russian speaker from the United States listen to the interpreters to make sure that they were not changing the message as they translated it.

Eugene brought with him the men and women who had been doing the interpreting for the trade negotiations with the US and some of the commentators from Radio Moscow. We didn't do everything perfectly in the conference, but the Russian educators appreciated the attention we gave to ensure the accuracy of the written materials and the professionalism of the interpreters.

Newspaper reporters began to crowd the hallways after the sessions. They were amazed at how the conference was run. They had never before seen time cards used to tell the speakers that it was time for them to stop their sessions. All of their articles spoke of the "highly organized Americans."

But the real impact of the first convocation was felt and seen in the small groups. The teachers had come in the first day wary and cynical. Some had been ordered by their principals to attend. For others, the conference had been a "payoff" for some favor rendered in the past. In the small-group meetings on the first day, many teachers announced that they were members of the Communist Party; they were atheists; they would not become believers; they had come only because they were interested in the teaching methodologies of the West. Many sat with arms folded. Some were large, imposing, intimidating Russian women with scowls of cynicism, hardened by years of hate, mistrust, and lies.

On the second day we showed the *JESUS* film, and I spoke for thirty minutes after the showing to explain how one begins a personal relationship with God. "It doesn't do any good to teach people to follow a system of morals and ethics if there is no motivation to follow the system," I said. "People need to do the right thing, even when no one is looking. We believe that if people make a commitment to the God of the universe, to follow His ways, they will do the right thing because they are motivated from within. This faith in God also will give them the supernatural strength to do the right thing— even when it is difficult.

"If we are going to place this kind of faith in God," I continued, "we need to know what He is like. That's why we have shown you this film on the life of Jesus. He said that He came to show us what God is like: He is like Jesus. Today, if you would like to become a follower of Jesus, if you would like to accept the payment that Jesus made for your sins so that you can live with the God who made the universe, I am going to help you to talk to Him in prayer.

FOR SOME, THEIR FIRST PRAYER

"I realize that for some of you, this may be your first prayer ever. Others of you were taught some of these things by your grandmother many years ago, but you pushed them aside. Perhaps you still have many questions, but you want to take your first steps toward God. I want to help you today to say a simple prayer to Him."

I then led them in a prayer of invitation to Jesus. It was a chance for them to receive Him as Savior and Lord. They would need so much more help to grow spiritually in their new faith, but this was a beginning.

By the end of the fourth day, it was obvious we would need even more time to get the materials out of customs. We reluctantly announced to the teachers that they would have to return in a few weeks to pick up the rest of their materials. They were skeptical. The government often promised them things and never delivered. There was never enough to go around. It was a fact of life.

However, they had received a Bible, some New Testaments, Gospels of Luke, a couple of Christian books and the *JESUS* video, so they were grateful. They would be unable to begin teaching the curriculum, however, until they could get the instructional manual. We got part of the materials a week later, and another part about two weeks after that. One entire truckload is still "lost" somewhere in a black hole.

But the convocation proceeded wonderfully. Most of our "guesses" about how the schedule should go and what content should be presented had been right. God had answered our prayers for wisdom and guidance, and, as usual, we were surprised.

What we were only beginning to understand—but a fact that would be emblazoned on our minds and hearts during the next five years—was that this was God's idea. He would keep the doors open and He would prompt the people to come. He would also encourage that one person on the city or area's educational committee to stand against all of the communist sympathizers, and He would carry this project forward. By the end of the conference, forty-eight percent of those who attended had indicated that they had placed their faith in Christ.

Despite every difficulty, an amazing ministry had been launched. The next generation of Russian children would learn of God in their classrooms, and the first impression many would have of Jesus, would come as they viewed the *JESUS* film. We gave thanks and left for the train station. Our agreement was to try the convocations in three cities as a test. The next two "test" cities, Vologda and Leningrad, were waiting.

A SPRINGTIME OF FAITH IN VOLOGDA

An all-night train ride took us out into the countryside. It was only May, but already the nights were short. I crawled out of my berth at 3:30 A.M., looking for the restroom as the Russian countryside raced by. Thickets of white birch trees were just coming into bloom, and I saw flowering fields, pine forests, and marshy swamplands.

Spring! A break from the long, bitter winter. Little patches of land were developing into gardens. Peasants struggled to raise some vegetables. Everyone tried to survive massive food shortages and the continuing economic collapse.

I marveled at the goodness of God. What an unspeakable privilege to be going into the heartland of Russia. As spring was breaking the cruel bonds of winter, perhaps God would use us to bring a springtime of faith and break the bonds of cold and barren lives. It was a time of awesome respect and worship, of unspoken thoughts, of high expectancy. We felt deeply thankful that the mighty, loving, hand of God reached out to such spiritually starved people.

Vologda, with its many houses built as log cabins, was a marked contrast to Moscow. There had once been more than fifty churches there, in the days before it became known as "little Siberia"—place of exile for those in political disfavor. Now there were two. A third was opening. Still not many for a city of more than 300,000 people.

The Minister of Education for the Vologda region met us at the train. This region encompassed 26 districts, 837 schools, and more than 500,000 students. Of the 26 districts, 23 would be represented and 350 schools would take part. Some leaders had come hundreds of miles and were staying in hotels. The fifty English teachers from the local teacher-training college would eat in factory lunchrooms.

We stayed at the Communist Party hotel. A bust of Lenin sat in the lobby. A party headquarters and meeting place for the whole region turned into the site for our convocation. In the same auditorium where teachers had been indoctrinated in how to teach atheism, we would teach the truths of God's Word.

But this was the countryside. People here were not as progressive and "liberal" as the folks in Moscow. Most of my life I'd leaned toward the conservative side of things in America. But in the Soviet Union, at this time, the liberals were the ones who thought about giving more freedom to Christianity. The conservatives were the old-guard Communist Party officials. I was glad to be a "liberal" here.

We were excited. Having learned a great deal in the Moscow conference, the small-group leaders were much more confident. More than 400 teachers packed the sessions. In the opening session, the head of the education committee for the region, a highly placed Party official in the area, came down to give the opening speech. We could tell that the teachers who were in attendance had misgivings about even being in the audience. They wondered if they would one day be called in for their attendance at a meeting about Christian morals and ethics.

The official began his speech by saying, "Of course, all of us here are communists and atheists. However, under *glasnost,* we are now allowing new ideas to be presented, and so we welcome our friends from America and this conference of educational ideas." Halfway through the conference, some of our materials were released from customs and brought up to Vologda by train.

We had worked hard to make the content of our conference of high caliber, educationally. No Russian educator would have to be embarrassed sponsoring our conference. They might not like the spiritual content, but they had to be impressed by the philosophical and educational methods taught. The expertise and credentials of the visiting university professors validated the educational experience to even the most ardent skeptics.

We had a fine line to walk. These had to be educational conferences or they would not be co-sponsored by the Ministry of Education. We had to prepare the small-group leaders to be especially sensitive in how to bring teachers to the point of commitment within this educational context. Several times in the conference, such as after the *JESUS* film showing, doing this would be especially appropriate, and we wanted to take advantage of these opportunities. We wanted to move carefully, but there was much hunger.

On the morning of the second day, my interpreter came to ask a question. "The members of our small group would like to know: 'How it is that we can open the door to our lives and get Christ in the way we heard one of the Americans talking about?'"

"That's a good question." I smiled. "I will tell you how each of you can personally invite Jesus to enter your life, right after we see the film this morning."

"Okay." She nodded. "We will be waiting."

Later that afternoon, as our small group of teachers met together, we learned that more than half of our guests had prayed to receive Christ, including my interpreter, the twenty-year-old daughter of the Deputy Minister of Education for the whole region.

As in Moscow, the final session brought wonderful reports, with many tears, of how the lives of the teachers had been affected in just four days. They returned to their classrooms with printed materials to use, as well as personal copies of the *JESUS* video. Most—even those not professing faith—had pledged to show the film in their schools and with neighbors, family and friends. We were doing important work, and we knew we needed to expand.

When the third convocation closed in Leningrad, the Ministry of Education officials were besieged with requests inviting us to other regions of the country. The showings of the *JESUS* film in the Russian public schools were off and running.

THE COMISSION

By the end of June 1991, all of our dreams and hopes had been surpassed. I was excited. We had actually negotiated with the Ministry of Education officials in Moscow, set up a test to train 1,000 teachers, developed, translated and printed an entire curriculum in Russian, and conducted four conferences. And the response was tremendous. They wanted us to do more conferences. It was intoxicating!

But some of those who had been there with us were not sure we should move so fast. Jerry Franks, Vernie Schorr, and others gave us a very clear message: "We don't want to keep moving on to new cities when these teachers are so eager to grow in the faith. We can't just go off and leave hundreds of teachers without any guidance or encouragement in these cities. It's like giving birth to a new baby and leaving it on the doorstep somewhere. We want to go back to the cities and follow up on them."

I didn't know what to do. They were right, of course. We couldn't just leave these new believers without any help. They had 1,000 questions about the Bible, Christianity, and how they could teach the course to their students. What should we do?

We decided to send a follow-up team back once a month to each city. We would also send the teachers a letter each month to stay in touch with them. Jerry organized all of this out of his apartment in Moscow, but we knew it wouldn't be enough. We needed full-time people in each city.

I pulled out my yellow pad of paper. And prayed. And began to write. We would have to move teams of people into each of the cities where we had convocations. There would have to be at least four people on a team – 150 x 4 = 600. We would need 600 people to move to Russia for at least a year to begin the discipleship process. Right away.

So that was my plan—at least to start with. I didn't announce it to any one; there were too many unanswered questions. Where would we possibly find 600 people willing to move to the uncomfortable housing, limited food, and difficult political conditions of the Soviet Union? I didn't know the answer.

The next six weeks were a blur of activity. New convocations were scheduled for the fall. Sufficient money had not been raised, and we were committed not to spend what we didn't have. More materials awaited translation, and we needed help for Jerry in the set-up work. Not enough people were available to train the teachers in the upcoming convocations.

Thursday, September 19, 1991, I was back in the office. About 4:00 P.M. I received an unexpected call from Bruce Wilkinson, president of Walk Thru the Bible.

"Paul," he began, "It's Bruce. Do you have a few minutes to talk?"

I was absolutely buried in work, but I wanted it to appear to others that I had everything under control and could take time for any call that came in. So I said, "Plenty of time. Tell me what's happening with you."

"Paul, I'm going through some things in my life, and I don't understand where they are leading. Let me tell you about one thing I believe the Lord is burdening me about.

"About a year ago," he went on, "I felt I had plateaued in my spiritual walk with the Lord. I went away for a week with my wife, Darlene, to think about the future and to pray. I decided to take seriously the command of the Scriptures to 'number our days.' I began to write down some dreams for what I wanted the Lord to do in my life and ministry," he continued. "Please don't laugh, but one of my private prayers was that the Lord would someday allow me to teach the Bible to millions of people each week."

"Does it matter where those people live?" I asked him.

"Not any more."

"Then there's something I have to tell you."

For the next hour I told him about the wonderful open door we had discovered into the public schools of the Soviet Union. I told him about the tremendous need for capable teachers to lead the convocations we hoped to sponsor. I told him of my vision to send workers over to each city to follow up the convocations and help the teachers begin teaching the Christian ethics course in their classrooms. And I explained the need for Bible-teaching videos for parents in adult Christian education classes that I believed we could set up in each school. These classes could help provide a place to grow in their faith for those being reached by the big media effort.

Bruce responded, "We'll help in any way. Let's meet."

The tears began to flow down my cheeks. I'd had such a burden that so much more needed to be done, and now God was answering my prayers. He was prompting others to get involved. I had no idea then what a big answer it would be. Bruce and I agreed to meet on October 11 to talk. But the Lord was not through pulling things together.

AND GOD PROVIDES THE PEOPLE

Three months earlier, Jerry and Karen Franks had taken two of the leading officials from the Russian Ministry of Education, Dr. Alexei Brudnov and Dr. Olga Polykovskya, with them to the conference of educators in Romania, sponsored by the Association of Christian Schools International. While there, these Russian officials expressed their need for help in training their teachers in the latest educational techniques and philosophy. Since that time, the ACSI leadership had been very concerned about the need.

About an hour after Bruce and I finished talking, he received a

Alexei Brudnov and Olga Polykovskaya meet with Jerry Franks in Moscow.

call from Dr. Paul Kienel, president of ACSI. This body is made up of the largest group of Christian schools in the world and includes more than 45,000 Christian teachers.

"Bruce," Paul said, "we've been invited to the Soviet Union to help give additional training to their public school teachers. We think your organization is especially equipped to do that."

Bruce told him about the conversation he had just had with me. "Have you two ever met?" he asked.

"No, but I know who he is."

"We're planning to meet in Atlanta on October 11. You probably should come."

"Well, it's obvious that the Lord is doing something big. Let me check my date book." And after a short pause, Paul Kienel said, "On that date I'm participating in a major teachers' convention in Northern California."

"I understand..." Bruce began.

"No, wait," Paul interrupted. " I'm going to get out of that commitment. I'll find someone to take my place. I'll be in Atlanta."

Bruce told him that he didn't know what we were going to do. We had no agenda for that meeting.

"I understand." Paul's smile communicated even over the phone. "The Lord knows what we need to do. I'll see you there."

On October 11, I flew in to Atlanta for the meeting. Curt Mackey, then director of international training for Campus Crusade for Christ, flew in from South America for the day. Paul Kienel came from California, Phil Renicks from Alabama, and we were joined by eight key staff members of Walk Thru the Bible. We began to talk about what God was doing in the Soviet Union and Eastern Europe. We prayed about what we should do now.

FIRST PARTNERSHIPS

I talked about the four-day convocations that we were holding in the Soviet Union. We were averaging 300 to 400 teachers at each one. We were taking forty to fifty North American Christians over to staff each meeting. We desperately needed additional qualified teachers and instructors for all the conferences that we were to conduct.

"How can we help?" Bruce inquired eagerly.

"You could send over some of your Walk Thru the Bible instructors to help with the conferences."

"How many do you want?"

"As many as you can send."

"Okay," Bruce promised. "We'll guarantee at least eight at each convocation. How much does it cost?"

"About $3,000 per person. We go for seventeen days. We do a convocation in one city, take the weekend off to travel, and then repeat the convocation the next week in another city. We want to do 150 cities, so we will need people for 75 trips."

"Done. We will send eight people per trip for the next 75 trips. Don't think about it any more. We will raise the money. It will happen."

Then Bruce asked me how the Christian school movement could help. I had never met Paul Kienel before. When Bruce first suggested that ACSI should join us for the meeting, I was not sure why. As our time progressed together, I saw the incredible fit. This organization could provide the professional educators needed to give our convocations educational credibility. So I said, "We could use three professional Christian teachers for each of the three groups we teach: elementary, secondary, and principals. We could use nine each time."

Bruce turned to Paul Kienel. "You need to send nine each trip. Nine times 75. At $3,000 each."

Paul didn't respond immediately.

Bruce said, "Paul, you don't know Paul Eshleman. I do. I want you to know you can trust him. You know me. Take my word for it."

Paul was interested, but hesitant. He knew he had to talk with his board.

Then Bruce said, "This isn't a committee. We are always getting committees together. There's always too much talk and too little action. We need to be an action committee. I have to talk to my board, as well. But I sense your board and my board will say 'yes' to this. Do you want to do it?"

"I've never done anything like this before," Paul smiled.

"Neither have I."

"Yes, I want to do it!" Paul Kienel affirmed.

I was shaking my head in disbelief. I had never seen organizations make decisions so quickly. I had never before seen them embrace and fund a plan they didn't develop themselves.

Then I told them that I believed that the biggest need in the Soviet Union was for Christians to teach the Bible. There simply weren't enough teachers—or pastors, or churches—to contain the spiritual harvest and disciple all the new believers. What we needed was a good video curriculum. We thought it would take about three years to take a person who knows nothing about Christianity to the point where he could lead a group. A video training could help accomplish this.

Bruce said, "We in Walk Thru will take the responsibility of developing up to 150 hours of video instruction, and translate it into Russian. Also, as a part of our commitment, we will train 2,400 teachers to conduct Walk Thru the Bible seminars in the schools and colleges."

Pat McMillan, a management consultant and long-time friend to many of us, had joined the meeting for a few hours. He said, "I think you should call your group the CoMission. You are cooperating to help fulfill the Great Commission." We agreed.

The meeting ended and we took a picture on the front steps of the building. Those were memorable moments. We had great enthusiasm. Would the Lord confirm our steps? Would He bring our dreams to pass?

JESUS film billboards appeared throughout the country.

THE VISION EXPANDS

In the weeks that followed, God amazingly confirmed that we had embarked on something dear to His heart. At this point, our three organizations were getting to know each other. While I was in Albania for the premiere of the *JESUS* film, the Lord confirmed the involvement in the Soviet Union to both Bruce Wilkinson and Paul Kienel.

We needed God to confirm to each of us individually that it was His plan for us to work together in this undertaking and that He was orchestrating it. In the days to come, we would be filled with confirmations beyond what any of us had ever imagined. The initial experience with the *JESUS* film in the Soviet Union was a personal story, but through the CoMission, God was about to do things that would unleash an avalanche of stories from everyone involved.

Bruce Wilkinson took the major leadership role, and I encouraged him to go as soon as possible and attend a convocation so he could see the possibilities in Russia for himself. He left a few weeks later on his first trip to the Soviet Union to serve as the main speaker at the Teacher Convocation in Pushkin, a beautiful city a few miles south of St. Petersburg, Russia. "A miracle happened in those four days," Bruce later reported. "We began to see that God had opened a door so large, and the field was so incredibly ripe, that we didn't know what to do with it.

"I remember a staff prayer meeting I was leading for our ministry team on Thursday morning at 6:30, before we began the first session of the day. Forty of us gathered together, including J. B. and Betty Crouse of OMS International, and Paul Kienel. After a short Bible reading, we broke up into groups of three or four as I led us in fervent prayer for the Russian people. It was a moving time. And then I said, 'I want you to tell the Lord that if he wants to move you to Russia, you'll go.' Silence. You could have heard a pin drop. No one said a word.

"'If we cannot pray that way,' I continued, 'and there are conditions to our obedience to Christ, the anointing of God will be hindered and it will stop. There must be no hindrances. If God says "Do it," our reaction must be, "Where, and when, and how do I do it?"

"People began to pray. Throughout that hour of prayer, it became obvious that thousands of people needed to move to the Soviet Union. It was the biggest open door to the gospel that the Christian church had ever seen."

We scheduled another CoMission meeting in January. Paul Kienel agreed to host the meeting at the Association of Christian School International headquarters in La Habra, California. When Bruce asked what I thought about inviting other organizations to join us, I readily agreed.

The meeting opened on Thursday morning, January 23, 1992, with twenty-two ministries represented. Most of the attendees were presidents or held key leadership roles in their organizations. Among those attending were the presidents of Moody Bible Institute, Biola University, Child Evangelism Fellowship, and Worldteam. Leaders from Slavic Gospel, Focus on the Family, Multnomah Bible School, Columbia Bible College, US Center for World Missions, and many others also attended.

The goal of the meeting was to join together in a way that Christian leaders never had before. Typically, we compete. Sometimes we cooperate. This usually just means that I do my thing and you do your thing, and we don't get in each other's way. We've never come together as an army, to make it happen *together,* to do God's work in a united way. The biggest challenge was whether or not this was really possible. If this open door proved to be the largest in the history of the church, then this was the time we had to attempt that cohesion.

The first morning Bruce Wilkinson led the meeting.

"By the time this meeting is over," he said to those gathered, "we'll know if God is in this or not. No one will have to tell us. We'll all leave saying, 'God did it' or 'He didn't.'"

So the goal became the development of a brand new vision that none of us had exclusively, that not one of us owned. It had to be one where no one could say, "That's my vision. Come help me do my thing." Every one one of us had to be able to say, "This is our vision. We're going to do it *together.*"

The Thursday meeting was somewhat frustrating. Several people had already heard about the convocations and about some of the ideas we had. They kept asking, "What's the plan? What's the strategy? How are we going to do it?" They seemed to say, "I know you're going to lay some plan on us at any moment, and I am prepared to tell you what is wrong with it. And, no matter what you say, I will probably be against it." Yet another group of people just wanted to know how they might fit into whatever was ultimately decided.

Beyond a Plan or Strategy

"Don't worry about the plan," Bruce kept saying. "If we work on a plan, what will happen if the plan doesn't work? We'll all quit and say God wasn't in it. Plans change. It can't be a plan. It can't be a strategy. It has to be God doing something in our hearts, so that if the plan doesn't work, or the strategy fails, we still keep going."

We broke for the evening. Bruce and I sat in his room from 9:30 P.M. until 1:30 in the morning, talking and praying and trying to figure out what to do. We didn't know. The next morning we looked at the pattern of Nehemiah when he went back to Jerusalem to re-build the wall that had broken down. Before he went back, he first repented of his own sin.

As Bruce again led the meeting on Friday, he began, "In the past, sin is what has stopped Christian leaders like us from work-ing together. That's why we haven't done it. It's the will of God that we do this, so the world may see that we are one, and right now we're not one. What are the sins that have stopped us from working to-gether?" He went to the blackboard and began to list responses as they were called out from around the table. He filled a whole board. Arrogance. Independence. Pride. Love of money. Love of power. Ego. Turfdom. Afraid someone will steal our donors. On and on. The room became quiet, and the quiet was sobering.

"What we have to do now is repent," Bruce suggested. "Repen-tance is not a feeling; it is a choice. We choose to repent. I don't want you to close your eyes. I want you to look at that list on the board and pick out one that convicts you. I want you to confess it on your own behalf, and then on behalf of all of us. We're all guilty of most of these to a greater or lesser extent."

It was hard at first. Some perfunctory prayers were prayed. Then one man began to weep as he asked God to forgive him for his pride and arrogance—and repentance came like a flood over the room. There were no dry eyes. When the repentance was completed, we turned back to the example of Nehemiah. He had a burden.

Bruce cleaned off the board and we started again. We asked what the burdens of the Soviet people were. We asked how they were feel-ing at this time. It was not difficult to imagine. They felt betrayed by their leaders. Their dream was gone. They felt lied to and em-barrassed. They were not a world class power. Their economy was in shambles. Most of all, they had to be feeling hopelessness. We asked God to allow us to feel, just a little bit, what the Soviets must be feeling at this point in their history. We asked God to give us a little of their burden.

Then Bruce erased the board again and asked how God felt about the Soviets. He loves them. He is not willing that any should perish, but that they all should come to repentance. He sent Jesus to die for them. He cares. He grieves. He forgives. He keeps seeking.

Then we asked God to put His burden on our hearts. We prayed, and the peace of God began to fill us.

A GOD NOT OVERWHELMED

But several men in the room said they just felt overwhelmed. "When I look at the size of the Soviet Union," one said, "I feel like we can't do it at all. I feel like it's a black hole, and no matter how many resources we pour into it, we won't get anywhere."

"But when God looks at the task," Bruce interjected, "is He overwhelmed with it?"

"No."

"Whenever we have our eyes focused on the task, we'll always feel overwhelmed. Tell me a couple of things God has done in the Old or New Testament that will make this task look like nothing." The answers flew quickly from the floor.

"He created the world."

"He raised Christ from the dead."

"He led the Israelites across the Red Sea."

"He fed two million people in the wilderness."

Each time someone else said something, God got larger in our eyes. We forgot about the task and started focusing on God. When we saw the task through His eyes, our faith grew and our fear disappeared. We prayed again. We acknowledged on the basis of His omniscience and His omnipotence that this was not a big thing to Him. At this point, we were ready to work. As we broke for lunch, Paul Kienel, Bruce and I sat at a separate table.

"What do you think we should do now?" Bruce wondered.

I said, "I think we should ask them to send people over as workers for at least a year."

Bruce turned to Paul Kienel. "How many workers could ACSI send over the next year?"

Paul said, "I think we could send 100 couples a year for the next five years."

People Pledges

If we could conduct convocations in 150 cities, we would need 150 teams of ten to follow them up. We would need 1,500 people to go. When the meeting resumed after lunch, we challenged those who were there to make a commitment of how many they would send. We encouraged them not to give any number unless the Lord was prompting them. We began to total them on the board.

"ACSI pledges 200," from Paul Kienel.

"Child Evangelism Fellowship pledges 75."

"Walk Thru the Bible pledges 100."

"Worldteam pledges 10."

"Slavic Gospel pledges 40."

"Campus Crusade for Christ will try to send 240."

"Moody pledges 100."

Bruce interrupted his good friend, Joe Stowell: "Joe, don't forget that you have *Moody Magazine* and the radio network."

Joe said, "You're right. Moody pledges 100 students, and another 300 a year from the community at large."

And so it went. When we totaled it up a few minutes later, the organizations had committed to sending 1,280 people.

A few weeks later, the Navigators, who had been unable to attend the meeting, unanimously voted to send 400 a year for five years.

We checked with missions experts, and none could recall any time in the history of the Church where more than 800 missionaries had been sent out in one year. We would have to see what would happen.

THE COMISSION LAUNCHES OUT

The next meeting of the CoMission convened on the evening of March 30. It was held in an upstairs classroom in the new Moody Center for Evangelism at Moody Bible Institute in Chicago. As usual, we began by tracing the origins of the united vision and the fact that none of us currently involved had set out to organize something new. The next morning, when we went to the time of confession, it was a much larger group.

Bill Bright sat in the front row. John Corts, president of the Billy Graham Association, sat in the back on the left. Bill Gothard was seated near the front. Many other presidents of organizations and Christian Colleges were also in attendance.

Several men arrived late, missing the time of personal confession. When it came time to discuss the strategy, they vehemently opposed the course of action agreed on in the LaHabra meeting. They felt like everything needed to be done in and through the existing local church in the Soviet Union. They also felt that our stated objectives for the movement had to be church planting.

By the afternoon, we realized that things were not going well.

It was discouraging. I got up and explained that I had met with the church leaders in Russia, and they had encouraged us to go ahead. They had told me that the communists had not allowed them to go to college or seminary, thus, they lacked credibility to work within the educational system.

In my meeting with Grigori Kommendent, president of the Evangelical Baptist Federation, he had simply asked that we make the same materials that we were giving to secular schoolteachers available to the churches. He also asked that we devote time to the preparation of indigenous Russian leadership. I agreed that we would do both.

We were at an impasse. Some of the men were ready to walk out.

Bruce Wilkinson, who was leading the meeting at the time, said, "I don't know what the Lord would have us do. If the Lord is impressing one of you with a direction for us, please come up and speak." He put the chalk down with which he had been listing ideas on the blackboard, and took a seat in the audience.

No one was leading the meeting.

"We Cannot Let That Happen Again"

Then a man got up and slowly walked to the podium in front. It was Andrew Semenchuk, a long-time veteran of the Slavic Gospel Association and Russian Ministries. He was a big, bearish man with a deep voice and a warm smile.

"About seventy years ago," he began, "just after the Bolshevik Revolution, Russia was open briefly to the gospel. On this very block here in Chicago where we are meeting today, a group of mission leaders met to discuss the idea of working together to send missionaries to Russia. The meetings ended with no agreement, and the workers were not sent. Gentlemen, we cannot let that happen again."

Then Jerry Franks, who was seated in the second row, opened his Bible and read the passage from Acts 16:9,10:

"During the night Paul had a vision of a man of Macedonia standing and begging him. 'Come over to Macedonia and help us.' After Paul had seen the vision, we got ready at once to leave for Macedonia, concluding that God had called us to preach the gospel to them."

"I believe that's the situation we're in right now," Jerry observed, "except, we haven't needed a vision. We have been to Russia, and they have personally begged us to come. I believe our only choice is to do what the apostle Paul did: get ready to go at once, because we conclude that God is calling us go."

It was a turning point. We realized that not everyone might join in the CoMission. That was sad, and we began a series of side meetings to resolve some of those differences. But, we could not allow ourselves to be deterred by those who were not in favor of our course of action. We needed to get moving. And more than eighty organizations joined the movement. (A list may be found in Appendix 2.)

In the next day and a half, the fastest organizational developments took place that I have ever seen in my life. We divided those at the meeting into working committees that would develop all the policies and procedures which we would all abide by as a part of working together. Our original Executive Committee was expanded.

THE EXPANDED TEAM

Paul Kienel, headed up the School Curriculum Committee, and began developing a plan to help the Russians rewrite their textbooks, and to provide additional training for their teachers. Paul Johnson, a businessman from Detroit, headed up the Arrangements Committee, which was charged with finding the housing and equipment needed for all of the CoMissioners who would move overseas.

In the weeks that followed, others were added: John Kyle, president of Mission to the World, headed up Mobilization. This team would wrestle with the issues of how to recruit thousands of people to move to the Soviet Union for a year.

Terry Taylor, US president for the Navigators, took over the Training and Materials Committee. He and his colleagues would decide how the CoMissioners would be trained and what materials would be used.

Peter Deyneka, president of Russian Ministries, would be our liaison with everything going on in the Soviet Union. Mary Lance Sisk, a businesswoman from Charlotte, North Carolina, headed up our prayer effort. Joe Stowell, president of Moody Bible Institute, cocoordinated our relations with the Russian Church.

J. B. Crouse, president of OMS, International, was in charge of those in other countries who wanted to cooperate in sending people to work with the CoMission in the Soviet Union.

School administrator Margaret Bridges joined the Executive Committee as Chairwoman of the Christian Cultural Exchange Committee. Ralph Plumb, president of International Aid, became our Chairman of the Relief and Development Committee.

I served as vice-chairman of the Executive Committee and headed up the Sending Organizations Committee. Our job was to determine the logistics of how all of the workers would actually get over there.

During the next thirty-six hours, a host of decisions was made. None of us believed the door of opportunity in the Soviet Union would stay open long; therefore, we realized we'd better not quibble about policies and procedures. We had better just get on with the task as quickly as possible.

The amazing story of the CoMission continued, of course, but I will leave it to my colleagues on the CoMission Executive Committee to continue the narrative. There is no doubt in my mind that the open door to Russia and the ministry of the CoMission has become one of the truly great experiences of my life. I'll always be grateful for the privilege of seeing God do the impossible, not only in the former Soviet Union, but also in bringing together such a diverse group of people and organizations to accomplish His purposes.

FROM WALL OF ATHEISM TO WILL OF THE LORD

Russia, 1998:

"I am an atheist and a Communist Party member. Here is my Communist Party pin. Communism did not fail Russia, the Russian people failed communism," spoke Katya before abruptly sitting down. I glanced at her. This was our small group's first sharing time. Katya was in her mid-thirties, outspoken, and already presenting our group leader quite a challenge.

All seemed to be going smoothly until Katya spoke. Each of the other members shared why they had come. One rather distinguished gentleman sitting close by stood and said that he was the head of a major training center and was delighted to be there to learn of the latest teaching techniques in the west.

Although Katya's statement was an abrupt start, each of the participants, including Katya, actively took part in the lessons. As the convocation proceeded, each of the participants heard the personal faith stories of several believers. They also heard accurate and sound explanations on the validity of a Christian worldview, watched the JESUS film, and discussed their specific questions.

During this time I wondered about Katya. What was she thinking, regarding the many presentations and the literature? The time slipped by quickly, and soon it was our final day together.

On this last day, each of the members of the small group had an opportunity to express what the convocation meant personally. The gentleman who was head of a major training center stood and spoke, "I have a new mission in life. I have become a Christian. Now I want to see believing teachers go to every school district in my country."

Another member stood up and said in a soft-spoken voice, "Many people have done things for me in my life." She mentioned her mother and a dear friend. "But," she continued, "no one has done what you have done for me. You have given me eternal life. Thank you." It was difficult to choke back the tears.

Then it was Katya's turn. She stood and looked at each of us.

In a somewhat quiet voice, she said, "I must tell you that last night I became a Christian. I am a believer. Today I stand before you and I renounce atheism and I renounce communism."

She reached down, removed her Communist Party pin and handed it to the group leader. Katya stood with poise and declared, "You can hold me accountable. Before school begins next year, I will share the Jesus I have come to know with one hundred of my students."

PRINCIPLE
FIVE

DO THE WORK UNDER A NEUTRAL BANNER.

Wherever we were doing CoMission work, we took off our "agency hats" and put on "CoMission hats." This meant we did not take our organizations' "agendas" to the CoMission, but rather that we left them at the door to serve the whole of CoMission. This allowed us to operate in a spirit of unity and purpose.

Dr. PAUL KIENEL, author of six books on Christian
school education, is the founder and president emeritus
of the Association of Christian Schools International.
ACSI is the largest Christian school organization in the
world. Dr. Kienel is one of two founders of the Evangelical Christian Credit Union that provides financial services to a wide range of evangelical ministries. One of
the founders of the CoMission, he served with Paul
Eshleman as co-vice-chairman of the CoMission Executive Committee. Paul and his wife, Annie, live in La
Quinta, California. They have three grown children and
seven grandchildren.

CHAPTER THREE

THE PUBLIC LAUNCH

School Textbook/Curriculum Redesign Committee

Dr. Paul A. Kienel, committee chairman and co-vice chairman of the CoMission Executive Committee

THE HISTORY OF things is important. One hundred years before Christ, Cicero, Rome's foremost thinker, underlined history's importance when he said, "Not to know what took place before you were born is to remain forever a child."

But how can historical events, religious or otherwise, be studied and learned by future generations unless written down by those who experienced them? This question was driven home to the members of the CoMission Executive Committee when one of our committee members, Peter Deyneka, passed to his eternal reward in December 2000. His passing jolted us to the reality that we, the remaining members, will in time, one by one, pass off the scene, potentially leaving the amazing story of the CoMission lost to posterity.

How important is the story of the CoMission? I believe very important, because of its uniqueness in the annals of Christian ministry. It is unique in the following ways:

UNIQUE DOOR OF OPPORTUNITY: After seventy years of atheistic communism, Russia, "a nation of 300 million people, blinking in the light of newly found freedom," as one observer put it, in 1991 became fully aware of her spiritual void and officially invited Western Christians to assist the Russian people in finding Christ, as their grandparents had known Him earlier in the twentieth century.

UNIQUE RESPONSE: The initial break-up of the hardened spiritual subsoil of Russia came through when the simple presentation of Christ's life and message, drawn from of the Gospel of Luke in the form of the *JESUS* film, was shown in theaters throughout the former Soviet Union by Paul Eshleman and his colleagues in Campus Crusade for Christ International. This ultimately led to the formation of the CoMission, initiated by Bruce Wilkinson, president of Walk Thru the Bible, Paul Eshleman, director of The JESUS Film Project, and myself. It quickly became evident to the three of us that the magnitude of the opportunity required a much larger response than our three organizations could possibly provide. In short order, we expanded the Executive Committee and invited a wide range of evangelical organizations, large and small, to join the CoMission. What began with three organizations in October 1991, quickly grew to include eighty-two parachurch groups, mission agencies, local churches, denominations, educational organizations and institutions, foundations and relief agencies. As far as we know, this unique coming together as a noncorporate organization, laying aside individual ministry agendas to work together to train and send thousands of Christians to minister in a former communist country, is a first in the history of the Church, at least on the scale of what the CoMission ultimately became.

UNIQUE HARVEST: Many came to Christ through the ministry of the CoMission, but without question, the greatest spiritual harvest occurred among educators in the former Soviet Union. Many of them were well trained, gifted leaders. To a large degree, they represented the intelligentsia of Russia.

Standing in sharp contrast to America's departure from Bible-based education in her public schools, we have these interesting words from Russia's Minister of Education, Dr. Eduard Druprov. He said, "Worldwide educational reform may actually spread from Russia, which is setting the stage and pattern for a return to moral Bible values in schools." Today in Russia it is permissible to teach the Bible in the schools, provided no one church is advocated. Would that it were it so in the US!

The history of the CoMission is important because it documents the fact that evangelical Christians can, indeed, work together, when working together is essential for success. The unique five-year commitment of the CoMission demonstrates that Christian organizations can partner together to accomplish what none could achieve alone. It is amazing what occurred under the CoMission motto: "Let's see what we can do for the cause of Christ in the former Soviet Union, and let's not care who gets the credit."

HOW IT BEGAN FROM MY PERSPECTIVE

Permit me to tell you about the man who laid the groundwork for my involvement with the CoMission: Jerry Franks. He is a godly entrepreneurial businessman who time and again throughout the five-year life of the CoMission was willing to set aside his duties as a US business leader to go to Russia with his wife, Karen. They lived there, working behind the scenes to advance the cause of Campus Crusade and The JESUS Film Project, and later the cause of the CoMission. When it became clear to Paul Eshleman and Jerry Franks that professional teachers were needed as trainers for the four-day teacher convocations in Russia, Jerry remembered an educators' convention he had attended in Ohio, when he served as the superintendent of Cuyahoga Valley Christian Academy in Cuyahoga Falls, Ohio. He knew that the convention's sponsor, the Association of Christian Schools International (ACSI), held similar conventions for thousands of Christian school educators across the US and in other countries.

In 1991, ACSI held the first conference for Christian teachers ever held behind the Iron Curtain. This conference, held in Timisoara, Romania, drew more than 300 Christian teachers that God had wondrously and miraculously preserved during forty years of harsh communist rule. Learning of the conference in Romania, Jerry Franks invited two officials from Russia's Ministry of Education to attend. Thankfully, they accepted the invitation and traveled by train from Moscow to Timisoara. The two officials were Dr. Alexei Brudnov, chairman of the Department of Alternative Education, responsible for training children in communist ideology in 65,000 Pioneer Palaces; and Dr. Olga Polykovskaya, Education Specialist for Moral and Ethics Curriculum for Russia's public schools. Both were members of the Communist Party. Dr. Brudnov had worked for the Central Committee of the Party. Both Russian officials were impressed with the two-day meeting. Dr. Philip Renicks, ACSI's vice-president of International Ministries, was in charge of the Timisoara conference. Both Russian officials were impressed with the two-day meeting. Dr. Renicks met with Dr. Brudnov after the conference. Of that encounter, Dr. Renicks wrote:

> At the close of the conference, Dr. Brudnov asked if he could meet with me. As we sat at a park bench working through a translator, he began to express his desire to have a conference just like this one for his teachers in the government schools of Russia. His rationale for the request was that for two generations they were a country that had forgotten God. He said, "As a result there are great chasms that run underneath all of our society. If we don't put God back into our society, it will collapse."
>
> I had told Dr. Brudnov that it would be impossible for such a conference to occur in Russia because his teachers didn't embrace the same values as the Christian teachers in Romania. He pondered that thought for a moment, then said, "Then come and make them all Christians."

Both officials, Brudnov and Polykovskaya, would soon play a significant role in God's plan for Russia. And best of all, both became strong believers in Jesus Christ! Jerry Franks was a godly example to both officials and to many others as well.

In July 1991, Jerry sent a four-page fax from Moscow to Phil Renicks at the ACSI headquarters, then located in California. The fax was an invitation to participate in two four-day convocations for Russian public school teachers and administrators. A portion of his fax to Phil Renicks follows:

> *Dear Phil:*
>
> *Thank you for the many courtesies extended to the Russian delegation at the Timisoara conference. Our delegates were very favorably impressed and grateful for the opportunities to interact with you and many of the capable staff.*
>
> *Mr. Brudnov is very interested in having conferences (or convocations, as he calls them), for his staff of 200,000, to train them to communicate Christian values to their students.*

Jerry Franks then described the excellent response to the first convocations, and then invited the Association of Christian Schools to send teachers to participate in the convocations and the follow-up program that would later be coordinated by the end of the CoMission:

> *Phil, these people are very committed to learning the truth and communicating it to their students. Even those who do not make a commitment to Christ say, "Our children need to know these things so that they can make a choice."*
>
> *Our next convocation is in Pushkin (near Leningrad), November 18–22, 1991, and will be followed the next week by a conference in Novgorod.*
>
> *Our sincere desire is that ACSI consider being represented at these two conferences to provide expertise on Christian education. Further discussions on the specific subjects and staff will be necessary after you have determined the receptivity of your board to this request.*
>
> *I believe that there is a major role for ACSI in the area of teacher training for Christian education. Each conference we hold creates a significant group of teachers in that city who have a sin-*

*cere desire to learn how to communicate Christian truth in all areas
to their students. ACSI has the expertise to train these teachers how
to do that better than any other ministry. Please ask your board to
pray about helping 21 million young people understand God's truth
through participation with us in follow-up training programs.*

*On the third of July, my wife and I were in the office of the may-
or of Pushkin to discuss the upcoming convocation with him and the
education committee, which is sponsoring the event. After I had described the Christian nature and content of the convocation, he said,
"You have come at an interesting time in our history. We are in a
post-revolution era. The ideas of the revolution no longer motivate
our people, and we are searching for ideas that provide inner motivation; perhaps Christian ideas are the ones we need."*

*Indeed, the leverage of opportunity goes beyond the governmen-
tal endorsement to the very void which men feel when they do not
know God and are disillusioned with all of life. It is truly a leverage
of timing: the filling of a vacuum which has been created by their
Creator and can only be filled by Jesus Christ. Please help us if you
can.*

What Jerry Franks did not know was that his now famous four-
page fax arrived at the ACSI headquarters in the middle of an ACSI
board meeting. I quickly made copies of it and distributed it to the
members of the board. After a brief discussion, the board approved
our participation in this amazing door of opportunity in the former Soviet Union.

Phil Renicks, Jim Braley, Henry Toews and myself were the first
from ACSI to participate in the Teacher Convocations that would ultimately span the eleven time zones of Russia and her republics.

If I live to be a hundred years old, I will never forget the many
evidences of God's grace in the lives of the Russian educators who
attended the convocation in Pushkin. My friend, Dr. Bruce Wilkinson, was the principal speaker. The response cards told us nearly half
had received Christ as their personal Savior by the end of the conference. My ACSI colleagues and I were responsible for the administrators' track during the breakout sessions. (There were other tracks

for elementary and secondary teachers.) Each of us was given twenty Russian administrators, along with a translator, for our small-group sessions.

When I met with my group for the first time, it was clear to me that one female administrator had assumed the role of spokesperson for the others. She was a jovial person, full of humor; I suspected the laughter she engendered among the group was at my expense. She made it clear to me through Igor, my interpreter, that they were all communists and atheists. What a way to start!

We talked about typical administrative problems common to school leaders worldwide. We talked about the changes they were facing in their schools. I must confess, I was impressed with them. It wasn't long before I realized how brilliant, well-educated and professional they were.

As we neared the end of the conference, I directed our discussions toward things spiritual. Much to my delight, they seemed anxious to talk about the basics of Christianity. In our final session I said, "We have been here four days. You have heard the message of Christ presented in a variety of ways. May I ask how many of you have received Christ as your Savior?" To my amazement and to my great pleasure, the woman who had made it clear at the outset that they were all communists and atheists stood up, and, with tears streaming down her face, said, "We have all become Christians!" Only God knows the accuracy of her remarkable declaration, but I know as we parted there were no dry eyes among us, including mine.

With experiences like these, it is little wonder that North American Christians who went to Russia as participants in the teacher/administrator convocations or served on year-long assignments as follow-up CoMissioners were deeply impacted spiritually. Most claimed their lives would never be the same again.

THE PUBLIC LAUNCH OF THE COMISSION

There were numerous high moments in the five-year life of the CoMission that will remain etched in my memory. I will never forget, for example, the secret baptism of Dr. Olga Polykovskaya; nor will I forget the safe landing of the charter flight from Odessa to Moscow in the rickety thirty-five-year-old Russian plane with the CoMission Executive Committee members and their spouses on board. And then there was the great news that Dr. Alexei Brudnov at the Russian Ministry of Education had received Christ, and publicly gave his testimony in Moscow.

The event, however, that stands out most dramatically in my mind was the public launch of the CoMission on November 2, 1992, in Anaheim, California. At that point only seven of twelve members of the CoMission Executive Committee had been selected, namely: Bruce Wilkinson, Paul Eshleman, Paul Kienel, Peter Deyneka, Paul Johnson, Joseph Stowell and Terry Taylor. The remaining five members— Margaret Bridges, J.B. Crouse, Mary Lance Sisk, John Kyle and Ralph Plumb—joined us soon after the public launch of the CoMission.

Press conference at the CoMission public launch during the ACSI convention. l. to r. Peter Deyneka, Bruce Wilkinson, Terry Taylor, Paul Johnson, Paul Eshleman, Paul Kienel

It became clear to the committee that a large-exposure media event was needed to help attract Christian volunteers to go to Russia. As the Executive Director of the Association of Christian Schools

International, I invited the CoMission Executive Committee to consider launching the CoMission media event in conjunction with the 42nd Annual Southern California Teachers Convention at the Anaheim Convention Center.

There were three reasons why this idea was readily accepted: (1) Bruce Wilkinson, our CoMission chairman, had already been selected to be the main speaker for the two-day convention. It would be easy for him to weave the challenge of the CoMission into his remarks; (2) The convention, the largest of twenty-three ACSI teacher conventions, provided an audience of 8,000 attendees; and (3) I had already invited four officials from Russia's Ministry of Education to participate as our special guests at the Anaheim convention. It was indeed an ideal setting for the public launch of the CoMission. Ideal as it was, we had no idea if members of the various press agencies would show up, nor did we know what the Russian officials would say to our audience and to the press.

Our Russian Guests

Like so many times during the CoMission, the Lord Himself went before us and opened doors that were beyond our abilities to open. That fact was evident in my invitation to the four Russian officials. Given their responsibilities in the Russian government, it was nothing short of amazing that they were available at the precise time we needed them in November 1992. In addition to their responsibilities in the Ministry of Education, they had ongoing duties in Russia's governing body, the *Duma*. Before I describe the public launch of the CoMission at the ACSI convention permit me to introduce them to you.

ALEKSANDR ASMOLOV. The foremost leader among the Russian guests was Dr. Aleksandr Asmolov, Deputy Minister of Education, considered Russia's leading psychologist, and he was a gifted public speaker and writer. The CoMission Executive Committee met with him a number of times in his office in Moscow. He, like the other three guests, had been a member of the Communist Party during the communist period. There is no question in my mind that he will continue to be an important political figure in Russia.

ALEXEI BRUDNOV. Dr. Alexei Brudnov, whom we met earlier in this chapter, was at that time the chairman of Russia's extensive program to indoctrinate Russian children in communist ideology. His program, carried out through Russia's Pioneer Palaces, an elaborate youth camp system, was, most likely, the world's most efficient children's indoctrination program in all of human history. Dr. Brudnov's Department of Alternative Education was the engine that drove communist ideology throughout the eleven time zones of the former Soviet Union.

The fact that Alexei Brudnov, in the last year of the CoMission, wholeheartedly gave his life over to Jesus Christ is one of the greatest miracles of God's grace I have ever seen. This former communist leader is now my brother in Christ! I must confess to you I am experiencing a few tears as I write about him. My emotions are stirred further knowing that Alexei Brudnov died suddenly of a heart attack in July 1999. The good news is that this former atheist is now and forever in the arms of the Savior of the world. I truly look forward to our reunion one day.

OLGA POLYKOVSKAYA. Dr. Olga Polykovskaya is another trophy of God's grace. Olga came to faith in Christ from reading a Bible given to her by an American visitor to the Ministry of Education in Moscow. She does not recall who the visitor was. Like many Russians, Olga's grandmother was a Christian who clandestinely read the Bible to her when she was a child.

In 1975, Olga Polykovskaya (now Lutsenko) graduated from Moscow State Gumanitarian University with a degree in history and became a high school history teacher in Moscow. She soon advanced up through the ranks and became a vice-principal and then principal of the school. To hold these positions of authority, it was necessary for Olga to join the Communist Party. She passed the exam on the history of the Communist Party, and then obtained two personal recommendations. The Party membership committee quickly approved her membership.

Upon completion of her Ph.D. in Russian International Relations in 1987, Olga was invited to become a member of Russia's prestigious Academy of Pedagogical Science, the brain trust for the Ministry of Education. It is also the center for curriculum development for Russia's school system.

When the communist government collapsed in August 1991, Dr. Dneprov, a professor at the Academy of Pedagogical Science, was appointed by Russia's Mikhail Gorbachev as the first Minister of Education in the noncommunist era. Having worked with Olga at the Academy of Pedagogical Science, Dneprov appointed her as his specialist for moral and ethics curriculum. "Now that communism is gone," Olga asked Dneprov, "what kind of morality will be acceptable?" He replied, "I don't know. You figure it out."

So Olga, the historian educator, did the educator thing and formed a committee made up of her scholarly friends from the Academy of Pedagogical Science. They, of course, knew the history of the Russian alphabet, how it had been created by two monks, Kirill and Mephodi, in Moravia (now Hungary) in the 9th century at the bidding of Slavic Prince Rostislov. In defiance of the Catholic Church, they translated the Bible into the Slavic language and established schools for Slavs so they could read the Bible for themselves. From the 10th century on, the Slavonic alphabet made its way to Russia and became the written language of the Russian people.

Since literacy had come to Russia through the translation of the Bible, the committee recommended that the Bible be accepted as the moral base for Russian education. Amazingly, the committee's recommendation was approved by the Ministry of Education and by the Russian *Duma*.

As Olga's faith grew, she expressed to me that she wanted to be baptized in an evangelical church in the United States. She made it clear that her conversion to Christ and any future baptism must be held in strict confidence or she would lose her position with the Ministry of Education. Olga has since given us her permission to share the following details of her water baptism. My wife, Annie, and I met with our pastor and his wife in Colorado Springs, Colorado, and explained the situation. Pastor Towell agreed to the unusual baptism and set the date for August 26, 1994, a date previously agreed to by Olga.

When Olga arrived in Colorado Springs from Moscow, we went immediately to Living Springs Church for an event the press would have loved to cover. The only observers of this mid-week, mid-morning baptism of this Russian official were my wife Annie, Mrs. Towell, and myself. Pastor Towell handled the occasion beautifully. Prior to the baptism, Pastor Towell, to make sure of Olga's conversion, led her through the sinner's prayer and then explained in detail the significance of water baptism. Olga was deeply moved by all the pastor said.

After prayers in the pastor's study, we went to the sanctuary for the baptism. With only three seated in the center section of that large sanctuary, we were fully aware that we may have been setting a record for small attendance at a baptism, but we were also aware of the hosts of heaven who were rejoicing that Olga Polykovskaya, an official from the Russian government and a former member of the Communist Party, was now a member of the family of God. Of this event Olga says:

> I will never forget this special day in all my life, from the moment I woke up until late night. I can tell you even now (eight years later) the color of the sky, the colors of the church room where we met. I even remember the furniture. I recall the friendly faces of Pastor and Mrs. Towell and Paul and Annie Kienel. I remember the questions the pastor asked me, and my answers. I remember the tears of joy in everyone's eyes. It seemed that Christ was standing right next to me through the entire baptism.

Space does not allow me to describe the many ways Olga assisted the ministry of the CoMission in Russia and in the United States.

ALEKSANDR ABRAMOV. At the request of Peter Deyneka, president of Russian Ministries and member of our CoMission Executive Committee, I included Dr. Alexandr Abramov in my invitation to Russian officials. While Dr. Abramov was not an official with the Ministry of Education, he was, indeed, a significant part of Russia's education establishment. As the director of the Moscow Institute for Development of Educational Systems, he was responsible for publishing textbooks for Russian schools. As the CoMission's chairman of the Curriculum Redesign Committee for Russian Textbooks, I was interested in working along side of Dr. Abramov.

As we will learn later, that part of our mission did not materialize, largely due to a lack of finances to carry it out.

THE MEMORABLE OPENING SESSION

With those introductions, permit me to describe the launch of the CoMission at the opening session of the 42nd Annual ACSI Teachers' Convention, held in the large oval arena in the Anaheim Convention Center on November 5, 1992. After a rousing band rendition of our National Anthem, I introduced the four Russian leaders with these words:

> *Ladies and gentlemen, it is my happy privilege to welcome to our 42nd Annual Convention our four Russian guests from the former Soviet Union, now known as The Commonwealth of Independent States. They arrived at the Los Angeles Airport from Moscow last Sunday afternoon. Since then it has been my privilege to be their host.*
>
> *Our guests are being escorted to the platform today by three young flag bearers carrying the American, Christian, and Russian flags, and flanked by sixteen young ladies representing the homecoming courts of three Christian high schools. And so now, ladies and gentlemen, I present to you:*
>
> *Dr. Olga Polykovskaya*
> *Dr. Aleksandr Asmolov*
> *Dr. Alexei Brudnov*
> *Dr. Aleksandr Abramov*
> *Please let them know they are welcome in the USA!*

Bruce Wilkinson describes the scene as the Russians made their way down through the audience toward the platform:

> *Who can ever forget the thundering applause and standing ovation by 8,000 American teachers as those four Russian delegates nobly strode down the center aisle of the Anaheim Convention Center behind the American, Russian, and Christian flags?*

Russian education officials speak at ACSI convention, November 1992. l. to r. Drs. Olga Polykovskaya, Alesandr Asmolov, Alexei Brudnov, and Alexandr Abramov.

Each of the four Russians spoke briefly at the four general sessions of the two-day convention. Dr. Olga Polykovskaya spoke first. Peter Deyneka, president of Russian Ministries, served as her interpreter. She said:

> *Dear Friends, I love you. I invite you to come to Russia to help us— our students, our teachers, the parents—as as we work together in the area of Christian education.* [Then, in English, she said]: *Thank you for your helpness—very much.*

Bruce Wilkinson says, "Olga was magnificent!" The vigorous applause of 8,037 Christian educators clearly affirmed his words. Olga's brief but powerfully delivered invitation to come to help Russia's public school teachers teach their students the principles of Christian education was strong evidence that the long cold war between Russia and the United States was over.

Prior to the public launch of the CoMission in Anaheim, the CoMission Executive Committee had hired the services of the Walter Bennett Public Relations Agency to invite the press to the event. Not only did the Walter Bennett people succeed with their assignment, but they won a major award (the De-Rose-Hinkhouse Award of Merit for a national media campaign) for the CoMission launch. Because of their efforts, more than 15 million people heard or read about the great cause of the CoMission.

After the opening general session, the Walter Bennett staff had arranged for a press conference with the four Russian guests and the CoMission Executive Committee. Dr. Aleksandr Asmolov led off with a statement that somewhat startled the press. Through the interpreter, Sophia Manikova, he said:

> I want to emphasize today that Russian education is open for Christian values. And it is a miracle that the Christianity of the United States is going to help their brothers in Russia. I want you to realize that the people who go to Russia can make a heroic deed.

A reporter for the United Press International Radio Network asked, "Is there some irony here that what you are doing in Russia is actually illegal here in the United States?"

Bruce Wilkinson answered:

> Yes it is. It is very ironic that these issues are against the law in our own country—to pray, to post the Ten Commandments on the walls. Yet, the Russians, who were not allowed to pray and teach Christian morality under communism, are now saying, "That flat out did not work."

The next reporter, a bit arrogant in his manner, asked the Russians this cynical question: "Are you concerned or are you comfortable with the fact that the CoMission is made up of a fairly small group on the spectrum of American religious life?" To which Dr. Asmolov quickly responded:

> I want to answer your question. When a person is in a waterfall and he wants to save his life, and when he sees a hand extended to him for help, can he think, 'Whose hand is that?' He will accept the hand which is first. The first hand was of the CoMission.

Dr. Asmolov's answer was excellent, and the reporter looked a bit stunned by it. Had it not been impolite, the Executive Committee members would have applauded. After numerous other questions from the bank of reporters, our capable chairman, Bruce Wilkinson, said the following to our Russian guests:

> We appreciate your words. And we do take seriously your invitation. We fully realize the significance of it. Our hearts are with you, and a lot more than our hearts. We're coming. We're coming to help.

THE WATERFALL VIDEO

The CoMission produced a number of excellent videos promoting the many opportunities for serving God in the former Soviet Union. I believe the video we called "The Waterfall," featuring the launch of the CoMission and the press conference with our four Russian guests, was the most memorable. The promotional videos were shown thousands of times in many venues, promoting the noble cause of the CoMission.

BREAKING NEW GROUND

As I mentioned at the beginning of this chapter, almost everything about the CoMission was breaking new ground. Permit me to list some of the features of the CoMission that were uncommon in the annals of Christian missions. I know my fellow members of the CoMission Executive Committee would want me to make it clear that any creativity or innovations in the structure or operation of the CoMission were not due to our collective cleverness, but rather to God's intervention, working through twelve individuals who were desperate for His direction.

With that in mind, and with the understanding that what I think is innovative may not be particularly innovative at all, I present my list. A list of these unique elements would include:

1. **The CoMission was a noncorporate, nonorganization organization.**

In fact it was not an organization at all. Paul Johnson, in his excellent chapter, points out that the CoMission was, "An affiliation of existing organizations banded together to accomplish a certain task and for a limited time, five years." More than anything else the CoMission was a cooperative with no central authority, no corporate headquarters and no centralized bank account. Monies were raised through the cooperating ministries and spent through those ministries. Operating policies were established by the CoMission Executive Committee, but the ultimate decision to cooperate or not cooperate was up to the corporate heads of each participating organization. When one looks at the nonstructure of the CoMission, it is amazing that it worked so well. Throughout the five-year life of the CoMission, not one of the eighty-two member organizations withdrew its membership, nor were there any resignations from the CoMission Executive Committee. In fact, the Executive Committee members and their spouses still meet once a year for fellowship and to recount God's rich blessing.

2. The CoMission responded to a unique door of opportunity unprecedented in human history.

That sounds like an overstatement, but when have you heard of a delegation from a foreign government coming to a large body of evangelical believers in the US or in any other country, as did the Russians in 1992, and inviting them in the presence of national and international media representatives to come and train their public school teachers in Christian ethics and morality? As far as we know, no invitation quite like it has ever been offered before. The great psalmist David says that it takes the training of only one generation for a nation to turn back to God. David writes:

> He decreed statutes for Jacob and established the law in Israel,
> which He commanded our forefathers to teach their children, so the
> next generation would know them, even the children yet to be
> born, and they in turn would tell their children. Then they would

put their trust in God and would not forget His deeds but would keep His commands (Psalm 78:5-7).

I shudder to think how sad the heart of God would have been had we not responded to Dr. Asmolov, who said to us and to the press in Anaheim:, "I want to emphasize today that Russian education is open for Christian values." Thankfully, thousands of Russian teachers and their students are born again believers at this very moment because we stepped forward and worked side by side with fellow believers from eighty-two ministry organizations to answer the amazing call of Russian leaders.

3. Lengthy prayers of repentance and prayers searching for God's direction were common at CoMission meetings.

Every great mission blessed by God is characterized by extensive prayer. There were, however, two aspects of prayer at CoMission meetings that I felt truly touched the heart of God. Under the strong spiritual leadership of our chairman, Dr. Bruce Wilkinson, our lengthy prayer sessions began with individual and corporate prayers of repentance. Bruce rightfully believed that unless we sought God's forgiveness for our sins and approached Him with pure hearts, God could not bless the work of the CoMission. We confessed to God and to each other personal sins and corporate sins. We confessed sins of "turf protectionism," sins of not respecting one another, and sins of not working together to build Christ's great body of believers around the world. We also prayed extensively for the Russian people, many of whom, we learned, felt embarrassed by all that happened during the long communist era. In some meetings, we spent as much or more time in prayer as we spent in matters of business. Consequently, I can honestly say that the five years of the CoMission were one of the great spiritual experiences of my life.

MARY LANCE SISK AND THE PRAYER COMMITTEE

One of the best decisions we made as the Executive Committee was to bring Mary Lance Sisk on as Prayer Chairman. Quite frankly, when Mary Lance Sisk prays, the room shakes. I had no idea that Presbyterians could pray like that! My wife, Annie, was a member of her prayer committee. On one occasion, I traveled to St. Petersburg and Pushkin, Russia, with Annie and the committee. In addition to a two-day prayer conference involving local Russian Christians, Mary Lance Sisk led us on a prayer walk in St. Petersburg and Pushkin. It was a first for me, but I must confess I felt God honored it. In fact, from the time Mary Lance Sisk joined our Executive Committee, the spiritual victories of the CoMission multiplied. I am convinced a strong emphasis on prayer by pure-hearted people makes all the difference in the world.

THE UPS AND DOWNS OF THE CURRICULUM REDESIGN COMMITTEE

When the long night of communist rule in Russia came to an end in 1991, Russian educators were faced with a dilemma. Their grade-level textbooks were suddenly obsolete! On December 10, 1991, Elizabeth Shogren wrote the following for the readers of the *Los Angeles Times:*

Branislava S. Fridman has been teaching history to Moscow school children for 41 years, but these days she has to spend three hours a night preparing her lessons.

That's because much of what she used to teach now looks more like fiction than history. And Fridman, along with so many other teachers, is searching for the truth.

"My students don't really have any heroes from our past because so many of their childhood heroes have turned out to be false heroes."

The dilemma faced by Branislava Fridman and her obsolete textbooks presented a unique opportunity for the CoMission. If somehow we could raise the millions of dollars necessary to assist the Russians to rewrite their elementary and secondary textbooks, we could, in one generation, replace communist ideology with Christian values.

The first ray of hope for the Curriculum Redesign Committee came to us at the public launch of the CoMission. Before Bruce

Wilkinson spoke in that opening session, he presented us with a check for $56,000 that had been given to the CoMission's Curriculum Redesign project from a generous anonymous donor. It was a great beginning!

On January 7, 1993, we convened the first meeting of our committee at the CoMission Pastors and Christian Leaders Conference in Phoenix, Arizona. We brought together an impressive array of capable people: Dr. Sharon Berry, Dr. Ellen Black, Dr. James Braley, Dr. Blair Cook, Jerry Franks, Dr. Gene Garrick, Dr. Ollie Gibbs, Dr. Loreen Itterman, Curt Mackey, Dr. Olga Polykovskaya and Vernie Schorr.

On April 14-16, 1993, we sent the first team from our committee to Moscow to assess the feasibility of developing a curriculum that was accurate and culturally sensitive for the 150 school districts of the former Soviet Union. Our team members, Drs. Black, Braley, Gibbs and Itterman, met with high-level Russian educators and were received with enthusiasm. After many hours of discussion through our capable interpreters, Ray and Cindy LeClair, it was decided that the new curriculum should initially be limited to forms (grades) 1, 2 and 3, and should include poetry and illustrations from Russian life. It was also determined that a teacher's manual and special teacher training sessions would be necessary. A total of five trips were made to Russia in preparation for the writing phase of the project.

The long process of grade-level writing got underway. It soon became clear the cost of production and printing of a project of this magnitude would require several million dollars. Consequently, a vigorous effort was made to raise funds through foundations, but to no avail.

In November of 1994, we thought we had the breakthrough we were looking for. At our Annual CoMission Executive Committee luncheon in Moscow with Ministry of Education officials, Dr. Asmolov handed Bruce Wilkinson an elaborate, copyrighted, beautifully bound proposal from the Transworld Mission Communication, Ltd., to print "schoolbooks for Russia" with a proposed budget of $21,500,000. Dr. Asmolov said he would agree to the project if the CoMission would provide oversight. Bruce assigned Peter Deyneka and myself to look further into this "too good to be true" opportunity.

At the request of Dr. Johannes Reimer from Germany, several members of the CoMission Executive Committee met with him at the ACSI Headquarters in Colorado Springs. As the meeting progressed, it soon became evident that it was up to us to raise the funds!

Just a portion of the first shipment of student school supplies provided by Christian school students in the US, Dr. Paul Kienel and Mark Webb.

With no funds in sight for production and printing of the new curriculum, the project was put on hold. Approximately $20,000 was left over from the gift given to our committee in Anaheim. After consulting with Bruce Wilkinson, these funds were used to translate Christian books for distribution at Russian teacher conventions—a very worthy project.

It is still our prayer that in the Lord's time, the door will open to make possible this noble cause.

CONCLUSION

The CoMission Executive Committee, throughout its five-year tenure, held numerous public meetings across the country to share the vision of the CoMission. These meetings were a key to the amazing growth we experienced. Bruce Wilkinson's exceptional leadership of these two-day events was inspiring to all of us.

Brief reports from each member of the CoMission Executive Committee were a part of the program. I always began my report with these words: "I am amazed that Bruce Wilkinson allows me to say anything at these meetings, because I have all the charisma of a speed bump!" It was meant to be humorous, and it always evoked laughter. Thankfully, Bruce and the other dynamic leaders on the CoMission executive committee overlooked my lack of charisma and through each of us the Lord accomplished His great purpose for the CoMission. To God be the glory!

IN HUMAN WEAKNESS, GOD REVEALS STRENGTH

Arkhangelsk, 2001:

Had it not all been a dismal failure? I wondered on the last night of the conference in Arkhangelsk.

I began the evening wondering whether my limited time with the small group of teachers was effective. Had I been able to communicate properly to them the concepts of Bible study and small-group interaction? Having to work through an interpreter had only made my task more frustrating.

We opened the Greatest Promise booklets. Each teacher began reading the Russian booklet, as I led them using my English version. The teachers were whispering among themselves instead of following along with me. The interpreter quickly helped me understand the problem.

The teachers kept turning back to the page with the picture of Jesus nailed to the cross. The text explains that Jesus was taking the punishment for their sins.

Helen, one of the teachers in the group, asked, "Why did Jesus have to suffer so? Why would God allow such a horrible death to be administered to His Son?" I realized that in my haste to get to the end of the booklet, I didn't give them the answers to the vital questions they wanted resolved. Some of the participants began to weep as they considered the answers for the first time.

As we spoke with one another, it gradually dawned on them what we had discussed every evening for nearly two weeks. In a spontaneous and heartfelt moment on this last evening, many of the group said they finally understood the meaning of the Christian message. Without hesitation, they all said they would continue to pursue a relationship with God and seek a better understanding of Christianity through Bible study.

God was accomplishing great things in the lives of these teachers, even in a weak vessel like me.

PRINCIPLE
SIX

EXPECT EVERY ORGANIZATION TO PAY ITS OWN WAY.

There was no central fund raising force for the CoMission. Every person involved paid his own way to every conference, committee meeting or task force—as well as a share of the ministry costs. If an organization wanted to provide literature, Bibles, videos, etc.— that organization paid for them. We had some organizations that were willing to join the CoMission if their material could be purchased or they could get funding. We had to decline their participation. We never spent funds that were not already raised. The CoMission ended without any deficits.

DR. PAUL H. JOHNSON is an active Christian business-man. For the past fifty-one years, his firm, Paul H. John-son, Inc., has constructed buildings of all sizes and types, including hospitals, schools, churches, airport ter-minals, office buildings, shopping centers, apartments, etc. He presently serves as chairman of the board of the Moody Bible Institute; chairman of the board of Walk Thru the Bible Ministries; and board member of the Maranatha Bible Conference in Muskegon, Michigan. He has traveled extensively throughout the US and to more than forty countries, largely in his leadership role with the Christian Business Men's Committee during more than forty years of involvement. With the CoMission, Paul served as chairman of the Arrangements Commit-tee. He and his wife, Marilyn, have three grown children and fourteen grandchildren.

CHAPTER FOUR

FINDING FOOD AND SHELTER

Arrangements Committee

Dr. Paul H. Johnson, chairman

IT WAS IN LATE October of 1990 when I received a call from my good friend, Peter Deyneka, Jr., the head of Russian Ministries. He said that a group of Christian leaders had been invited to go to Moscow to interact with various government leaders and to possibly meet with Mr. Gorbachev, then head of the Soviet Union. Russian leaders had asked for the group to include a businessman, and he would like for me to be the one.

The last place I wanted to visit was Russia. Those awful people! The ones who had threatened to bomb us with nuclear bombs and whose leader in days gone by, Mr. Khrushchev, had promised to "bury us"! Why would I want to go see *them?* But, with some encouragement from my family and my secretary, I decided that maybe it would be an educational trip. It was, indeed, that and a lot more. One of the others on the trip was the author, Philip Yancey, who took many notes and, when we got back, wrote all about it in a book called, "Praying with the KGB."

We not only had visits and meetings with the new KGB, who said they wanted to reform, but also with top government officials, the leaders of Parliament, ministers of education, commerce, representatives of the newspaper "Pravda," leaders of the media and arts and, finally, with Mr. Gorbachev himself. It was an eye-opening experience, to say the least.

Dr. Paul Johnson meets with then President Mikhail Gorbachev, October 1990.

We found the country to be in shambles politically, economically, socially and spiritually. The one bright spot was that most of those we met knew they needed help. But they didn't know what it was. Therefore, they were most open to suggestions and to help of any kind. I came away with a heavy heart for the good people of that great country, misled by a handful of radicals for over seventy years and now left bankrupt in every area of life. I thought of it in a business sense of having a fast-talking financial advisor taking all your assets and promising great returns, but coming back one day saying, "Well, I guess my schemes didn't work. You have lost everything."

A Loss of Hope

Actually, in the case of Russia, they lost a lot more than their money. Many had lost their lives, and the ones left had lost family, jobs and, most of all, hope. A few who had trusted the Lord through all this chaos provided the one bright spot on the horizon for their own future and for the entire country. The question was: could it be turned around? Such an enormous task! In my opinion, only God was able to handle a situation like this.

After my first exposure to Russia, I came home educated but frustrated. I concluded that there was little I could do to help except perhaps to support financially Peter Deyneka, Jr., and his ministry and perhaps a few others who were finding open and receptive hearts to the gospel. Maybe we could reach a few for Christ, but it would be an uphill and slow process.

At that time I had been chairman of the board of Walk Thru the Bible Ministries for twenty years. Ours was a small group, as boards go, with only seven members. We were selected back in the early 1970s by Bruce Wilkinson, the president and founder of Walk Thru the Bible, to give him advice and counsel. We were his friends. He was a young, gifted and creative individual with tremendous enthusiasm and potential for great ministry in the area of Bible teaching.

One day in 1991, Bruce called to say that he felt the Lord's leading to be involved in teaching the Bible in schools in the former Soviet Union. It seemed that since the wall had come down, some of the wiser leaders in the Ministry of Education believed that the only hope for survival of their society was to start over with the children. They concluded that the present Communist Party generation was pretty far gone, and that communism, with its foothold and personal value system and lifestyles, would be too difficult and would take too long to change. They doubted if the adults could be changed at all in their lifetime. After my visit, I certainly agreed.

As a result Bruce said that a group was being formed to study the issue, because of the unprecedented invitation from the education leaders to come and to teach the nation's children in the public schools about the need for morals and ethics in order for a society to be successful. When some of our Christian leaders explained to the Soviet educators that the foundation for this system was based on Judeo-Christian ethics, God and the Bible, the Soviet educators as much as said, "So be it! Do whatever it takes to teach our children to be honest, moral and responsible citizens." An amazing turn of events from a few months earlier!

This was to be a major challenge, but an unprecedented opportunity. As Bruce was talking to three or four others and dreaming about what could be done, he felt strongly that Walk Thru the Bible could have a key role. When our board met to discuss the situation, they asked me, as chairman, to attend some of these early meetings and to sort of look out for our interests as an organization; to be sure it was something that we (and Bruce) should be involved in, and examine what our role would be, what it would cost, etc.

THE HAND OF GOD

It didn't take long for me to see, after a meeting or two of interesting, innovative discussions, that this was, indeed, the hand of God moving in a most unusual way. I recommended to our board that we do all we could to be supportive. The idea developed to involve several organizations, since it would be impossible for any one or two organizations to handle this huge undertaking. It would take an unusual amount of cooperation among existing agencies and a willingness to give priority to their venture, as well as millions of dollars to finance it, plus hundreds of volunteers to actually go and do the teaching.

As the discussions progressed, each agency was to take responsibility for one segment of the strategy. For example, Campus Crusade for Christ and The JESUS Film Project, under the leadership of Paul Eshleman, was the "door opener" with their convocations; ACSI, under Paul Kienel, would help supply teachers to go; the Navigators, under Terry Taylor, would train the volunteers who would go;

and Walk Thru the Bible would provide video tapes for training in Russia on a variety of subjects. Twelve committees resulted, including a prayer committee and several others. One organization would take on each area of responsibility and be responsible for it in its entirety, including funding, etc. Ultimately, eighty-two organizations were involved. The name chosen was the CoMission, and the motto became, "Let's see what we can do for the cause of Christ in the former Soviet Union, and let's not care who gets the credit." As a member of the board of trustees of the Moody Bible Institute, I encouraged its president, Joe Stowell, and the board to endorse the CoMission. They did so wholeheartedly, and Joe became a member of the Executive Committee.

At one of the early meetings, the Executive Committee saw the need for an "arrangements committee." This team would be charged with finding housing for the hundreds of volunteers who would go, giving a year of their lives to teaching the Christian Ethics and Morality curriculum to the teachers who, in turn, would teach the pupils. An office for coordinating activities would be required, probably in Moscow, and a small staff would likely be necessary. Someone said, "We need a businessman to head up this committee." We all looked around the room, and it soon dawned on me that they were all looking at me!

My response was, "Wait a minute. I'm just here for a few days as an observer and counselor, and maybe to supply a little help with some organizational suggestions, etc. What do I know about the former Soviet Union and living and doing business in Russia? I'm a building contractor and a real estate developer from Michigan. Besides, all of you head up large organizations with staffs, offices, budgets, fund raising capacities and so on. My people are all busy full-time running the real estate management business. I'm one guy with a personal secretary who would help me, but...hold on here! Not so fast!" But they said, "We believe you are the one for the job."

How Could Things Get Worse?

I thought to myself, "How did I get into this? What did I do to deserve this? How could things get worse?" But they did!

Dr. Paul Johnson joins art students in Russian class-

As the job description unfolded, it was overwhelming. I almost had a heart attack just thinking about it. They were talking about sending hundreds of volunteers for a year, in teams of ten, with two people living together in an apartment and all of them, hopefully, in the same building, or at least close enough for fellowship, etc. Some would be married couples, others single. Hopefully, many would be schoolteachers. But it was decided that many non-teachers could do the job, with our special intensive three-week training program. It was incredible to think that I was going to be responsible for all those logistics. I remember someone saying, "You know, some of the apartments in Moscow and other places don't have refrigerators, since the people go to the market every day to buy fresh food. So therefore, they don't really need a refrigerator." I knew that was true, but our people would be too busy teaching to go shopping every day, so we needed to supply each apartment with a refrigerator. Also, there were few apartments with washers and dryers, so we would need to supply washers and dryers as well. Now we were getting into the appliance business! While I did know something about that, as I owned hundreds of apartments in Michigan, the former Soviet Union was another story. Just buying them from other countries and getting them shipped in and installed was an overwhelming prospect.

But it got worse! They were not talking about just Moscow, but the entire country: eleven time zones, an area three times as wide as the United States. "Oh, my goodness!" I thought. "I'll probably go broke and die trying to fulfill this assignment." I guess I looked as bad as I felt, when someone said, "Don't worry. We will include the cost of the rent, the appliances, and equipping the apartments in the funds that each volunteer will raise before he or she can go."

"Well," I thought, "that will help. At least I won't have to pay for everything." They discussed the difficulty of getting materials through customs, getting money into the country, dealing with Russian printers and other business people where we might encounter a lack of integrity, in terms of keeping promises as to delivery and fulfilling commitments. Things that we take for granted here were not necessarily so over there. For example, it was not unusual to agree to buy a refrigerator from a local store and agree on a price and pay half down. After waiting sometimes three or four months, the delivery truck would show up and the driver would say, "Before we can unload the refrigerator, you have to pay the other half of the purchase price *plus* a $200 delivery fee." If you refused, someone else got your refrigerator, and you were out half of its cost.

These were not encouraging things to hear when contemplating this assignment. And, worst of all, I knew from my limited experience it was all true. I remember leaving the meeting saying, "Lord, how did *we* get into this? Obviously You had something to do with it, so You'll have to be the One to see me through." And, indeed, He did!

Mission societies began recruiting lay volunteers for a short-term (one year) service with the CoMission. People began to sign up and take a leave of absence from their jobs and to rent out their homes. It was amazing how some of the least likely individuals would be impressed by God to go, including my own son Kevin and his wife, Lisa, who served in Moscow under OMS International.

Kevin Johnson, official photographer, with wife and fellow CoMissioner Lisa.

One aspect of the CoMission that impressed me early on was that there would be no new organization formed. It was to be an affiliation of existing organizations banded together to accomplish a certain task and for a limited time, five years. There would be no CoMission bank account, as such. The necessary money would be raised by each agency, as required to perform their part of the task. The Executive Committee was simply a coordinating group, with very little authority. Guidelines were agreed to by each agency, but the only authority was what was given by the leaders of the agencies. It was sort of like the early days of our country when the thirteen states gave up some rights to the federal government, except that the CoMission never had a national treasury. This approach avoided a lot of duplication of administration and associated costs, and kept our expenses down. As a businessman, I liked this efficient arrangement.

Since each agency recruited and sent its own people, it was logical for each to provide a small salary, insurance, housing and supervision for its own people. But all happened under the larger banner of the CoMission. This was the only way that the Arrangements Committee could possibly accomplish all the "arrangements." We had to have the help of each sending agency, of which there were several.

Our job was to seek and find possible apartment opportunities; then each agency would make its own arrangements. We also had to coordinate all travel and activities in the former Soviet Union. It was obvious I had to find a staff and open an office in Moscow or go myself, and that wasn't too practical. I did wind up going over seven times during the five-year period, but early in the process I began to pray for "my man in Moscow."

Beverly and Andy Bishop, executive director or the CoMission Arrangements Committee, with Dr. Olga Polykovskaya.

OUR MAN IN MOSCOW

At one of our early meetings in Phoenix, my friend, Peter Deyneka, Jr., said to me, "I've got a fellow here that you should meet. He may be your man." At lunch he introduced me to Andy Bishop and, as they often say, the rest is history. Andy and his wife, Beverly, were missionaries with the Christian and Missionary Alliance (CMA). They were visiting the meeting to find out more about the CoMission and the opportunities in Russia. As Andy puts it:

> Getting to Russia, for Bev and me, started with one of our CMA donors asking me to go look at a plan called CoMission in Russia. I traveled there in September of '92 with Paul Eshleman to attend a convocation for Russian public school teachers at Orlyanok. I came back convinced of the possibilities and recommended to CMA that they join, which they did.
>
> A few weeks after I submitted my report, Bev woke me at 1 A.M. She said, "I think we ought to go to Russia." I said, "But you just said after thirty years of marriage that twenty-six addresses were enough."
>
> "Every time I pray," she said, "I see Russia. We should go there too." So I spoke with my boss. "If we're going to go to Russia, we need you here to raise money," was his response. God will supply the money, was my feeling. I asked again, and the answer was, "Wait a year!" Bev wasn't satisfied. Neither was I. I was asked a week later to go to Phoenix with a pastor and layman from CMA. Russia was on the horizon big time. After Bruce Wilkinson gave his famous "Caught in Elijah's Chariot Wheels" sermon, over 900 people were pledged to go. Later, my pastor friend came into the room and said, "Let's pray."
>
> "What's the subject?" I asked. His reply: "The CoMission board wants you and Bev to go to Russia to arrange for the program of CoMission there." We prayed. I called Bev. She said, "Let's go." I said, "We have to raise our own support." She said, "Okay." We agreed to go for five years.
>
> The next morning, after getting clearance from CMA, I met the board. Paul Johnson would be my boss, and all we had to do was raise $200,000 and open an office in Russia for CoMission...by April – about 90 days away! As I was leaving, slightly challenged by all this, a donor and friend of mine came up and said, "I've just pledged half a million to one agency for the CoMission. I'm glad we have you going to set things up." "Pray," I requested, "that we find the support. We are going for five years!" He thought a moment and

then said, "I'll do one fourth of your support for the next five years." Well, God worked, and when I flew to Moscow in March to do the preliminary work-up, we had five years of support from seven people. God is amazing!

Indeed, God is amazing! Andy was a "get it done" type of guy, if ever there was one. He could speak some Russian and was the perfect man for the job. He became the "man in Moscow" for the entire CoMission and all the agencies. He helped them find apartments, washers and dryers, as well as steel doors and locks for apartments to keep burglars out. He arranged airport pick-ups, hotel rooms for temporary layovers, transportation to other cities, equipment repairs and printing and determined where to buy just about anything. He was a "can do" man, and he did it!

But it was soon apparent that he needed some extra help, having only a couple of office staff. He called me from Moscow and wanted to know if the Arrangements Committee (my secretary and I) could afford a helper for him. When I found out all he was doing, I was surprised he didn't ask for two or three, and I quickly approved the added expenditure. Here is an excerpt from Andy's report about his new helper, Vlad:

> In Moscow I was with Missionary Aviation Fellowship's man, Bob. He introduced me to Vladimir Gagavyshev, whom they'd met in Mozambique, Africa. We got on well, and by the time I left he had agreed to work with me. We'd rented an office which had been used by Campus Crusade, and I felt much better about how God was going to bring it all together.
>
> By June, the office was up and running. Vlad and I were scouring Moscow for apartments, washing machines, water filters, TV and VCR units, as well as transformers for people who didn't believe that Russian irons and hair dryers would work. But they did!

Among our many duties was transportation for the CoMissioners from Moscow, where they all landed first, to wherever they were going to serve for the year. Andy recalls his first transportation crisis:

The first big consignment of CoMissioners was scheduled to arrive in July 1993. Two weeks before, the US travel office sent us a panic flash. All the in-country travel plans had collapsed. We were to go out at the height of travel season and book 400-plus seats to about 20 destinations.

I called in the staff for a reading of James 1 and prayer. One of our key workers was out sick, so we prayed for wisdom, seats and her health. As we finished, she walked in. Vlad exclaimed, "See how prayer works!"

Next, we broke up the group into teams to find bus, train and plane tickets. Vlad and I called a charter company and began negotiations to charter a flight to Novosibersk, Russia, and Almaty, Kazakhstan. The next few days were busy and productive, and by the time the CoMissioners arrived, we had secured the needed seats to go everywhere!

For a portion of them, Vlad and I chartered a plane, a 1950 vintage JL-18. We went to the airport at 7 P.M., but didn't get on the plane until officials had collected their "cut" of the charter fee. Finally, at midnight, we took off with nineteen CoMissioners and ten tons of goods, including washers, books and baggage. In the back of the plane, I found a nice office and slept on the couch. Later the crew told me it was President Yeltsin's old personal plane that he'd given the crew to use to earn a living.

We landed in Novosibersk and off-loaded the team and their goods. The airport was crowded with planes going nowhere! "No fuel," we were told. Valentine, our charter agent, took my briefcase of money and disappeared. Things did not look promising. Suddenly a fuel truck pulled up and Valentine got out. He said, "There's fuel, if you have cash."

After some arguments with the flight center, we were in the air and on our way. I went up to the cockpit to see how everything was going. The whole crew was asleep! With visions of wandering into China or Afghanistan, I woke the navigator. He busied himself with details, then woke the pilot. We immediately began our landing at Almaty. After dropping off our second team and their stuff, we headed back for Moscow. I was glad to get home, and even happier that all CoMissioners were where they were supposed to be. God's arrangements are always the best.

Although Vlad was not yet a believer, he was a devoted and faithful employee. During my several visits to Moscow, I spent some time with him, and realized how important he was to our cause. Andy wrote me about his importance to the effort:

> God provided in various ways. We had finally found sources for everything. We had a bank account that worked, and almost everything we'd planned for worked as advertised. We were short of all kinds of materials, but with no copyright laws, we could duplicate almost everything. Walk Thru the Bible's "7 Laws of the Learner" videos were the most popular of the tools, and we loved to see the teachers respond. But then video projectors, bought in Germany and sent in with the luggage, began to fail. Bob Ehle said Sharp would fix them if we sent them to Germany. We could not do that without first showing they were properly imported, etc., etc.
>
> One day I said to Vlad, "We have eight units that have failed. Russia has a space station and qualified engineers and technicians. We should be able to find someone who can fix these video projectors." Vlad said, "Yes, I will see." Two days later he came back and said, "I've found a technician who is out of work. He will do it." I figured we could sacrifice a unit to see, so we did. It took him one day to fix the Japanese projector assembled in Poland. He soon fixed all of them and everything else that failed in the next five years. We even sent him to Vladivostok to fix equipment and train a local technician there, and then to Ukraine to do the others.
>
> Vlad helped do anything necessary to make CoMission work, and along the way began to take note of what Christ in a person's life meant in practical ways. He would go to airports at all hours of the day and night to help CoMissioners with problems, and he negotiated with people who smelled money on foreigners. Increasingly he gave out Bibles or Christian books since, as he explained, "these people are bringing Russia what it truly needs." His father was a KGB engineer. "But," Vlad said, "we were raised heathens, so the

Bible is suspect to us. My mother was a Christian until she married my father. She could not practice her faith the rest of her life, but we buried her as a Christian."

The CoMission Executive Committee made an annual visit to Moscow for one of our regular meetings, but also for the purpose of encouraging the "troops," letting us see firsthand some of the activities that were taking place. Most of us looked forward to the visits, although the accommodations often left a lot to be desired. It was not unusual to be housed in a hotel with little or no hot water, and sometimes no heat.

I remember one trip where I took my grandson up to Vladimer in ten-degree weather. In a hotel without heat, we slept with our clothes on and under so many heavy, army-type blankets that we woke up tired from the weight!

One trip with the Executive Committee was planned to go first to Odessa in the Ukraine to see the work going on there, meet some Ukrainian leaders, then go on to Moscow. We asked Andy to make arrangements for a charter flight, as there were more than thirty of us, including wives and families, and it would be safer than the national airlines Aeroflot, quicker than the train, etc. Andy had used this charter company before, with good planes and good results. His report on the trip shows the state of transportation in the Soviet Union:

When it was time to go, we went to the airport on a nice bus. Our baggage was whisked away to be put on the plane. We were served soft drinks and snacks in the VIP lounge, and after a while, a customs man appeared and stamped all of our passports. Then, with great courtesy, we were ushered out to the airplane. There sat a 35-plus year Antonov 24 (similar to an old American DC3). Beside it was a pile of luggage, and standing by, a few surly-looking men. I was informed they would not load without some serious cash. The plane was weatherbeaten and had small puddles of oil and fuel under the engines. The tires were bald with threads showing! On the side was a painted-over "Aeroflot." When I saw this, I said to myself, "Paul Johnson is going to fire me! These are not the kind of arrangements he likes." Paul Kienel said, "We're all going to die, but at least we'll die in good company!" I responded, "First, we load the luggage." Overcoming shock and fear, Bruce Wilkinson began to pitch bags into the cargo hold, and Joe Stowell began to stack them.

We got on the plane, with fervent prayer, and awaited developments. The crew arrived and casually began the flight. When the pilot came on board, we were all on the plane waiting to go. He entered from the rear and came up the aisle, which was a steep incline, through the passenger cabin and through the cargo room and into the cockpit. He was wearing a brown leather jacket with a red scarf around his neck. Before entering the cockpit door, he turned around, smiled at all of us and said in broken English, "Red Baron!"

There was one cabin steward, a young man dressed in a unique flight attendant's uniform. He served us warm yellow punch and cucumber sandwiches. He used the loudspeaker system and all of us to practice his English. He announced everything from the weather to the time of day. After several announcements and interruptions to our sleep or conversations, he began to apologize, and each time he came on he would say, "Now I am again!" It did help to keep our minds off our anxiety of the flight. Three hours later we landed in Moscow, and after unloading our luggage we boarded a new Mercedes bus to town for board meeting "part two." We were all still alive, and I still had my job!

Andy was very diligent about his job and took it very seriously, but he also had a lighter side and often reported on the humorous side of things. He shares some here:

> Our committee sometimes played a role not envisioned by the planners. We were, in the mind of the Ministry of Education, the "authority" for the CoMission in Russia. They'd never had a voluntary consortium operating in Russia before and firmly believed someone besides God was "in charge." This led to many funny incidents.
>
> Papers had to have signatures, and signatures had to have a stamp. No amount of explaining that from our perspective this was unnecessary would do. I finally had a stamp made saying, "CoMission Russia." It cost $3.00. One day Dr. Olga Polykovskaya came in

all flustered, which was unusual for her.

"I must go to America," she explained. "I have a letter of invitation from Paul Eshleman with his signature, but the Minister of Education said I must have a stamp. I must go to America and get it officially stamped." So I got out my $3.00 stamp, affixed it properly smudged and signed my name across it and, voila, an acceptably official letter! Just another arrangement!

We also handled emergencies. One time it was, as Snoopy says, "a dark and stormy night." About 11 P.M. came a knock on our door. Upon opening the door I beheld three very weary and wet travelers, one looking rather disconcerted. Eddie Broussard had gone to the airport to pick up his boss, Stacy Rinehart, and a friend. He had succeeded in locking himself out of his apartment and wasn't sure what to do, as he could not remember his landlady's name or number. I had some keys, so we went over and tried again. No luck!

By now it was midnight, and the newly arrived were bushed, so Bev rolled out the beds and tucked them in as Eddie went off to find someone who knew the landlady. At breakfast over pancakes, we learned he'd finally asked his neighbor, who called the landlady, who opened the apartment. Next day, Eddie brought an extra key to my apartment, which joined the others, so that when he got locked out again.... I still have a few odd Russian keys lying about.

On another occasion we were preparing for simultaneous convocations in Kiev and Moscow. I was busy with setting up things like hotel and travel (no charters!) when, a month prior to "show time," I had a mild heart attack. Vlad stepped in and did the calls and contacts. After three weeks I was up and working half days. I went to Kiev with a briefcase full of money and air tickets. Carrying cash in Russia in those days was necessary, because very few businesses accepted credit cards or checks.

Two days before the Executive Committee was to arrive, I left my briefcase in a taxi. I called Vlad. He rushed to the airline, cancelled the tickets, got new ones and put Irina, our Russian helper, on the train to Kiev with new tickets. Right after she arrived in Kiev, the cab company called and said, "We have your briefcase." Everyone had told me, "You'll never see it again." But I prayed anyway. I picked up the briefcase from the cab company and, lo and behold, all the money was still there!

Even though I was a bit slow due to the heart problem, everything went well. Finally we had the Executive Committee and Walk Thru supporters safely at the Novotel Hotel at the Moscow airport, ready to leave and satisfied with the whole trip. It was always a relief when they all left safe and sound. The next morning John Hoover called. Everyone was on the flight except him and one of the donors and him. The donor was carrying $6,000 in Walk Thru funds and had neglected to declare it. Vlad and I went over, extracted them from the police and arranged a later flight. The customs confiscated the money and then let them go. John also had $6,000, which he left with me. As Walk Thru and Paul Johnson financed the arrangements office, it was deducted from the next amount sent. Vlad was amazed at all this, but glad they weren't charged and held.

I'm convinced that Andy and Vlad were sent from the Lord to do the outstanding job they did for the CoMission during our five-year run. They, along with a small office staff, were the real arrangements committee. Andy could never overstate Vlad's value to the CoMission.

Over the years, he had seen the good and the not so good of the CoMission. He'd passed out Bibles and books and spoken up for CoMission whenever any questions were raised. We trusted his judgment and benefited from his experience. A graduate of Moscow State University in foreign trade and of the Foreign Affairs University, he had degrees in Portugese and English, and twenty years working in and out of Russia. He was a godsend.

He joined in Bible studies and looked for answers. He loved to talk to Bruce Wilkinson and read the materials we used. At one Executive Committee meeting, during a break, he indicated that he was ready to receive salvation. I asked Bruce to talk with him. I walked the hall and prayed with Paul Johnson. After about an hour, I heard Bruce exclaim, "Yes!" We went into the office, and Bruce said, "Tell them." Vlad smiled and said, "Well, now it seems I have eternal life!" We all praised God for this fine brother in Christ.

Vlad continued on after the CoMission ended to supply

arrangements for missionaries and visitors to Russia. Working with CMA and Mission Aviation Fellowship (MAF), he is able to bring in short-term teams, help find anything one needs to live and work in Russia, and still signs his e-mails and cards "Your brother in Christ."

His advice was always good. When we first arrived and decided to buy a car, he picked out an insurance company. All the foreigners scoffed and said, "Hah! If you have a loss, they'll never pay." But $250 for a year of full coverage didn't seem bad. We had the car about 48 hours. It was stolen without a trace. But Vlad went to the insurance company and recovered eighty-five percent of the price with no problem.

I do remember Vlad's shock at his first visit to America. He kept repeating, "So many choices!" The second trip was good, too, as we took Larrissa, his wife. She loved church, and after a couple of days during morning devotions said, "Now I will pray." And she did, trusting Christ.

The CoMission's five years changed thousands of lives in Russia and America. It will be the thousands of children who were exposed to "Christian Morals and Ethics as a Foundation for Society" who will change the nation.

The Arrangements Committee, with the help of Andy and Vlad in Moscow, played a very important role in the behind-the-scenes activities of the CoMission. We were the support team for the many agencies and CoMissioners who so faithfully served during the five-year period. The overall accomplishments of the CoMission effort were very impressive. We on the Arrangements Committee were pleased with the total results, and glad that God allowed us to have a part in such a productive venture for the cause of His Son, the Lord Jesus Christ.

For myself, I can truthfully say, "I, being in the way, the Lord led me." When I first heard about the duties and responsibilities of the task, I felt unable to do it. But as is most often the case, the answer the Lord wants to hear is not whether we're able, but if we are available. When I finally said that I would be "available," the Lord more than supplied all that was needed to get the job done. To Him be the glory!

GOD USING
THE HEART
OF A CHILD

Kiev, 1995:

Why had eleven-year-old Mariana come to the Leadership Conference? This conference was for future leaders. With her friend Olya, she had been sneaking into an elementary level class to participate and learn the curriculum.

As I spent some time with Mariana, I was deeply humbled to realize that Mariana was indeed a leader, even at her age. Due to a shortage of teachers, there was no available secondary curriculum in her region. I learned that she had come to help address this need herself.

By the end of the conference, Mariana and Olya made plans to work with the elementary teacher to prepare a proposal. The proposal would allow them to teach a voluntary after-school morals and ethics class to their peers. Once the plan solidified, the girls spent the remainder of their summer studying the Bible and preparing to teach in the fall.

How powerfully the Holy Spirit was moving in the hearts of these people, even youth like Mariana and Olya, to lead their peers to a knowledge of Christ.

PRINCIPLES SEVEN AND EIGHT

RESPECT THE UNIQUE GIFTING AND CALLING OF EACH ORGANIZATION.

We asked those people who were strong in a particular area of ministry to lead us and teach us in that area. This made our training and preparation very strong, since it was led by the best practitioners in the area. We centered our teaching and materials on the person and work of Christ—where there was little disagreement.

BE FLEXIBLE.

Throughout the time of the CoMission, conditions changed continually. Strategy changed as more needs were discovered. We listened continually to those on the field in order to make our policies and supervision relevant. We realized we needed to train people with both practical ministry skills and general principles. We trained in specific skills, but allowed adaptation on the field as needed. We learned the importance of having field supervisors regularly visit the team of laymen. Since the teams were there for only one year, we had to help them solve problems quickly if they were to be effective. And we needed to train each team in the essential tools and systems to be self-feeding and sustaining on the field.

DR. TERRY TAYLOR and his wife, Carol, lived in Orlando, Florida, for seven years, where he practiced optometry. Beginning in 1972, the Taylors served Christ with the Navigators. Terry became the US president of the Navigators in 1984 and continued in that position until 1997. A member of the CoMission's Executive Committee, Terry directed the Training and Materials Committee. This team was particularly instrumental in preparing CoMissioners for their year-long assignments in the former Soviet Union. With two other couples Terry and Carol also founded Second Half Ministries. They live in Colorado Springs, and have three adult children and eight grandchildren.

CHAPTER FIVE

THE CoMISSION TRAINING SCHOOL

Training and Materials Committee

Dr. Terry Taylor, chairman

MANY OF US that night in April 1992, unable to sleep, prayed the hours away after we heard about the CoMission. Earlier that evening, in the Pink House at Navigators headquarters, Bruce Wilkinson had challenged us, thirteen leaders of the Navigators, to join the massive effort, along with our overall ministry.

Stacy Rinehart and I walked the hotel parking lot for hours talking. Years later Stacy still recalls the deep burning in his heart, the excitement. God called us to the ministry of CoMission that evening in Colorado Springs, and to accept Bruce's challenge to take the lead in training all the CoMissioners that all the agencies would recruit and send.

This was an enormous task, and a great honor and show of respect for what the Navigators had done in training multitudes of laymen and laywomen for practical ministry throughout our history. The impact of the vision and the potential to reach the former Soviet Union through a partnership of ministries moved us deeply. For all of us, the decision was almost, in Stacy's words, "a no-brainer." We unanimously agreed to participate as a sending agency and also take on the responsibility to train all the CoMission people. I took on the role of overseeing the Training and Materials Committee (TMC).

Our commitment to assist came almost immediately after the first large organization meeting of agencies, held in March 1992 at Moody Bible Institute. There the first task force on training was chaired by John Hoover of Walk Thru the Bible. Among the handful of experienced trainers who brainstormed with John on what the parameters of this training might look like were: Phil Renicks of ACSI; Anita Deyneka of Russian Ministries; and Myles Lorenzen of World Team. Foundational training concepts were sketched out, but an obvious key to the success of such a training venture was missing. Needed would be a large agency with a training history that would give leadership to a multi-agency training team. Within weeks God would lead the Navigators to fill this vital role.

FORMATION OF THE TRAINING AND MATERIALS COMMITTEE

I soon convened the committee of representatives who gave initial shape to the training that would be needed. They were tasked with making formal proposals to the executive committee by the end of May 1992. It was apparent from the beginning of the CoMission that the strategy needed to be very training intensive. Mobilizing lay people to minister in the former Soviet Union would demand that they be equipped well for their "adventure of a lifetime."

God's love for the Russian people is clearly demonstrated in the people He called together to carry out the noble mission of the CoMission. Dr. Stacy Rinehart was one of those champions God used to prepare hundreds of CoMissioners for ministry in what is now primarily the Russian Federation and Ukraine. Stacy's role in the CoMission as executive director of the Training and Materials Committee was crucial to the effectiveness of the CoMission teams.

In early May Stacy began to recruit trainers from both inside the Navigators and from CoMission agencies. The idea was: Yes, the Navigators are responsible for training, but we do not have the breadth of skills and knowledge to train in the broad areas of ministry needed for CoMission. Beyond that, no ministry had ever thought of training hundreds of lay missionaries over a five-year period, going to an unknown field and starting the first training cycle in just five months. No ministry had utilized laymen as the primary work force of pioneer missionaries. No ministry at that time had much experience in openly ministering in Russia or training people to minister in the former Soviet Union. And no ministry had ever thought of taking average people of all ages, from all walks of life, from about every conceivable Christian background, and turning them into "educational consultants in Christian ethics and morality." This was pioneer training, and needed the best trainers the agencies could provide.

Over the next several years, perhaps one of the most talented group of trainers imaginable assembled to conduct training for the CoMission. Various trainers contributed for a few training cycles; others for much longer. Some had field training responsibilities; others had only training design responsibilities. The key, though, was the diversity, experience, godliness, giftedness, eagerness and wisdom of the training team.

Dr. Stacy Rinehart, executive director of Training and Materials Committee, meets with colleagues.

I am not only indebted to Stacy Rinehart for taking the overall leadership in the CoMission training, but I am equally indebted to my friend Bob Sheffield and his lovely wife Nancy. They responded to God's call in a latter season of life to go and live in Russia and lead the Navigator ministry there. They sacrificially loved and gave their lives. With Stacy and Bob carrying those two major leadership roles, I was free to devote my energies to overall leadership with the CoMission Executive Committee.

Practical Training Design for Laymen

The result was what we called "Just-In-Time Training." This included the basic vision and training in how to serve with the CoMission ministry, how to develop and keep a spiritual life, how to draw on your team, how to begin understanding the host culture, and how to conduct ongoing training for the CoMission ministry in the field. The principle of "just-in-time training" drove us to come up with the following training functions for each training cycle:

1. CoMission Orientation and Fundraising Training (three days), run by each sending agency.
2. Team Leadership Training (three days).
3. Primary Training Institute (ten days). The Team Leadership Training and Primary Training Institute were held back-to-back at the same location.
4. In-country Orientation (three days).
5. Ongoing Training (half day per week while on the field).
6. Sixth Week Training (five days in country). This training event was conducted regionally in the field, with several going on at the same time, e.g., one in Moscow and one in Kiev.
7. Rest, Refuel & Refocus (six days in Western Europe).
8. Scriptural Roots of the Ministry—a year-long, weekly team Bible study with a two-day summary seminar at year's end.

9. Debrief (occurring the last three days prior to the CoMissioners' return to their home country).

THE IMPORTANCE OF THE PRIMARY TRAINING INSTITUTE (PTI)

TMC had the very large task of conducting training in eleven time zones in the Soviet Union while simultaneously planning the launching events in the US for the next cycle. We launched our CoMissioners in eleven training cycles spanning October 1992 through July 1997.

One event stands out as the most important event in each training cycle—the PTI. Not only did the CoMissioners come to be trained, but they also came with their bags packed, literally, just before getting on the plane and going as teams to their cities and waiting ministry.

During the PTI, the DNA—that is, the values, vision, mission and strategy of CoMission—was set for each cycle. Leaders from all the sending agencies and committees were present. The CoMissioners got to see the heart and soul of their home agency leadership and the CoMission leadership at the same time. Servanthood, teamwork, and deference to one another were on display for them at all times.

The final event of the PTI was the commissioning service. TMC member Eddie Broussard served as the regular master of ceremonies for this event. All present members of the Executive Team attended, sitting on the stage, and had a part in the program. The commissioning service culminated with the ritual of "The Handshake," where each CoMissioner, TMC member and Sending Agency leader pledged to keep himself sexually pure in the next year, shook hands with Bruce Wilkinson and then took communion. They were then commissioned as a group by the laying on of hands. This memorable event was like no other in the CoMissioner's year.

ON-FIELD RESOURCES

The CoMission strategy called for a resource team specifically trained for the tasks each on-site CoMission team would face in the constantly changing ministry environment of the former Soviet Union. Remote trainers based in the US could not provide relevant training, nor keep abreast of the changing ministry demands required for training the next cycle of CoMissioners. For this reason we had numerous trainers who lived and traveled in the former Soviet Union to observe and resource the teams in their cities. Among these in-country trainers were Tracy Jensen Mancino and Rebecca Bramlett Goldstone, who served as our in-country educational specialists. Tracy and Rebecca worked side by side with national teachers, creating character development and Bible lessons that they could incorporate in their classrooms.

"The teachers were surprised," Tracy recalls, "to find out that they could study the Bible for themselves and use lessons they learned from God to pass on to their students. The light bulbs went on for them when they were able to take 'ownership' for their own understanding of the Bible. They loved Scripture, and seeing them enjoy the newness of it was like watching your own children learn new things."

Eddie Broussard served as our in-country training director, and Ralph and Jennifer Ennis served as our cultural specialists. (Ralph and Jennifer wrote a book entitled *An Introduction to The Russian Soul*, which, in my opinion, still serves as the best layman's Russian ministry orientation available.)

THE ROLE OF TMC IN COMISSION

The TMC served to implement the training of the overall CoMission vision, mission, values and strategy. We were responsible for the training events where all members of the CoMission converged for two weeks semi-annually. So a broad role emerged for TMC, including that of serving as a bridge between the executive committee and the sending agencies. As the CoMission matured, the TMC chose to begin to diminish its role and to turn over more and more training events and functions to the Sending Agencies Committee.

There was an intense commitment within the CoMission to work as one, with TMC and Sending Agencies working alongside each other. We had not done this before in a ministry partnership environment, so we all had a lot to learn. Key people making the TMC and Sending Agency interface work were Curt Mackey (executive director of the Sending Agency Committee, who also served as a member of TMC) and Andy Weeks (operations director of TMC). For two weeks at all PTIs, we had daily lunch meetings so that the Sending Agency leaders and TMC leaders could talk about issues in training and ministry delivery. These meetings were usually led by Andy, a man with unusual wisdom and credibility in the eyes of Sending Agency leaders.

Strong friendships resulted from the days and weeks spent in each other's presence. Stacy Rinehart recalls unexpectedly seeing David Graffenburger, OMS's agency leader, in Chicago's O'Hare Airport. The two of them picked up right where they had left off several years earlier. There was a satisfying joy and pleasure of seeing and fellowshipping with each other, if only for fifteen minutes in an airport. One of the hardest things in ending CoMission, many say, was not seeing our CoMission friends anymore. TMC and Sending Agency leaders, almost to the person, count their CoMission experience as a highlight of their careers.

Major Crisis in Cycle 3

There were many "bugs" to work out in our ministry, some resulting in misunderstandings. This is normal. There were many areas of growth for each TMC member and Sending Agency leader. This was understandable. But all of us remember Cycle 3. This was our first training cycle with a large number of CoMissioners, teams and agencies. It lasted twelve full days. The previous two training cycles were much smaller, allowing us to field test our ministry strategy and build our training team and infrastructure. But a 760-percent growth in the number of CoMissioners being trained will stretch anyone's limits.

Two things added to the challenge of this training cycle. First, the TMC was unprepared for the growth and complexity of the logistics required to serve the 450-plus people who came to the training

facility. Second, we were in the midst of some major strategy fluc-
tuations, with the strategy sometimes changing from one hour to the
next, creating confusion among the trainers, agency leaders, team leaders and CoMissioners. It was hard for all to live through at the time,
but we still laugh about it. We are now able to stand back with the
perspective of history and see what God did. Many of our best Co-
Missioners and agency leaders still serving internationally came from
Cycle 3. Hardship and flexibility were built into them by the hand
of God through the limitations of man.

Our winter training cycles were always interesting because of the
weather. We had a major ice storm, snow and record cold in our Cycle 4 training in Charlotte, North Carolina. Two years later, a record
blizzard hit during Cycle 8 at Sandy Cove, Maryland. Our summer
training location was at Olivet Nazarene University in Kankakee,
Illinois. One summer we experienced a record heat wave, and many
of the dorm rooms where our CoMissioners stayed had no air con-
ditioning. During another summer cycle, we had a tornado touch
down nearby, creating a major disruption in our training for a short
period of time.

**Dr. Terry Taylor (l. front) gathers his training team in
Kankakee, Illinois.**

IMPORTANCE OF PRAYER

We experientially learned the importance of prayer. We saw God work in miraculous ways throughout the CoMission. Two notable examples:

Early in the preparation for CoMission Cycle 3, Bruce Wilkinson and Paul Eshleman met with Curt Mackey, Dick Katz, Myles Lorenzen and Stacy Rinehart. We only had one day of meetings planned with a long agenda. Contrary to our natural leanings, we spent two-thirds of the time in prayer and sharing, led by Bruce. With only a third of our time left, we still finished our agenda on time.

Throughout the years of serving together, many things coincidentally happened to key trainers and events that reminded us of the reality of spiritual warfare. Just before the Cycle 3 Primary Training Institute, for example, a trainer had a car engine blow up, a water heater go out, an air-conditioner go out, a dryer go out and several other small things at home stopped working—all within a one-week time span. We prayed and interceded for each other, but not until the CoMission Prayer Committee was formed did we see a large-scale difference. There really is such a thing as a gifted intercessor. Mary Lance Sisk, chairwoman of the Prayer Committee, was God's gift to the CoMission.

LONG-TERM RESULTS FROM OUR TRAINING APPROACHES

The many ways that God worked through the CoMission continue to leave a legacy.

Bill Wolfe and Alan Nagel, who both carry major responsibilities in Campus Crusade, testify of the lessons learned that they carried back to their home organization. David Dick, current executive director of International Ministries for OMS, reports that numerous training principles learned in CoMission were implemented. The same is said of many other trainers and their home ministries. I know of no one on the TMC who was not permanently changed by this experience. Many years of wisdom and experience were gained in only five short years.

Perhaps the most satisfying long-term result for many of us was to see the growth and development of Nick and Maia Mikhaluk's ministry, International Partners, working in Ukraine. Nick and Maia served on the TMC from Cycle 7 to Cycle 11, taking increasing responsibility with each cycle.

In January 1997, we commissioned them to start their own ministry to serve their fellow Ukrainians. They started with just the two of them. Five years later they had forty-five national staff working in ten Ukrainian cities. Here is Nick and Maia's testimony, written in Kiev, Ukraine, August 2001:

> It was a real blessing and great training for us to visit cities of the former Soviet Union where CoMission teams worked and see how God is working in the lives of our people. Over the period of three years we visited thirty-five different cities. We could observe what was working, what was not working. Gerald and Mary Parker, who have been and still are our mentors, taught us to always think how things can be done better. The lessons that we learned from observing so many teams in ministry gave us the preparation that no seminary or university could provide!
>
> In the summer of 1995 we were invited to be trainers in ministry track in the 7th Cycle of CoMission training. We really appreciate the trust that TMC showed us by allowing us to do some training. We were not experienced trainers; we were very young and we were young believers. But having an opportunity to share with CoMissioners what we believed was going to help them be effective evangelists in our country was very important to us and gave us a much greater feeling of ownership of CoMission ministry.
>
> We learned so much from being a part of the TMC team:

- The value of a team of trainers versus individual trainers.

- Emphasis on equipping equippers.

- Ongoing evaluation of training process and content.

- Importance of interactive training.

- Importance of an application process during the training.

- Crucial value of cooperation of supervisors and trainers on the field.

In January 1997, with the encouragement of CoMission and TMC leadership, we started a Ukrainian ministry called International Partnerships. IP continues carrying out the vision of CoMission for reaching the influencers of society for Christ. The mission of IP is to "touch the ones who will bring to Christ thousands." In January 1997 there were just two of us. Now we have forty-five people on staff who share our vision and passion for reaching Ukraine. IP has teams in ten cities of Ukraine now: Kiev, Cherkassy, Zhitomir, Zaporozhye, Sevastopol, Lviv, Sympheropol, Kherson, Kharkov, Yalta. Our goal is to have teams in all twenty-six regions of Ukraine.

Our strategy involves evangelism, discipleship, raising leaders and church planting. The staff and lay leaders are leading over 140 Bible discussion groups. Most of the people in those groups are not believers when they first come, and they have many negative stereotypes about Christianity. We see these convinced atheists finding Christ through studying the Word and submitting their lives to Him. In four cities we have new churches planted (Sympheropol, Kherson, Cherkassy and Yalta). Ninety percent of the members of these new churches were not even believers three years ago.

The vision of IP, philosophy of ministry, [and] some values and strategies, were born out of our CoMission and TMC experiences. We saw the uniqueness and crucial importance of CoMission's vision to reach the educators of [the] former Soviet Union for Christ, and through them reach the whole society that they are influencing. We don't know of any other ministry that is targeting this audience. As we worked with CoMission, God gave us a burden for this strategic and yet most untouched segment of our society.

KEY LESSONS LEARNED FROM OUR TMC EXPERIENCE

Much wisdom was learned from our experiences, including this brief list:

1. Training shapes vital ministries at a shoe-leather level.

2. With appropriate training, lay people can make an enormous ministry contribution.

3. Team ministry is a must in training and ministry.

4. Partnering in the body of Christ is God's way in our day.

5. We must train not just cognitively, but with both practical ministry skills and general principles. Train in skills and expect modification of the skills and tools to fit the local situation.

6. Train each team in the essential skills, tools and systems it needs to be self-feeding and self-sustaining on the field.

7. Don't try to be "omnicompetent." Live within the limits of your gifting and rely on others' gifting.

8. God is the "just-in-time people manager." He brings the right person to make the right contribution at the right time, just in time. We saw this happen many times with His timely provision of a person to fill our need. One of these was Christine Weddle of OMS. She joined our TMC office in Raleigh, North Carolina, to provide the administrative support and leadership for all our training events. Her large capacity for service gifting was obvious to all and particularly appreciated by TMC.

9. Train to be servants, not Christian culture exporters. Serving the nationals' growth and development is of utmost importance. Turning the ministry over to the nationals can be done faster than one thinks, if we come to serve them.

10. When huge doors open, prepare to go through them, even when it appears impossible.

CONCLUSION

I hope this has given you an inside look at the TMC and those who served on it, along with how they worked. Those wishing to examine the training process in more detail will find additional principles and strategic elements spelled out in the Appendix.

Only the Lord knows exactly how many people He raised up of the original 12,000 we wanted to recruit to minister in the former

Soviet Union. Perhaps, through the CoMissioners, thousands of nationals still carry the torch of the CoMission ministry in their own country. If so, TMC did multiply its training through the CoMissioners.

Dr. Terry Taylor (center front) with fellow hat-wearing CoMission team members.

As president of the US Navigators for thirteen years, I had many wonderful experiences serving the body of Christ, but never have I enjoyed serving God more than in my role as a member of the CoMission Executive Committee. It warms my heart to know the work begun by the CoMission was only the beginning. The long-term results of the CoMission are now in the capable hands of nationals like Nick and Maia Mikhaluk and their rapidly growing ministry of International Partners, along with a host of other ministries that will be reviewed elsewhere in this volume.

Like so many others, I thank God for allowing me to be a part of the CoMission. To God be the glory!

FORTY YEARS
OF WAITING

Monchegorsk, 1995:

When I was five years old, my family was sentenced to the gulags because we were Christians. We were separated during our interminable stay. My sister, who was ten at the time, was raped and eventually died in the gulag. My father also died there. But my mother and I survived.

Decades later, in my eagerness to learn about the Christian heritage for which my parents had risked their lives, I attended the convocation. Following the first session, I slipped on the steps and broke my arm above the elbow. Many people recommended I see a doctor immediately, but I refused. The pain was not enough to stop me from attending the convocation.

"I have waited forty years for this — and I will not miss it," I said to those urging me to seek a doctor. I would go after the lunch break.

Later in the convocation, God worked deeply in my heart. I learned about the Christian faith I had longed to understand. I became a believer.

Now, forty years after my imprisonment, I have the light of Christ and can share it with the children in my school. Through the Foundations of Christian Ethics *curriculum* and the JESUS *film*, I can share the light I waited forty years to see.

PRINCIPLE
NINE

DIVIDE THE TASK AND THE TERRITORIES.

In our practical ministry we genuinely attempted to count others more important than ourselves. One of the first questions occurred when five organizations all felt "led" to place their CoMission teams in Moscow. That would have created great duplication of effort there and left other major cities without a team. But the leaders, in the spirit of cooperation, offered to place their teams in cities most in need and began ministries in places that virtually no one had heard of— and could not spell or pronounce. They were places like Dnipropetrovsk, Chelyabinsk, and Nizhny Novgorod. Some places were high in radiation levels from nuclear accidents. One organization sent older CoMissioners past child bearing ages to go to these places of high radiation.

PETER DEYNEKA, JR., like his father before him, was a champion for Christ among the Slavic people. For many years he served as a missionary—and later as president—of Slavic Gospel Association, a mission founded by his father. In 1991 Peter began a new organization, Russian Ministries. Through these two organizations, and by serving as a consultant to many others, he helped expand numerous ministries to his own Russian people. He performed a valuable service to the CoMission Executive Committee as chairman of the Russian Federation/Commonwealth of Independent States Liaison Committee. Peter Deyneka's CoMission colleagues, along with the entire evangelical community, mourned his death on December 23, 2000. He will not be forgotten.

ANITA DEYNEKA, the author of this chapter, serves God as the president of Peter Deyneka Russian Ministries. The author and co-author of seven books about the church in Russia, she speaks and lectures in many venues in the evangelical community. She has been a valuable resource to the CoMission.

CHAPTER SIX

THE RUSSIAN CONNECTION

The Russian Federation (Commonwealth of Independent States) Liaison Committee

Peter Deyneka, Jr., chairman
Written by Anita Deyneka

MY HUSBAND, PETER, said that when he walked into the room, he had to pinch himself to believe where he was and what was happening. The CoMission Executive Committee had been invited to the Ministry of Education in Moscow to meet with Dr. Alexander Asmolov, a Deputy Minister of Education, Dr. Olga Polykovskaya, an education specialist for morals and ethics, and Mr. Evgeny Kurkin, also a Deputy Minister of Education. Dr. Asmolov told the executive committee, "Please come quickly while the doors are still open."

Not only was Dr. Asmolov's 1993 invitation astonishing, but so was the place where the meeting was held. Dr. Asmolov told the CoMission Executive Committee that the building was the location of the first Ministry of Education after the Bolshevik Revolution in 1917. Lenin's wife, Nadezhda Krupskaya, had served as the Deputy Minister of Educational Policies, Literacy and Psychology. She believed that libraries and education molded the nation and its children, and said, "The children's book is one of the most powerful weapons of the socialist character—education of the growing generation."[1] Peter told me he had sat in Krupskaya's chair, reflecting and reveling at the ways God works.

The Russian landmark, St. Basil's Cathedral in Red Square.

From the day the communists consolidated their power in 1917, they never wavered in their certainty that education of children was a foremost goal. They saw clearly and correctly that the future of the communist Soviet Union depended on the education of its children. Bolshevik education invariably included indoctrination in communism and its atheistic foundation. As Christians in the United States speak of integration of faith and learning, communist leaders intentionally integrated atheistic teaching in educational curriculum from kindergarten through post-doctoral studies.

"As early as 1918, a decree was passed forbidding religious instruction in public schools. Eleven years later, in 1929, another law expanded the prohibition even further by forbidding religious associations to conduct religious education with minors… Soviet educators were instructed to never bring up religion in the classroom."[2] Instead, atheistic literature was enshrined in the national curriculum. Lenin, Stalin, and other communist leaders became role models for Soviet children.

Devotion to Lenin acquired a religious aura. "In most schools, one could also find a picture of Lenin hanging above the blackboard with the slogan, 'Lenin even now is more alive than all of the living.'"[3]

"Educators were encouraged to organize special programs for students to discuss how communism might meet humanity's most important needs, such as the meaning of life, or how to find happiness. Youth groups called Youth Atheists' Clubs published magazines and newspapers, circulated literature, oversaw atheistic museums, and gave advice to other students about atheism. The most zealous participated in atheistic 'evangelism' by organizing atheistic cultural activities, distributing literature or seeking to convert classmates from religious homes."[4]

In 1925, the communists formed a League of Militant Godless, founded by Bolshevik Emelian Yaroslavsky, who had been publishing an atheist newspaper called "The Godless" for three years. By 1930, its nominal membership had risen to 5 million. This organization was led by communist intellectuals and took a hard line toward religion and churches. It began a highly organized campaign to promote atheism and destroy Russia's religious culture. It produced much anti-religious propaganda in the form of films, radio programs, books, and pamphlets to demonstrate the foolishness of religion and the wickedness of the church.

Interestingly, the founder and first chairman of the League, Emelian Yaroslavsky, observed that "religion is like a nail; the harder you strike it, the deeper it goes."[5]

Because Marxism considered any transcendental reality illusory and also deemed it diverting and detrimental to the molding of "the new Soviet person," atheism propagation was systematic in all of society—including the educational system. When Peter and I entered the Soviet Union, we saw signs of atheism everywhere. Many cities had museums of atheism, including one that we visited in Kiev, overcrowded with displays, but not visitors. I recall the elderly caretaker telling Peter, "Thank God, we may soon have a new building."

There were atheism posters, intended to be prominent in all classrooms and posted elsewhere. A typical poster might show a cosmonaut floating in space and triumphantly announcing: "There is no God." As other countries have Christian youth clubs, the Soviets had Marxist, atheistic youth clubs and camps. (Now many of these communist youth campsites and clubs are being used for Christian clubs and camping—another activity the CoMission helped to promote.) Children six to nine years old were expected to be enrolled in the Octobrists; children ten to fifteen years old in the Young Pioneers; and youth fourteen to twenty-eight years of age in the Komsomol, or the Communist Youth League. Membership in the Komsomol was necessary to receive favored treatment and was also a stepping stone to full membership in the Communist Party.

Rosy-cheeked children with red scarves, and sometimes toy military weapons, were expected to demonstrate their loyalty to communism. Teachers told them to imitate the Young Pioneer hero, Pavlik Morozov, who betrayed his own bourgeois parents to the communist authorities. The statue of Pavlik Morozov that stood in Moscow was constantly visited by children who covered it with fresh flowers.[6] Although Lenin said that "religion was unutterable vileness," communist ideology often took on a religious complexion to attempt to fill the God-shaped vacuum in people's souls. For example, to promote a stable society, the Communist Party evolved a moral code that was remarkably like the Ten Commandments, but with no mention of God.

The saturation of atheism was sometimes counterproductive, often producing unintentional spiritual searching, which became apparent when communism collapsed, and even before. In Soviet days, Peter and I met students who would tell us that bold classmates would sometimes ask their teachers of atheism, "Why, if there is no God, is it necessary to speak against Him so much?"

I also remember the man Peter and I met who said that he had been an atheistic propagandist, officially trained and equipped. In order to be informed against Christianity, he had been permitted to read the Bible, a generally prohibited book in communist days. Through his reading, he became a believer.

**Anita and Peter Deyneka meet with General
Nikolai Stolyarov and other government leaders.**

There were others, like the elderly woman caretaker at the atheistic museum, who had not been deeply etched with atheism and may have been secret believers. Even Stalin himself once said, "You can tear down the churches, but the people will build them in their hearts."

The number of human lives that communism took in its campaigns to eliminate all perceived opposition was horrendous. Alexander Solzhenitsyn said, "In addition to the toll of two world wars, we have lost, as a result of civil strife and tumult alone—as a result of internal political and economic class extermination alone—66 million people!" Solzhenitsyn also said, "I myself see Christianity today as the only living spiritual force capable of undertaking the spiritual healing of Russia."

Russia, which had approximately 50,000 Orthodox churches and chapels, as well as a few Protestant churches on the eve of the Bolshevik Revolution, had only four Protestant churches and perhaps 500 Orthodox churches remaining open by the eve of World War II. To enlist the support of the populace to fight the Nazis,

Stalin reopened some churches, but Nikita Khrushchev, often perceived as a liberal reformer in the West, launched a vitriolic anti-religion campaign in the 1960s. Once he hyperbolically said that he would eradicate all Christians, but save one believer to preserve in a museum so future generations "could view an extinct species."

Especially agonizing was the dilemma of Christian parents forced to send their children to public schools, where they knew they would be force-fed atheism. Some parents faced prison when they refused to allow their children to attend atheistic schools, camps, and clubs. Most Christian children did attend public schools, but were shielded through the example and faithfulness of their families—and grew up to become the next generation of church members. I remember one Christian telling us how his parents defied the authorities and brought him to church. Since communist authorities were especially opposed to children attending the limited number of churches permitted to remain open, his schoolteacher dutifully stood at the church gate and told the parents he could not enter. He remembers the teacher pulling him away and his parents holding on to him, pulling in the other direction.

At the request of Soviet believers, Peter and I wrote some books about the situation of Christians in the former Soviet Union and—primarily because of this—were denied visas for thirteen years. Even so, during that time in our mission work, when Peter was organizing such programs as strategic prayer for Politburo leaders and Christian prisoners, short-wave radio broadcasts through the Iron Curtain from stations around the world, publishing and distributing Christian literature, and many other outreaches, we kept in close and constant touch with the country. We knew that both disillusionment with communism and spiritual hunger were widespread. But not until we were again able to enter the country in 1989 did we realize how rampant the corruption of Marxism was and how cavernous the spiritual hunger.

Peter and I once saw an article in a Russian newspaper after the collapse of communism that seemed to us to symbolize the situation of millions. The story included two photos: one of a young child sitting on Stalin's lap, and another of the same person, now a grandmother (*babushka*). As a child this woman, like all children, had been thoroughly indoctrinated in communism. She had been selected for the high honor of presenting Stalin with a bouquet of flowers and having her photo taken with him on one occasion. So strong was her belief in communism and her hero, Stalin, that even when her parents were sent by Stalin to Siberian prison camps as enemies of the people, she continued to believe in Marxist ideology. Now the article described the pathos of an old woman, who had suddenly discovered that all she had been taught was a crumbling scaffold of lies.

The Deynekas meet President Mikhail Gorbachev as part of a delegation of western Christian leaders.

Nowhere was this vacuum greater than in the school system, the foundation of which had been atheism and communism. In 1992 Peter and I moved to Russia with our two college-age children. A school was located directly behind our apartment. When Peter and the children visited and offered their services teaching English, the vice-principal welcomed them eagerly. She said that only recently the principal had bemoaned the collapse of communism. "On what do we help the children base their values now?" she asked. The vice-principal told us that the principal had increased trips to art museums and cultural events to try to fill the void.

As our children taught English at the school and made friends with the students and the vice-principal, they were soon invited to have a Bible study each week after school. Elizaveta, the vice principal, began to visit our little apartment and devour every Christian book Peter gave her. It was a joyous day for all our family when she became a follower of Christ.

In 1992 Peter was invited to join the Executive Committee of the CoMission. Home from Russia that spring, I remember the first meeting we attended at Moody Bible Institute. The room was bursting with people who cared about the former Soviet Union and wanted to walk through doors that God had opened.

Peter told me he could scarcely believe it was true. "To think that so many people care about Russia and are going to do so much to help," he told me.

In 1992 the principal of one school told us, "The footprints of atheism are everywhere in our schools." Repeatedly, I heard Peter thank God for the footprints of the CoMission, including the 1,300 committed Westerners who went to hold 136 four-day convocations with 41,618 teachers, most of whom then taught Christian values to students and teachers in hundreds of public schools and beyond.

The legacy of CoMission in the expansion of the gospel in Russia lives—and will live forever.

The Great Commission

Jesus, when you asked us
to take your good news
to the end of the earth,
it wasn't very far,
for all your finite followers knew.

Even then
it was a great trust,

a challenge of Goliath girth,
to reach every soul on earth.

Now, we humans
teem in the billions.
The command to carry your good news
to the ends of the earth
seems beyond any horizon, any view.

But over the centuries,
since you came among us
and lived and died,
your followers have tried,
with successes and failures
(ultimately determined only by
your eye).

A chapter, at least a page,
maybe only a punctuation mark—
Lord, how can we evaluate
what was written
when you organized the CoMission?

To see your followers banding together,
must have been a pleasure, a treasure
for you who carried salvation
at the cost of the cross.

Jesus, if we learn no other lesson,
from the formation of the CoMission,
from those few 20th century years,
may it be etched forever
what your followers do,
when we strive for your kingdom together.

—ANITA DEYNEKA

Notes:

1. Encyclopedia, Online, "Krupskaya, Nadezhda Konstantinova," accessed on May 23, 2001 from http://www.encyclopedia.com.

2. Perry Glanzer, "A Critical Analysis of The CoMission: A Study in the Loss, Replacement and Establishment of an Ideology of Moral Order," Dissertation, University of Southern California, August 1998, Ch. 1, p. 14.

3. Ibid., Ch. 1, pp. 8-9.

4. Ibid., Ch. 1, p. 14.

5. Trevor Beeson, *Discretion and Valour: Religious Conditions in Russia and Eastern Europe,* (Philadelphia: Fortress Press, 1982), 100.

6. Urie Bronfenbrenner, *Two Worlds of Childhood: U.S. and U.S.S.R.,* (New York: Russell Sage Foundation, 1970), 37.

7. Alexander Solzhenitsyn, *Letter to Soviet Leaders,* (New York: Harper and Row, 1974), 30.

8. Ibid, 57.

GIFTED
TEACHERS
LEAD ON

Latvia, 1997:

Little did we know that when we left our teaching and course management responsibilities in the capable hands of Laima, that she would be instrumental in having the course receive full accreditation in the University.

Laima, a teacher in my first class at the University of Latvia, was exceedingly talented and resourceful. I witnessed her becoming a key leader and saw dramatic growth of our initial work.

Laima and her husband, Arijx, have three sons—Matiss, Fabians, and Davids. They live out their lives in the economic uncertainties found in Latvia, undaunted by the economic turbulence.

Even with the rigorous demands of transferring the course and securing its accreditation, Laima has seen the enrollment in the year-long course jump from twelve students to sixty students last year at the University, with an additional ten students in a satellite program.

In her remarkable skill and effectiveness, she provided leadership for transferring the course from the pedagogical faculty to the theological faculty of the university. Little did I realize that God had even greater plans for the course. Eventually, with significant labor, Laima adeptly guided the course through an intensive and successful review by the university, resulting in nothing less than full accreditation.

Laima's goal is to devote herself full time to managing, teaching and developing the program at the university. In the hands of the Lord, the existing foundation we began years ago now has the potential to reach into every elementary and secondary school in all of Latvia.

God creates many immense opportunities as He uses remarkable and gifted teachers like Laima.

PRINCIPLE
TEN

RESPOND TO OPEN DOORS QUICKLY.

Every organization already had more than enough to do when the new opportunities opened up in the former Soviet Union. All of us lacked the manpower needed, to say nothing of the leaders and finances that would be necessary. We believed that just as there are critical periods where individuals seem more open to the gospel, there are similar times that occur to cities, nations and peoples. We were finding an unprecedented spiritual curiosity in Russia. Whether it was true spiritual hunger or not would be discovered later. But while people were interested in hearing the message of Christ, someone should go and tell it and live it so that they could respond. This meant, for everyone, that we had to make decisions quickly and train people on the job. What other opportunities have we missed during the centuries because we were too slow to respond?

MRS. MARGARET BRIDGES, British-born, is the founding director of Tabernacle School, Inc., in Concord, California. During her thirty years of experience in Jesus-centered education, she has assisted in founding schools in France, Poland, Russia and Romania. She is a gifted conference speaker and fund raiser for schools, orphanages, outreach projects for street children and for church buildings overseas. Margaret played a major role in the founding of the CoMission. As a member of the CoMission Executive Committee she served as chairwoman of the Christian Cultural Exchange Committee. She and her pastor husband, Tom, have four children and live in Concord, California.

CHAPTER SEVEN

THE EXTRA-ORDINARY ROLE OF AN "ORDINARY WOMAN"

Christian Cultural Exchange Committee

Margaret Bridges, chairman

WHEN WE ACCEPT the invitation of Christ Jesus to take His hand and follow Him, our response is to repent, commit, walk by faith and embrace the life of Christ in us with great passion. An authentic follower of Jesus realizes the importance of pain, suffering, and hardship. If these are responded to with the right heart attitude, they can produce perseverance, character and ultimately brokenness. In so many ways, our response to these things will get us ready to be willing to trust, obey and deeply love our Heavenly Father. All of us who felt the definite call of God on our lives through the CoMission can honestly say that this experience—which often included many of these elements—changed our lives.

The CoMission's challenge was for followers of Jesus Christ to cooperatively accomplish His direct command: take the gospel to the uttermost parts of the world. God worked in a powerful way in all of our lives to prepare us for this task. The CoMission was a clarion call of obedience to a radical paradigm shift from traditional thinking.

Many now say that they never want to go back to the old ways again. The motto of the CoMission was, "Many voices, one calling," meaning: many evangelical Christian organizations working together toward one cause—sharing God's love with the people of Russia.

The CoMission was also a personal story for everyone involved. We were swept up in a movement of the Holy Spirit of God. God always prepares His followers for the task ahead. More often than not, the preparation is a test of spiritual maturity.

PREPARATION OF AN ORDINARY WOMAN

As an ordinary woman married to an ordinary pastor and working as a school administrator, I was, to my shame, a typical, lukewarm, "Laodicean" believer. With them I could have said: "I am rich, I am increased with goods and have need of nothing" (Revelation 3:17). My problem was that I did not know I was blind, poor, miserable and a spiritual coward.

This reality became apparent to me when I had an encounter with a very evil man who was known for his satanic rituals and abilities to cast spells. I remember vividly his phone call inviting me to listen to his curse. Worse still, I remember my own response as I dutifully quoted a Bible verse to explain that the power of God in me was far greater than the power of evil in him. Although this was the truth, my spiritual arrogance and lukewarm attitude would prove to be severely tested in the ensuing months.

Unfortunately, I arrogantly assumed I could win the fight he had started on my own. However, after a few months, my weariness was obvious and my Laodicean attitude turned into a spirit of bitterness and retreat. I became self-absorbed in my own misery. My desire to give up was overwhelming. I no longer wanted to hold the hand of the Lord Jesus; I preferred to passively acknowledge Him from a distance. Thankfully, all of that changed, and changed in a dramatic way that was clearly God's intervention.

One Sunday in October 1989, I was sitting in our evening church service. I was there because it was my duty to be there as the pastor's wife. The auditorium was darkened as a film from Underground

Evangelism began. My heart was cold, my attitude disinterested. As I watched the film, my complacent heart was stirred, and I was suddenly challenged with the suffering of God's people in Eastern Europe. The longer I watched their oppression, the more ashamed I became of my selfish attitudes, self-pity and self-absorption. The Holy Spirit moved me to repentance.

I was weeping out loud, asking God for forgiveness and asking His permission to leave the room and seek His face privately. His answer was "No." I was to sit still, listen and watch. As I continued to apologize to God and ask for forgiveness, out of the depth of my heart I was moved toward obedience. I expressed to God that I was willing to go to these people, to take Bibles and offer to help in some way. As an afterthought I mentioned that perhaps God would want to send a man. However, if it were made plain to me as an ordinary woman that it was God's desire, I would certainly go.

God spoke volumes to the whole world in 1989 when there was a revolution in Romania. This revolution had deep roots in the underground church of Romania, filled with brave followers of Jesus Christ. They proved to the world that not only would they live for Jesus, they were very willing to die for Him. The revolution spread through Eastern Europe. The gates of those countries opened wide, giving spiritually hungry people a way to know God.

At a school administrators' conference in February of 1990, God's challenge to me began to unfold in a very personal way. Dr. Phillip Renicks, the missions director for the Association of Christian Schools International (ACSI), asked if I would be interested in going to Timisoara, Romania. I would travel with a team of people in response to an invitation from a Baptist pastor there, to encourage the starting of Christ-centered schools. God had already answered that question during the showing of the Underground Evangelism film the year before. I enthusiastically told Dr. Phil Renicks, "Yes!"

On my two-hour drive home from the conference, I reflected on my quick response. I thought it wise to truly make sure God wanted me to do this. Out loud I simply expressed to my Heavenly Father that I needed confirmation. If I could meet two Romanians from this city called Timisoara within the next three days, it would assure me without a doubt that God was pleased with my quick response to Dr. Renicks' invitation. That evening, I did not meet any Romanians. The following day, Saturday, I decided to thoroughly clean my house. Obviously I did not meet any Romanians that day.

On the third day, Sunday, as I sat in the choir and observed the congregation, I noticed several new couples. I picked one of them to quickly greet and express my appreciation for their visit to our church. As I thanked them afterwards for coming to the service, I could tell that they were quite excited. The gentleman started to explain that God had spoken to them as they drove past the church. He told them to turn their car around and go back. I immediately remembered my Grandmother Musgrave telling me how God spoke to her out loud. I inquired if indeed they heard God's voice. To my surprise and without hesitation, they said yes, God had spoken to them out loud in their car.

I commented about their accents, assuming they were from South America. At once they responded in unison with their country's name: Romania! I covered my mouth with my hand in utter amazement, but one other question remained. I asked, "Which city are you from?" The gentleman said that he was a pastor's son who had escaped from the city of Timisoara and recently came to America. I have to tell you, I was startled, pleased and honored all at the same time that God would answer the conditions of my fleece so completely.

God had definitely confirmed my decision. Later, when I answered the Lord's call and went to Romania, these dear people would become some of our best friends and supporters. The gentleman urged me to stay with his parents in Timisoara. His sister worked at the food shop, and that way I would at least have something to eat! This amazing, God-arranged opportunity for ministry was a faith-building experience for me that would prove to be but a preamble of what He was going to do through others and me in the larger cause of the CoMission. I will forever be grateful for the simple faith of those Romanian believers.

GOD'S PLAN UNFOLDS

The summer of 1990 was very productive for furthering God's kingdom in Romania. In a matter of weeks, I had partnered with a pastor to assist in building a church in the city of Arad. Another partner, Professor Cantana, and his wife, successfully opened the first Christ-centered high school in Timisoara. I traveled around the country just encouraging God's people to open small kindergarten schools in their homes. I learned to love the Romanian people and appreciate their steadfast joy and enduring faith in the midst of great suffering.

In 1991 I was asked by officials at ACSI to speak at its first Eastern European teachers conference. People came from numerous countries in that part of the world. We worked hard to provide translators for the numerous languages represented by the delegates. We did our best to teach those dear people the importance of starting Christ-centered schools in their countries.

A visitor asked if we had anyone who spoke Russian who could translate for some visitors. Eventually we found a German man who spoke Hungarian, and a Hungarian man who spoke Russian, yielding a relay-team translation effort. The most exciting part of this story is that these Russian visitors were from the Department of Education in Moscow. They had been studying education in several countries to determine what they needed to do for their children. I watched these Russian officials listen very intently to all the speakers at the conference. The Russian people love their children. Since the wall came down, they were ready to develop a new world view. I observed a beautiful Russian lady with blonde hair and blue eyes leaning forward listening attentively, and responding positively. I never dreamed we would become good friends and form a strong alliance in ministry. This beautiful lady, Dr. Olga Polykovskaya, would prove to be a crucial ally in opening doors for the gospel of Jesus Christ in Russia.

I was interested to learn that Jerry Franks of Campus Crusade for Christ was responsible for inviting these officials to the conference. Jerry, along with Paul Eshleman, was a pioneer in developing relationships with these officials. God used so many of His people, with their various gifts, to be part of His story. Through them, the gospel of Jesus Christ was taken to the Russian people, who had been essentially cut off from the world for three generations.

Before leaving Romania I visited with Priscilla Pop in Cluj Napoca, Romania. Priscilla became a very special friend. In the course of our conversation in her small kitchen, she told me that one man in America was ready for what God wanted to do, not only in Romania, but also in greater Eastern Europe. I was very interested that a lady such as she would know of someone, when indeed I as an American had no idea who would be eligible. She told me someone had sent her a tape of this man speaking. I anxiously waited for her to name this person. But Priscilla wanted me to first read the notes she had made from the tape.

It is important to note that the Romanian people have developed an incredibly strong faith in response to answered prayer and witnessing miracles. In fact, when I met Anna Gruesco, a Romanian believer living in Timisoara, her first comment was that we needed to start counting the miracles. What Priscilla did next was an expression of her strong personal faith in God.

She gave me instructions that when I met this man and sat next to him, I was to beg and plead for him to come to Romania. She felt he was the one person who was ready and able to make a significant difference in Eastern Europe. Priscilla assumed that I knew everyone, and in simple faith she told me, "Dr. Bruce Wilkinson is prepared and needs to be told to come to Eastern Europe. And you are the one who needs to tell him, Margaret."

I promised Priscilla that I would respond to her challenge. However, I did not think for one moment that I would actually meet Dr. Wilkinson. Nor did I feel it was appropriate to telephone him with the message. British-born people like myself do not call people they do not know to relay invitations from other people thousands of miles away!

As I reflected back to that Sunday night in 1989 and the film in my home church, I was not quite sure what the next chapter would bring into my ordinary life. Priscilla's request was filed away in my mind. Since I did not know Dr. Wilkinson, I was satisfied to think that if God wanted this to happen I would not need to manipulate the situation.

DIVINE APPOINTMENT AT ACSI

The next event would challenge my faith and confront the small-ness of my thinking. Dr. Paul Kienel, an important mentor in my life, sent me a copy of a fax from an official at the Department of Education in Russia. As a result of attending the conference in Timisoara, Romania, this official sent an invitation to ACSI to visit his country and introduce biblical morals and ethics to the children in the public schools. The opportunity was enormous. I was literally beside myself with excitement, knowing that God's story was expanding into numbers that were beyond my imagination, but not, by the grace of God and power of the Holy Spirit, beyond possibility. No question, God was at work.

Every year, believers who teach in Christ-centered schools meet for two days at an ACSI regional convention. In October 1991 at the Portland, Oregon, ACSI Teachers' Convention, God put together the beginning of what can only be described as the amazing CoMission story. As I was finishing up a seminar presentation, a young man came into the room and handed me a note which read, "Our missions director is sick. Will you please come to the platform and give the missions report?" Running down the hallway to the auditorium where about 3,000 people were waiting, I did not take time to look on the platform to see who was seated there. I simply walked past all the gentlemen and sat on the end seat.

My heart was immediately moved to speak about the Romanian people and God's work there, knowing no one could be dry eyed when hearing about God's grace and the power of the Holy Spirit in their lives. In those early days, we were seeing an unusual movement of God's Spirit, and the response of God's people was always compassionate and generous. As I quietly talked to these dear teachers, who by no means were financially rich, there was a deep silence among them. Suddenly there was the sound of 3,000 people tearing checks out of their

Margaret Bridges speaking at the ACSI convention held in Timisoara, Romania where she met Dr. Olga Polykovskaya and Dr. Alexei Brudnov for the first time.

checkbooks and depositing them in the ACSI missions offering!

I turned to go back to my seat on the platform. Wiping my eyes, I sat down. There was a gentleman sitting next to an empty seat. He motioned, inviting me to sit next to him. Looking up at him, I could see my promise to Priscilla was about to become a reality. It was Bruce Wilkinson! Before Dr. Bruce Wilkinson could say anything to me, I bravely spoke out and told him I had a message for him from Romania, that he should be the main speaker for the next conference. I commented that all of Eastern Europe is open and they need God's Word. I said I hoped he would say "yes" to this invitation.

There was no time to say anything else, because his name was being announced to come to the podium. His message was on brokenness. We were invited to leave the platform and move to seats on the convention floor. As I stepped down from the platform of the convention center auditorium, I had the strange yet wonderful feeling that this was a crucial moment, not only in the life of Bruce Wilkinson, but in the larger Christian community. I was speaking out loud to my Heavenly Father, and could not stop weeping. I sat on the front row, ready for this message on brokenness.

Dr. Wilkinson approached the microphone and was overcome with emotion, unable to speak. He took a step back and looked at all of us. He tried again, and still could not speak. Once again, he backed away from the microphone. I sensed that the Holy Spirit was at work in Dr. Wilkinson, and prayed that he would respond to His call to Eastern Europe.

After a powerful message, Dr. Wilkinson came and politely asked who I was and what I was doing at the conference. My reply was a simple one. I stated I was no one important, but I did want to know his answer to the invitation I had given him. Dr. Wilkinson explained that he felt God had called him to the American people. My honest response was that I felt the American people were already overfed and lukewarm in their attitude. He also commented that Paul Eshleman with the *JESUS* film had been asking him to take part in an outreach to Eastern Europe, and his answer had previously been "no." Now, however, without hesitation he told me he would speak at the ACSI convention in Romania. At that moment Dr. Wilkinson did not realize that the mantle of leadership for the CoMission had fallen around his shoulders, and that God would use him mightily. He was to be a prophet, not only to the American people, but also to the people of the Eastern Block countries, and eventually to Africa, India, China, and the whole world.

Dr. Wilkinson's obedience has since been rewarded by the success of his *Prayer of Jabez* book, which has sold into the millions in the US His heart's desire has been fulfilled beyond his wildest dreams.

What we did not know then was that there would be difficult tests ahead, and an intense fight with Satan over the souls of the Russians. This intensity would build in us spiritual maturity and perseverance against all odds.

To be quite honest, part of me did not expect to hear from Dr. Wilkinson again. I had some doubt about whether he would value the role of an "ordinary woman" in a ministry of this breadth and scope. Although Jesus, in His earthly ministry, valued women greatly, not all men in ministry do.

To my surprise, I received an invitation to the headquarters of Dr. Wilkinson's Walk Thru the Bible ministry. He also invited me to one of the first strategy meetings where we prepared for the challenge of addressing 120,000 Eastern European teachers, who would collectively reach 21 million students throughout the former Soviet Union and Eastern Europe. Dr. Wilkinson eventually asked me to join the CoMission's Executive Committee. I am so grateful to my Heavenly Father for allowing this to take place. What I experienced during those years of involvement has changed my life forever.

Dr. Wilkinson did indeed speak at the ACSI convention in Romania. There was a very unusual movement of God's Spirit in that meeting. During the reign of Ceausescu, long time dictator of Romania, some pastors collaborated with members of the secret Romanian police. This compromise meant that the police learned the names of followers of Jesus, and as a result many Christians were arrested, put in prison and tortured. These events caused much bitterness and fighting within the body of Christ.

At the convention Dr. Wilkinson spoke about repentance. It was so powerful to watch some of those pastors on their knees, weeping over their compromise and asking forgiveness. The Holy Spirit confronted me that day with my lack of love towards some of God's people who had deeply wounded me. I realized that forgiveness is the only release from bitterness. If not confronted, it threatens to cripple us emotionally. In that hall in Romania, God's grace was powerfully working in every heart, including mine.

THE CHALLENGE TO UNITE

Dr. Bruce Wilkinson invited the leaders of several large ministries to a planning meeting at the ACSI headquarters in La Habra, California. He realized that it would take a dramatic move of God's Spirit to allow powerful ministry leaders to commit to working together and sharing expertise, personnel and financial resources. God certainly was at work. As the last prayer was finished, we all realized God was bringing together an army of His people to answer that most unusual invitation from the Ministry of Education in Moscow.

As mentioned earlier, I was asked to become part of the Executive Committee. At first I was reluctant. I was not the leader of a large national or international ministry like most of the members of the CoMission Executive Committee. I did not have financial resources. I was an "ordinary woman," a follower of Jesus Christ. My husband's response was quite different. He encouraged me to think beyond my own inadequacy and step outside my comfort zone. With his encouragement and faith, in the Lord's equipping, I accepted the invitation.

My assignment on the Executive Committee was to partner with Dr. Olga Polykovskaya, Chief Specialist with the Ministry of Education of the Russian Federation. Dr. Polykovskaya worked with the cultural centers in several major cities across Russia. She also served as the coordinator for the International Project for Christian Moral and Ethical Education, as well as other forms of moral education in the Russian federation.Dr. Polykovskaya established what she called the "Kindness Foundation," to transform the cultural centers into centers for spiritual education. Her dream was to see families grow and develop morally and spiritually, and their communities become better equipped to deal with the challenges of the new Russia.

I deeply appreciated the work of Mr. Bill Wolfe, Dr. Ron Braund and Mr. John Geiger, who gave generously of their energy and creativity to this project. We had endless meetings, many flights to Moscow, numerous fundraising efforts and times of great joy and learning together. Only heaven will reveal the impact of their efforts. Thank you, dear friends.

Family life in Russia has long revolved around the Cultural Center. Under communism, the centers majored in political indoctrination for the whole family. With the collapse of communism, God opened the doors of opportunity for us to convert these into Christ-centered places. The purpose of our committee was to equip and support these centers within the Russian communities. Our objective was to make sure the truth of the Bible would impact all areas of their family life, and would further impact their educational system with Christ-centered values.

The cultural centers also operate the camps throughout the country. Once again, under communism these were used to indoctrinate the thousands of Russian children, who got on trains during the summer to attend camp. By God's grace we can say that those children heard, and still hear, the message of Jesus. It only takes fifteen years to change a nation when you begin with the children. We have had a wonderful beginning.

Russian children captured hearts at every turn.

With Dr. Polykovskaya as my teacher, I began to understand important cultural differences and the traditions I needed to embrace. We had meetings with the directors of the cultural centers to encourage their involvement with spiritual issues. We met in the Department of Education in Moscow. As I entered this large building and walked through it to our meeting hall, I saw a large portrait of Lenin. It reminded me of how far God's story had penetrated the Russian society. Children are always the prize in a spiritual battle, because if Satan controls how children are taught and trained, he controls their future ideology and the future of their nation.

It was ironic to me that in Russia I was participating in something that would never be possible in the United States. Dr. Polykovskaya could not understand why we were unable to teach morals and ethics in our government schools. She would shake her head in disbelief as I would try to explain this to her. May God forgive us for what we have allowed to happen to the children of the United States!

There is no question that I had a lot to learn about Russian culture. I learned, for example, I had to present every participating school director with a gift. On one occasion I learned that I was also responsible to provide lunch for everyone. Luckily a Russian McDonald's was nearby, and a Big Mac, fries and a drink for everyone was acceptable. When we did run out of gifts, I took my vice-principal aside. We decided to take off our own jewelry to make up the difference.

The children displayed an eagerness to learn.

THEIR HUNGER TO KNOW GOD

Some of my most enjoyable times were in schools with the students. I joined a group of college students in Estonia, formerly part of the Soviet Union, a country in the Russian Federation, during a visit to a high school. We had an Estonian gentleman show the *JESUS* film to 900 students in their auditorium. I was not quite prepared for what happened next. A very well dressed principal approached me just before the film started. He asked if I knew God. Then he went on to say, "If you know God, would you come to the staff meeting room? All the staff members are waiting for an introduction to God so they can know Him." I was rather nervous, yet excited to realize that during the two-hour period for students to see the *JESUS* film, I would have ample time to share with the school faculty an introduction to the God of the Bible.

As I wondered where to begin, it seemed obvious: I should begin at the beginning, with the book of Genesis. It was good to know everyone could speak and understand English except one teacher, whose friend quietly translated as I spoke to them. I later understood that it was not good to begin with the cross of the Lord Jesus. The Russian people have had so much personal suffering that it is upsetting to them, and they get off focus when thinking about someone else's suffering.

Our two-hour session began, and my knees were knocking as I thought about being the first person to speak the truth of the Lord

Children engrossed in *The Greatest Promise* booklets.

Jesus to these high school staff members. Their eyes were focused intently on me as I explained that God wanted a relationship with His children, and that He loves His children. Adam and Eve had the best Father, a Father who was waiting for them to make the choice to love and obey Him. We talked about sin in the Garden of Eden, and everyone started to weep uncontrollably. I decided to wait until someone could become composed enough to speak.

One articulate teacher asked this question: "Will God ever forgive us for teaching the children at the beginning of every day that God did not exist and the State provided their bread?" Oh, the pleasure of telling them about the complete forgiveness of sin in the Lord Jesus, and seeing the joy of the Lord come into that room!

As we walked through the story of the Bible, from the birth of the Lord Jesus to His death, they began weeping again. This weeping, however, was not from regret, but out of appreciation for the Lord Jesus' sacrifice. The story of the resurrection of Jesus brought them to tears of joy. Their response was to accept that Jesus was the Christ, and to repent of their sins. Like a fisherman pulls in his net full of the day's catch, we saw a collective response from everyone in the room. These were deeply intelligent people longing for the truth, who had waited twenty-five years to hear this message.

As I went back into the auditorium, the film was at the place where an invitation to trust Jesus Christ was being given. The response was once again overwhelming. After the room cleared, I sat down on the platform steps and wept, thinking of the privilege of following Jesus.

It is hard to paint a picture of the spiritual hunger of the Russian people, let alone explain the joy of discovery at their first reading of the Bible. The following letter from a Russian teacher will give you some idea:

> When I came home on Friday, I opened that big bag with wonderful presents. Among bright, tasty and aromatic things, I found the tiny blue book containing the New Testament, Psalms and Proverbs. My joy and delight knew no limits. It has always been my dream to have such a little book and treat it as my friend, as a living being. We never part; the book is always with me. I enjoy reading and

memorizing the most striking verses from it. As I read the first few
sentences of the introduction, which explained in simple and very
beautiful poetic language the role of the Bible in this life of people, I
felt tears pouring down my cheeks. Those were tears of happiness.

As I read her letter, I had to ask myself if I could remember the
last time I wept over the Word of God and expressed such delight
over having a Bible to read.

Members of the Executive Committee made a five-year commitment to the CoMission. During that time we met often at commissioning services for those who committed to live in a Russian city for
one year. There they developed relationships with teachers, students
and parents in the schools, and neighbors in their apartment houses.

We had several meetings in Moscow to meet with directors and
other workers in the field to see everything firsthand. I appreciated
their integrity and passion and all the things they taught me, an in-
experienced missionary and ordinary British woman who got swept
up in God's story in Russia.

During this time, there were events and circumstances that just
amazed me:

- I was amazed at the incredible amount of money that
  passed through my hands. It came from both friends and
  people I did not know, often in the mail with a note saying, "God told me to give you this." I was careful to create
  a fund under the church umbrella for these gifts, which
  was watched over by the leaders of the church.

- I was amazed at the unity created among influential men
  in ministry as they submitted to one another and deferred
  when there was disagreement.

- I was amazed at the power of the gospel of Jesus Christ in
  an atheist country, and the hunger of people to know God.

- I was amazed at the multitude of North American lay people who could not wait to go and live in Russia for one
  year, and who, upon returning home, often went back

again for another year. It is not an easy country to live in because of the lack of everyday sustenance.

- I was amazed at the impact of the *JESUS* film and the faithfulness of Paul Eshleman. This film was a key component in reaching people with the never ending story of eternal significance.

- I was amazed at the impact of videos produced by Dr. Bruce Wilkinson. These videos were an important element of the far-reaching impact of CoMission. Teachers' lives were impacted. They in turn influenced their students, and the students took the message home to their parents, who went to cultural centers in the evening hours to hear more. As I sat next to a young CoMissioner at a celebration banquet, he explained more about this process. In the morning hours he would go to the town marketplace where the older men and women sit and talk. He could not grasp their whole conversation, but he did know they had watched the Walk Thru the Bible videos, because he heard them constantly using Dr. Wilkinson's name.

Over the years of my involvement with CoMission, there have been many lessons learned and tests to move through. Once, on a trip to St. Petersburg, Russia, two Christian professors took me to Main Street to do some shopping. As they moved aside to look in their bags, suddenly a gang of street youths surrounded me. They literally grabbed everything—my arms, my bags—and within seconds disappeared as the professors started shouting at them. It did not take long to realize that my passport, visa, money and gifts were gone.

With my knees knocking, I simply prayed out loud, "Father, please bring back my passport and visa. The rest does not matter. Please, Father, within the next five minutes?" Almost at once a very young, blonde-haired boy in gray flannels stood in front of me. Our eyes met. He said, "Surprise!" and held out my passport and visa, which I promptly grabbed. He said, "Reward," and the young lady next to me gave him a piece of gum. Instantly he was gone. The grace and power of God and His Holy Spirit to answer my prayer so quickly was astonishing. No one wants to get caught in Russia without a passport and visa. I learned that God is in control no matter what happens.

The Importance of the Local Church

When visiting another country, I typically ask God to lead me to a pastor and his wife to whom I can be helpful in some way. Sometimes we partner in providing a building or assisting in opening an orphanage. In Russia I was asked to assist with a building. Second Baptist in Moscow was in need of a place to meet. It was a privilege to raise money for those dear people. Today they have a nice new auditorium due to the faithfulness of their pastor, Oleg Zedulov.

As we continue to work in Russia, it becomes evident that there is a great need for local churches to be started. In a 1991 survey conducted by Andrew Greeley, a University of Chicago sociologist, it showed that forty-seven percent of Russians believed in God. By 1998 this number jumped to sixty percent. "In a remarkably brief period of time, Russia has become one of the most God-believing countries in Europe," claimed Greeley.[1]

The Russians are quick to tell us that they want a church to touch their Russian souls. They appreciate an intellectual pastor expressing biblical truth. They want poetry to be read in services, and to hear classical music. May God help us pray and seek ways to train Russian teachers who feel called to the ministry, and assist them in starting small house churches that are Russian, and not Western, in their culture.

God's Story Continues

The five-year cooperative venture called the CoMission ended on December 31, 1997. I count it a privilege to have worked with the Executive Committee members and their spouses. All of them were obedient servants of Christ as leaders in the CoMission.

But numerous spin-off ministries have emerged from all this that bless the heart of God. For example, Dr. Ron Braund continues his ministry with CoMission for Children at Risk. Many of us became concerned with the problem of children on the streets of Russia. In the city of Moscow alone, there are hundreds of street children. Pray for us as we continue to bring God's story into their lives. I count it a privilege to add my support to this fine program.

It has been my privilege to sit on the board of Global Outreach with Dan DeGroat. This ministry is connected with Christian Camping International, working with Russian camps. Dan DeGroat and Bob Kobalish were part of CoMission. God's story continued to unfold on a plane headed to Orlando, Florida. A lady started a conversation with me as a gentleman listened in. He introduced himself as a person in ministry. I invited him to attend our CoMission meeting that evening. Wow—I have never seen a man so deeply moved with compassion for God's story. He immediately responded and told me he was going to speak to his board about becoming part of CoMission. Dan DeGroat was a director of a camp in Texas, and responded to God's call to live in Russia. After returning he became the director of Global Outreach, a worldwide outreach to Christ-centered camps.

In 2001, I was privileged to travel to Romania again to encourage nationals who are opening a shelter for street children in the city of Arad. Pastor Doru Popa of Maranatha Baptist Church had been appointed the mayor of the city. He has invited us to come, and will provide the building for this shelter. There are an estimated 200 million street children around the world who are the poorest of the poor, who are severely mistreated in every way possible. We pray that the Lord Jesus will empower us to reach some of these children in Arad with the message of salvation, along with food, clothes, and shelter.

Please pray with us as God continues to bring His message to these needy people through the extended impact of the ministry of CoMission.

NOTE:

1. SOURCE: EastWest Ministries.

PRAYER AS THE KEY

Nizhniy Novgorod, Autumn 1996:

"I do not believe in God, and I do not believe that God answers prayers," Julia said as she shifted uncomfortably in her seat. Julia, an atheist attending the convocation small group, puzzled over my words. She could not understand, nor accept my remarks.

I heard a tender voice respond to her from a nearby seat. "What is your greatest need as an educator? If we pray for it, and God answers, you would have a change of heart," spoke Nadia, one of the Russian teachers, a Christian who wanted to help her colleague.

"Well," Julia answered hesitantly, "I am a biology professor and work with adults here. I need equipment. I need a computer and software that would do scientific computation."

Julia paused, looked at us and then declared, "But that would be impossible, because no such computer is available. I have been searching for several years and, even if I could find one, it would be economically out of the question."

Immediately Nadia said, "We shall pray . . . we shall all pray." Spontaneously we all began to pray.

This was a real prayer of faith. Would God reveal Himself to Julia and to the others in the group through this prayer?

That night I pleaded with the Lord to reveal Himself in this way.

As thousands of intercessors prayed for the entire CoMission, so it was fitting that in the prayers of our small group God would prove Himself and open yet more doors.

The next morning as Julia walked into her office, to her utter amazement, a brand new computer with everything she needed to do her work sat on her desk. She inquired about the surprise. Yet even her supervisor had no idea where it had come from.

At lunch Julia approached me with joyful excitement and declared, "On my desk . . . a computer for my department . . . it had my name on it!" Her face radiant with a smile from ear to ear, she hugged me. Then she said, laughing, "Now, shall we pray for a house where I can live?"

When Julia came back to our group that afternoon, she came with a new attitude. Instead of being hostile and antagonistic, she came with an open heart. She began to ask many probing questions about how God relates to the world we live in and to her personally. Later Julia said she would definitely use the Bible stories in her teaching. Without hesitation she said, "After all, people need to know where they came from and why they are here!"

In a microcosm of what was happening across the nation that year, God revealed Himself and His power through many answered prayers.

PRINCIPLE
ELEVEN

MOBILIZE PEOPLE TO PRAY.

The Prayer Committee rallied over 20,000 people to pray daily for the CoMission. Each CoMissioner recruited prayer teams. Weekly newsletters contained the latest reports of praise as well as the challenges being faced. We prayed for ourselves. We prayed for the Russians. We prayed for the Church. We prayed for the workers. We prayed for the new believers. We had prayer walks, prayer seminars and prayer days. There were so many obstacles in the CoMission effort, that without the hand of God involved, we had no way to recruit the workers, raise the resources and get permission for the ministry in every school. Every participant in the CoMission saw the miraculous hand of God at work continually.

MARY LANCE SISK serves on many boards and committees related to prayer and evangelism and is highly regarded as a bridge builder in the body of Christ around the world. She travels extensively as a prayer leader and teacher of the art of friendship evangelism—a lifestyle of love, with an emphasis on one's own neighborhood. Over the years she has been closely associated with Leighton Ford Ministries as the prayer coordinator, and now as a lead teacher with Arrow Ministries, which works to develop younger leaders. In 1996 she served as one of the vice-chairmen of the Carolinas' Billy Graham Crusade, as well as its prayer chairman. She served the CoMission as chairwoman of the prayer committee and is now chairman of Mission America's Lighthouse Council, a national movement to pray for, care for and share the gospel with every man, woman and child in the United States. She and her husband, Robert V. Sisk (Bob), are the parents of five children (one of whom is with the Lord) and the grandparents of nine.

CHAPTER EIGHT

PRAYER—THE KEY TO THE CoMission

Prayer Committee

Mary Lance Sisk, chairman

"IT IS MY OPINION that prayer was the central means God employed for the success of the CoMission operations," said John Kyle of the CoMission's Executive Committee. "As the CoMission moved into the formerly hostile Soviet Union, all of us involved were plunged far beyond our experienced abilities in other Christian ministries. Without the continued prayers that bathed the CoMission—with all of its challenges and complexities—I know that we would not have experienced the great victories that were realized for the honor of Jesus Christ."

THE CALL AS I RECALL IT

Far beyond our experienced abilities was the beginning; challenges and complexities were encountered along the way; and finally, the great victories realized for Jesus Christ. But where did the great adventure in CoMission prayer all begin?

Paul Kienel says, "I recall very well the CoMission Executive

Committee in Atlanta when our chairman, Bruce Wilkinson, expressed concern that of all of the subcommittees we had formed to carry out the administrative planning of the CoMission, we had yet to form a prayer committee. Mary Lance Sisk was the unanimous choice for chairperson of that committee. As we look back now at all that happened from that point on in the life of the CoMission, one can only say that the formation of the Prayer Committee was the most important."

Even as the Executive Committee was moving in this direction, the Lord was preparing me. On May 8, 1993, I was spending a day in prayer and fasting, seeking the Lord for guidance regarding a question that lay heavily on my mind: Was I to continue ministering overseas as a missionary to the nations from my local church, Forest Hill Church in Charlotte, North Carolina? Or was it time for me to switch my focus to my own nation, where God seemed to be opening so many doors?

I didn't have to wait long for an answer. Late the following afternoon I received a call from Paul Eshleman, vice-chairman of the CoMission. When Paul invited me to serve on the Executive Committee of the CoMission as chairman of the Prayer Committee, I knew it was the Lord's response to my seeking Him the day before. Indeed, there was no shadow of doubt in my mind that the Lord Himself was calling me to this particular task.

A few months later, I attended my first official meeting as a member of the CoMission Executive Committee. As I listened to Bruce Wilkinson, chairman of the Executive Committee, cast the vision for the great work to which God had called the CoMission, and as I heard the other members express their hearts as well, the Prayer Committee began to take shape in my heart and mind.

GETTING STARTED

My prayerful inclination was first to invite the wives of the CoMission Executive Committee. These were godly women who had been supporting their husbands in kingdom work for years at the place of prayer. When I brought my plan before the Executive Committee, I asked members to recommend either their spouse or a member of their ministry staff to serve on the Prayer Committee.

An exceptional group of committee members, representing nine organizations, met for the first time in my home in Charlotte, North Carolina, in December 1993. God blessed us with a tremendous spirit of unity and a prayer strategy for the work. The mission to the former Soviet Union took flight on wings of prayer.

We saw our personal prayer mission as having multiple objectives: to undergird the Executive Committee in prayer; to pray for the CoMission team members—and also train them in effective prayer; to provide resources to aid their personal prayer lives and larger prayer ministries; whenever possible, to pray on site where the teams served; to mobilize informed prayer support for the CoMissioners; and to pray for the fruit of their ministries.

Executive Committee welcomes Mary Lance Sisk as the Prayer Committee Chairman.

SERVING THE EXECUTIVE COMMITTEE

One of the first and most important tasks at hand was to bathe the Executive Committee with prayer as they strategized, built relationships, opened doors of ministry and gave leadership to the CoMission. Lois Kyle took the lead and encouraged every Executive Committee member to gather around himself or herself twelve people who would commit to pray for them in depth, daily.

Recalls Lois: "I assured them that God had avalanched His blessing upon the ministry of the CoMission, and that Satan would avalanche his work upon the CoMission also, making each member of the Executive Committee and his or her family prime targets. I encouraged them not to count upon their spouse and fellow committee members to serve as one of their twelve, but to trust God to expand their prayer base by enlisting others."

Additionally, each member of the CoMission Prayer Committee prayed daily for one member of the Executive Committee. For four years, each Executive Committee member gave his or her prayer warriors personal prayer needs, as well as requests for their family members. Travel itineraries were regularly communicated, and we covered the leadership in prayer, moment by moment and mile by mile.

It was the custom of the Executive Committee to have one of its meetings each year in the former USSR, and they once invited the Prayer Committee to accompany them. While there, the Executive Committee would usually visit a CoMission team on site, letting the leadership see the ministry first-hand and also encourage both CoMissioners and new believers. The main meetings were always held in Moscow, where leaders serving in the field joined the Executive Committee to share their ministry reports.

In addition to Moscow, at that time the Prayer Committee traveled to Odessa, Ukraine, to see the work of the CoMission team sent by Mission to the World. While in Odessa, both committees met with CoMissioners and rising leaders among the new Ukrainian Christians, and also visited the work of the CoMissioners.

"One outstanding visit," recalls Lois Kyle, "was to Public School 15, where we were able to see a Christian school teacher using the

Bible-based curriculum introduced by the CoMission. We held a banquet for the new believers while we were there, and Bruce Wilkinson brought a message of hope and encouragement. What a joy it was to see the new Ukrainian Christians coming forward for a prayer of commission!" The Prayer Committee attended every Odessa event, backing up the visit with prayer and rejoicing in what God was doing.

Many teachers in the former Soviet Union have been prayed for and influenced by the CoMission. Here is one of their stories, as published in volume 3, issue 1, of *The Chariot*:

WOULD YOU COMMUTE SEVEN HOURS ONE WAY?

When Kurt and Elke and their team arrived in Ukraine, they were treated almost as heroes. They were the first Westerners ever to set foot on the campuses where they worked. Elke appeared regularly on the local television news and interview shows to explain what they were doing in the city and how people could live by the moral and ethical teachings of Jesus taken from the Bible.

But it was not an easy assignment; they had left a lot of conveniences behind. They were in a city with no supermarkets, no malls, no laundromats and no McDonald's. And they lived in a tiny apartment where they rejoiced when the elevator worked and the water ran hot.

During the day they held classes for teachers in various schools on teaching the Christian Ethics and Morality curriculum. One wonderful result of these classes is that many teachers came to faith in Christ. So Kurt and Elke also held Bible studies for converted teachers to help them grow in their own personal faith. In the evenings, they showed the JESUS film to parents, and began follow-up Bible studies in the parents' homes.

In one of the schools where Elke worked, a new teacher (we'll call her Olga) showed up about four weeks into the class. Elke introduced herself and learned that Olga had traveled seven hours to be there because she had heard about Elke's class.

Elke handed her a copy of every resource she had—the Christian Ethics and Morality curriculum, Josh McDowell's books on the resurrection, and finally a Bible.

Olga started to weep. She said it was the first time she had ever held a Bible in her hands. She didn't know what to say.

Week after week, once a week, Olga traveled the seven hours in the morning, stayed for Elke's hour-and-a-half class, and then traveled the seven hours back to her home. When Elke asked her what she was doing with the information she was gaining, Olga said that each Monday she taught the other teachers in her school what she had learned from Elke!

Eventually Elke and Kurt actually got to visit Olga's school and showed Bill Bright's video, Man Without Equal. *The response was wonderful, and Olga is continuing to teach the Bible to those who have responded. Elke commented, "I have never seen people so hungry to know God."*

Our trips into the former Soviet Union served not only to provide prayer coverage in-country and for the Executive Committee, but they also served to burden our hearts for the Russian people and to enlarge the vision of the Prayer Committee for our work in the former Soviet Union. The trips also gave us the opportunity we needed to link up with nationals, and were the beginning of God's fulfillment of the vision He gave us to raise up a prayer movement in the Commonwealth of Independent States (CIS). We returned home from these trips with hearts full and a much clearer vision of how we could best help CoMissioners—even before they left to serve in-country.

SERVING THE COMISSION IN TRAINING

Each year, the CoMission provided two Primary Training Institutes (PTIs) at which CoMission team members were trained to live and serve in the former Soviet Union for their one-year assignments. At these the training was intense, key meetings were held, and CoMissioners began the process of separating from their friends and family members. On-site prayer coverage by members of the Prayer Committee was crucial to the smooth training and transition of CoMissioners and their teams.

Milton Monell gave leadership to the Prayer Committee's support during CoMissioner training. This included having several members of the Prayer Committee on hand at the training site, both to pray and to train in prayer. We also spent time praying for specific meetings, including the Executive Committee as it met and made decisions; for specific requests, as when a needed visa hadn't come in or a team member was sick; and for each team's specific prayer requests before the members left for the former Soviet Union.

"As we spent time praying for and over each CoMission team as they prepared to leave for the former USSR," Milton recalls, "the Lord always had the right word of encouragement or instruction for each team to deeply touch them and delight us. Over and over, God showed Himself faithful to answer requests of CoMissioners as they took time to pray with us, for themselves and for one another."

One particularly exciting incident, he remembers, involved brain surgery scheduled for the "spiritual mom" of a CoMission team leader away from home for training: "Early in the morning of her scheduled surgery, the Prayer Committee members called a time of prayer for this loved one. Over 100 CoMissioners and others gathered to lift her up to the Lord, and saw Him respond in a very special way. The surgery was much shorter than anticipated, and the tumor was

Some members of the Prayer Committee and CoMissioners with Mary Lance Sisk.

much smaller than the pre-surgery tests had revealed. The entire procedure was successful and this believer, who was so important in the life of the CoMissioner was able to talk to him on the phone within 24 hours of her recent brain surgery!"

The Prayer Committee not only undergirded the training efforts with prayer, but taught the practice of prayer as well, led by Betty Crouse of OMS International and myself. Together we equipped the CoMissioners with the biblical foundations of prayer by leading them through a study of God's Word and our own practical experiences of preparing for and serving on the mission field. CoMissioners learned the importance of recruiting and assembling an organized personal prayer support team that would not only pray for them, but would join the CoMissioner in leaving a "gift of prayer" in the former USSR. We also instructed them in the discipline of journaling so that they could record and remember God's faithfulness and grow in their relationship with Him.

SERVING THE COMISSION WITH PRAYER TOOLS

One of the most important tools developed by the Prayer Committee and given as a gift to the CoMissioners was the "Prayer Preparation Manual and Journal." This covered five weeks of study designed to enhance the CoMissioner's ever-widening spheres of relationship and potential influence.

Topics of instruction included:

Relationship with God—*How to Have a Quiet Time*

Relationship with Others—*Forgiveness: The Key to Extraordinary Prayer*

Relationship with the Body of Christ—*How to Intercede for Your Teams*

Relationship with the World—*How to Intercede for Your City and Nation*

Spiritual Warfare—*How to Stand in the Battle*

I had a deep burden for each CoMissioner to understand that prayer is simply a relationship with God. As we grow in the knowledge of God, His character and His ways, as revealed through His Word, we become one of God's closest friends—an intercessor. He desires to share with us the burdens that are on His heart for the nations of the world.

The journal portion covered the purposes and power of journaling: recording, reacting, reflecting and problem solving through journaling and spiritual growth through journaling. It contained basic principles and helpful resources. Along with the manual and journal, Bette Crouse offered new CoMissioners the following advice, learned from her long and distinguished experience on the mission field: "Sometimes, when confronted with an entirely new culture, we have a hard time making sense out of what is going on inside of us. Journaling is a way to sort through your experience so that you can make the most out of it and are able to piece together your experience before you even come home."

The "Prayer Manual and Journal" is still enjoying a life beyond the CoMission, as I have happily granted requests from like-minded organizations to reprint and use it. These have included Campus Crusade's Macedonian Project, a short-term mission to the least evangelized parts of the world. Bette Crouse continues to use it as a resource for the training of all OMS International missionary candidates as they come in, and says: "I still have people ask for copies of the manual and journal, so it continues to be used in a very effective way." The responses from CoMissioners who were new journalers then, as well as those continuing the practice, were so inspiring that OMS uses them as examples for new missionaries. Many former CoMissioners say that they now can't imagine a life without journaling, as their lives are enhanced when they combine this rich devotional time with their prayer time and reap real growth in their spiritual lives."

Did prayer make a difference? Definitely. Consider the following glimpse excerpted from a letter written by Russian believers in Kislovodsk:

FROM RUSSIA WITH THANKS

Dear Christian friends,

As Russian Christians, we would like to thank with all our hearts the members of "our team of Americans." We would also like to thank the people who helped them organize their activities in our country by giving them their sponsorship. We think that there is no higher mission than to share the Word of God with those who need it. . . .

At first we doctors, teachers, engineers, housewives and students used to be just attentive listeners. But from the very first discussions of Christianity and its essence . . . our teachers helped us through the Word of God, to help us understand the spiritual laws shaping our relationship with God. Their inspired prayers for the Word to penetrate our hearts reached God, and all the members of our group received Jesus Christ as Savior. . . .

"Our Americans" were not only our teachers, but they were the very example of God of the Christian way of treating people. These people, always smiling and benevolent, kind and open hearted, were always ready to find for everyone words of consolation when we needed it. For all the time of their being here, we felt that they shared our joy and sorrow like true human beings, like true brothers and sisters in Christ. . . .

We thank you, those who gave these people the opportunity to come to Russia. . . . They directed our souls to the Kingdom of God. . . . Thank you for giving us the Bible, the most important book for every Christian. Reading this Book of books, we reveal Christ to ourselves and others. . . . We desire to follow His example daily and become the vessel of His presence for people around us. We try to bring to God those who have not yet received Jesus Christ, and we do our best to encourage them to make their choice, the greatest choice of their lives. . . .

With our hearts filled with faith, we feel ourselves happy because we know that God is always ready to rescue and protect us... Now we are not alone in this world. The moment we invited Jesus into our lives, God made our hearts His home. . . .

We thank our Lord for those who are beside us and for you who trusted our friends to carry the Word of God across the ocean. The seeds of faith sown by them gave "good shoots. . . ."

In the Holy Name of God,
Ludmilla

Another tool for prayer used to great effect in the former Soviet Union was the *Fast Fax Facts (FFF)*. The brainchild and labor of love of Prayer Committee member Anne Crow, the *FFF* was compiled from prayer requests sent from CoMissioners, their prayer captains and other interested individuals, then assembled by Anne at CoMission headquarters and sent out by the Prayer Committee.

Perhaps the most visible prayer tool offered by the Prayer Committee was the quarterly newsletter *The Chariot*, edited by Elaine Springer. According to her, "*The Chariot's* mission was to encourage prayer support for the many facets of the CoMission ministry in the former Soviet Union and Eastern Europe." In it we regularly featured articles detailing CoMissioner experiences; reports on how many, when and where CoMission teams were traveling to the CIS; invitations to participate in on-site intercessory prayer opportunities in the former Soviet Union and Eastern Europe; a teaching article on prayer; beautiful photos; and encouraging reports from CoMissioners of answered prayers. Mailed by request to over 8,000 people in multiple countries around the world, *The Chariot* informed and encouraged those who had a desire to help the people of the former Soviet Union rebuild their society on the truths of God's Word.

The Chariot did a fabulous job of keeping us all informed and connected. The following is just one of my favorite articles published there to encourage those praying for the people of Russia. It shows that God is always about the business of responding to prayer and revealing Himself to ordinary men and women like you and me.

AN ANSWERED PRAYER FROM STALIN'S TIMES

In the 1930s Stalin ordered a purge of all Bibles and all believers. In Stavropol, Russia, this order was carried out with a vengeance.

Thousands of Bibles were confiscated, and multitudes of believers were sent to the gulags—prison camps—where most died for being "enemies of the state."

Last year, the CoMission sent a team to Stavropol. The city's history wasn't known at that time. But when our team was having difficulty getting Bibles shipped from Moscow, someone mentioned the existence of a warehouse outside of town where these confiscated Bibles had been stored since Stalin's day.

After much prayer by the team, one member finally got up the courage to go to the warehouse and ask the officials if the Bibles were still there. Sure enough, they were. Then the CoMissioners asked if the Bibles could be removed and distributed again to the people of Stavropol. The answer was, "Yes!"

The next day the CoMission team returned with a truck and several Russian people to help load the Bibles. One helper was a young man—a skeptical, hostile, agnostic collegian who had come only for the day's wages. As they were loading Bibles, one team member noticed that the young man had disappeared. Eventually they found him in a corner of the warehouse, weeping. He had slipped away, hoping to quietly take a Bible for himself. What he found shook him to the core.

The inside page of the Bible he picked up had the handwritten signature of his own grandmother. It had been her personal Bible! Out of the thousands of Bibles still left in that warehouse, he stole the one belonging to his grandmother—a woman persecuted for her faith all her life.

No wonder he was weeping—God was real. His grandmother had no doubt prayed for him and for her city. His discovery of this Bible was only a glimpse into the spiritual realm—and this young man is in the process of being transformed by the very Bible that his grandmother found so dear.

This story has been repeated with a variety of details all over the former Soviet Union, where God has done amazing things on a regular basis, making Himself known and real in thousands of lives. Many *Chariot* stories, as well as *Fast Fax Facts* prayer requests, began life as an e-mail from a prayer captain. These were the individuals who assumed "back home" leadership on each CoMissioner's personal prayer team.

SERVING THE COMISSION TEAMS

A vital part of each CoMissioner's preparation and continuing ministry was the formation of a personal prayer team and appointing of a prayer captain. Pat Wentink, a CoMissioner to Petrozavodsk with World Team and a member of Calvary Church in Charlotte, North Carolina, invited several women she first met in her Sunday school class to be on her prayer team. She asked one of them, Susan Lindsey, to be her prayer captain because, she said, "I knew she was a real prayer warrior." Pat stayed in contact with Susan via e-mail, and Susan then communicated to the others on the prayer team. Each one committed to pray for Pat daily while she served in Russia. Susan also brought the whole team together once a month to pray, not just for Pat, but for the entire CoMission team and the whole CoMission effort.

"The Lord used my prayer team in a mighty way to support me while I was away," continued Pat. "And it was never more evident to me than on a certain trip from Petrozavodsk, Russia, to Kiev, Ukraine. I was taking quite a few Russian teachers to a conference in Ukraine where they could interface with other teachers using the CoMission's curriculum on morals and ethics, and learn new teaching methods and tools. My interpreter Natalia secured the necessary one-in and one-out visas so I could travel between borders, and then she set off with us.

"Little did we know as we traveled on July 3, 1998, that the Russian government had changed the rules on July 2. The result was that, as we traveled back to Russia from Kiev by express train, we were stopped and boarded by customs officials and denied entry back into Russia. Natalia spoke to the officials and learned that I was suspected of being a Chechnyan spy! The Russian teachers who were traveling with us were allowed to continue their journey, but Natalia and I spent an entire day sitting on the ground between the railroad tracks as the customs officials appealed to their authorities.

"I was eventually sent back to Kiev, and would have been stranded there for five days had I not been miraculously led on foot to the off-the-beaten-track CoMission offices in that city. There the team serving Kiev put Natalia and me up in their apartments and allowed us to establish contact with the rest of our Petrozavodsk team members, who were quite concerned about us.

"Many months later, when I returned to the US, I was surprised to see an entry in Susan Lindsay's prayer journal dated July 3, stating that she felt I was in urgent need of prayer, although she did not know why. That day she called my prayer team together, and they were praying for my safety as I sat on the ground between the train tracks in Russia. I praise the Lord for my prayer team."

Bette Crouse adds, "The results of requiring every CoMissioner to develop a prayer team were so effective that I set up the same requirements for all OMS missionaries who go out. We require it as firmly as the financial support, and insist that they do not go out into service without their team of daily intercessors. What a difference this has made in the preparation and ministry of our missionaries! In fact, one OMS missionary in Japan has twenty-four-hour prayer network coverage made up of intercessors from the US and co-workers and ministry partners in Japan. They report that they are seeing miracles happen."

Another gift to CoMission teams took shape when the CoMission Alumni Network (CAN) was formed in 1996 to recruit new workers for the CoMission and pray for those already there. The usefulness of this new network was multifaceted, as it drew upon the excitement and experience of individuals who had participated in convocations or had taught for the CoMission while living in the CIS. As CAN served to keep CoMission veterans in touch with one another, it also encouraged a continued sense of mission and purpose—and a vital part of that was prayer. Who would better know the deepest needs of CoMissioners still in service than those who had gone before them? Those in the Network began to receive *The Chariot* and *Fast Fax Facts,* as well as invitations to pray as ready-to-depart CoMission teams attended the Primary Teaching Institutes. Their contagious enthusiasm and unique position as alumni were integrated into our prayer efforts to serve the CoMission teams.

The CoMission teams were also encouraged to leave behind a "deposit of prayer" as they left the former Soviet Union. Sometimes this "deposit" was the result of holding large conferences where prayer was taught and relationships among nationals were forged. At other times the gift was more personal, as when Pat Wentink began to gather Russian women in small groups to study the Bible and pray.

"The thought of praying for one another was alien to these women," explains Pat. "They had been born into a culture where it was unwise to share your problems with others or to stand out in a crowd in any way. They learned early to keep their heads down and blend in, because it was just too dangerous to involve themselves in the lives of others. As we studied the Bible and the women began to trust each other, they began to pray for one another.

"These relationships are ongoing even though the CoMissioners are now gone. We still sometimes send money that these trustworthy, believing women use in-country to feed hungry families and perform other acts of mercy—Russian to Russian."

SERVING THE COMISSION IN COUNTRY

The Lord led several intercessors to a more in-person involvement on site in the former Soviet Union. Three Prayer Committee members were eventually led to give a different kind of gift to the Russian people as they answered God's call to be trained as CoMissioners, and live and serve in the CIS.

Ruth Holmsten, on staff with the Navigators, traveled into Russia twice a year for the purpose of prayer. She took two or three other women with her to pray for the cities in which the Navigators had placed CoMission teams, staying for about a week in each city. In 1996 she moved to Pushkin, where they had an all-ladies team. Each woman on the team had already spent at least one year elsewhere in Russia, and was now volunteering to spend another two years ministering in Pushkin. Ruth was asked to mentor this team, training them in the use of ministry tools.

At the end of two years, some of these women were dispersed to other ministries, while others joined a co-ed team in Pushkin led by Mike Bedient. "I joined Mike's team and was finally able to minister to the Russians themselves," says Ruth. "I asked God to give me some 'thirsty' English-speaking Russian women whom I could recruit for Christ and help to grow." God faithfully answered that prayer.

Ruth's health now allows her to travel in and out of Russia less frequently and for shorter periods of time, but, undaunted, she says, "I believe God is in the timing of all of this, since these women I had the privilege of mentoring are now ready for leadership and don't need me looking over their shoulders."

"The highlight of my time," she continues, "has been working with the Russians themselves, and seeing their deep hunger for God and commitment to Him. We now have two whole families who know the Lord, as well as many others where one spouse knows Christ. We've been praying for Christian families to model the Christian family life to their fellow Russians."

This "prayer deposit," although a small beginning, can grow and multiply. Another "deposit" is evident as we see Russians leading their own Bible studies and discipling other Russians. This too will multiply as Russians take responsibility for their own cities and nation.

Another gift of our Prayer Committee to Russia came in the form of Michael and Elizabeth Darby, who spent 1997 in Rostov-on Don. There they hoped and believed they would one day "work themselves out of a job," and be able to place themselves locally under a thriving unified, believing church. What they found in Rostov was not unlike the situation in most of the other places God scattered His CoMissioners: no unified, believing church—just missions and national churches trying to hold their own and keep their individual heads above the growing flood of persecution from political and religious sources. But this is where God's strategy surprised and delighted them. Elizabeth Darby says that "God used the CoMission model of different organizations and denominations working together for His glory—not caring who got the credit—to show the national pastors and Christian organizational leaders how their gifts and talents could be multiplied by standing, praying, believing and working together. It remains their only hope and the only way to claim their cities for Jesus Christ."

UNITING NATIONALS IN PRAYER

The other part of God's strategy in Rostov was to unify the nationals in prayer. The Darbys identified, equipped and left behind appointed representation from each church and Christian organization in the Rostov region to "pound the gates of heaven" for their region, their country and their people. "Because we believe that the prayers of the saints are foundational to everything God wants to do there, we realize that for them to be moving forward under that banner of unity is incredible," says Michael. "It will be a joy to watch God's plan unfold there, and to realize He invited the CoMission to play such a vital role in Russian history."

As many prayed that national leadership would develop in the CIS, CoMissioner Janna Shipley gave a thumbnail sketch in volume 4, issue 3 of *The Chariot* of a few emerging Christian leaders in Rostov:

> *Alla is witnessing to Muslims where she works. She is also taking over the leadership of the CoMission-initiated conferences that are held every few months.*
>
> *Valya leads a weekly Bible study for many of her fellow teachers.*
>
> *Ludmilla provides leadership for a Rostov Al-Anon support group and is influencing her friends, ex-husband and alcoholic son towards Christ.*
>
> *Luda, who struggled with Mormonism last year, is now doing well in her walk with Christ. Several of her neighbors have asked her to help them study the Bible.*
>
> *Larissa, a sixteen-year-old, initiated a Bible study for her friends, and now works with some of those girls in an orphanage each week.*

These ladies are the fruit of three prayer-saturated years of CoMission teams in Rostov. Their stories—and others like them have been duplicated in cities across the former Soviet Union.

Other gifts we left in Russia included two major prayer conferences hosted by the CoMission Prayer Committee, one in St. Petersburg and another in Rostov. In April 1996 we hosted a "Pray for the City Conference" in St. Petersburg, with the teaching leadership of the European Prayer Link (EPL) team. What resulted was a tremendous outpouring of God's blessing as participants sought His face to learn how to develop a prayer strategy for a city.

More than a conference, the four days gave participants a unique opportunity to get on board God's unfolding plans for Russia—and unity in increasing measure marked all that was accomplished. Submitting to the teaching leadership of the European Prayer Link was key. With a vision of serving and supporting God-ordained prayer initiatives across Europe and the CIS, those working with EPL began sensing an urgency of the Holy Spirit on them to help develop prayer for Russia and Eastern Europe, long before the St. Petersburg conference. I was sure that CoMission prayer efforts could be multiplied if the committee made a joint trip to the CIS with the EPL.

The goals of the conference were to learn how to strategically pray for a city, using St. Petersburg as a model, and to leave a deposit of prayer to spread to other CIS cities. Johannes Facius, German prayer leader of the EPL, began by unfolding the need to understand intercession—how it differs from other types of prayer, and how it relates to cities. Pieter Bos of Amsterdam led the participants in a strategy to see cities, as well as the church, as corporate personalities. He demonstrated how our prayers take on new meaning when we see that the church has a crucial role in interceding for her city of residence. Rick Ridings of Belgium then showed how praise and worship, repentance and reconciliation, intercession, proclamation and blessing all have a place in prayer for a city. As the conference drew to a close, European Prayer Link Chairman Brian Mills from Great Britain presented a strategy for mobilization of city-wide prayer.

Prayer Walks in St. Petersburg

Our prayer walks around the city solidified that sense that God was directing prayer specifically for St. Petersburg for purposes of His own. The location took on increasing significance, as one of the city's key intercessors gave us a brief historical background of St. Petersburg. Known as the "City of Bridges," it was an ideal place for God to construct the interdenominational council of forty-two area pastors who began to meet together there.

"I will never forget the prayer walk in the city square of St. Petersburg, Russia," says Annie Kienel. "I look on that 'prayer adventure' as one of the most important things I have ever experienced."

"That was the day we all saw St. Petersburg through God's eyes," Milton Monell adds, "a city with a tragic history, yet a place where God wants to reveal His glory, and a gateway for showing that glory to all of Russia."

Another gift we gave to the country was the October 1997 "Heal Our Land" prayer conference in Rostov, co-sponsored by the CoMission through the Navigators and the Rostov Area Association of Christian Churches and Organizations. Michael and Elizabeth Darby were instrumental in coordinating the timely conference. In September 1997, a new religious freedom law was passed in Russia that had the potential to make it very difficult for many Christian churches and organizations to continue their ministries. It was a very tenuous time for new Russian Christians, who wondered what would become of their new "church families," as well as what it might mean for their own Christian lives.

What a testimony to the faithfulness of God it was to recognize that He had begun to prepare for this period of trial months before it occurred. In October His plan culminated in the Rostov conference, where we gathered for united prayer with an almost capacity crowd. These more than 200 believers came from at least twenty-three different churches and six organizations, and represented nine denominations. As Michael Darby observed, "What better way to combat uncertainty and fear? These new Christians realized that they were not alone, but that God had surrounded them with brothers and sisters in Christ to stand with them in prayer against all difficulty."

Messages and seminars by Bill Lewis, Church Resource Ministries, Dan Peterson, Campus Crusade, and myself sought to encourage, enlighten, admonish and challenge those attending. Through constant, united prayer, all of these were forged into the strength and hope needed to drive away the seeds of doubt and despair Satan hoped to plant through the new legislation. We sent participants home to their congregations with a new understanding of and commitment to pray for their fellow Christians, their cities, country and world. Many Christians from different denominations entered into a forty-day prayer fast and others formed interdenominational prayer groups to continue the vital ministry of united prayer.

Comments Milton Monell: "It has been said that the gift that the CoMission has for Russia is the unity of the body of Christ. I believe that is true to this day."

THE PRAYER COMMITTEE'S VISION FULFILLED

From God's call to the CoMission, to the vision of the Prayer Committee to function as servants to the Executive Committee—in CoMission training, in development of prayer tools to give away, to supporting CoMission teams in prayer, to providing prayer support in-country—in all these, God was faithful both to will and to do His good pleasure in the hearts of those of us privileged to be a part of His great plan.

The CoMission Prayer Committee officially ended in February 1998. While there is no way to know the actual numbers of those praying regularly for the CoMission, with integrity we can say that we established a prayer support base exceeding 20,000 intercessors. To God be the glory. Great things He hath done!

HIGHLIGHTS OF THE PRAYER COMMITTEE
1993-1997

- Appointed a CoMission prayer coordinator from within each of the CoMission's member churches and organizations.

- Assembled and maintained a database, complete with e-mail addresses, of Prayer Associates for the CoMission, including prayer teams and former CoMissioners.

- Raised $200,000 from the Philip Lance Van Every Foundation to fund the work of the CoMission Prayer Committee.

- Distributed the Fast Fax Facts to the prayer coordinators in member organizations and churches, the Prayer Associates and CoMission leadership each month, with the publication strengthened and redesigned in 1997.

- Provided on-site prayer for Pastors and Leaders Conferences in Orlando, Florida, in February 1994, and Colorado Springs, Colorado, in March 1995.

- Accompanied the Executive Committee to Moscow in November 1994 to provide on-site prayer support.

- Coordinated/conducted on-site prayer during preparatory training of CoMissioners for the January and July PTIs for four years.

- Conceptualized, produced and distributed twelve issues of the quarterly prayer newsletter, *The Chariot,* whose circulation grew to a database of approximately 8,000.

- Trained CoMissioners in prayer and journaling at the January and July PTIs for four years. Each new CoMissioner received a regularly updated "Prayer Manual and Journal." Continued to encourage the new CoMissioners to build a personal prayer support base of twelve prayer partners who prayed daily for their needs.

- Sponsored a very successful "Pray for the City" prayer training conference, with the help of the Navigators, in St. Petersburg, Russia (April 13-16, 1996). Highlights: over sixty American missionaries and Russian pastors attended; teaching was provided by European Prayer Link members Brian Mills, Pieter Bos, Johannes Facius and Rick Ridings; a missionary prayer movement was significantly strengthened. In addition, a Russian pastors' call to prayer on behalf of the Russian government was issued worldwide and a task force was appointed to develop an in-country prayer strategy. The conference built vital relationships with leaders of European Prayer Link and Campus Crusade Eurasia in order to provide prayer training for the CoMissioners while in-country, as well as to begin city-wide prayer movements in CoMission cities.

- Saw three committee members, Michael and Elizabeth Darby and Ruth Holmsten, answer the call to serve on in-country CoMission teams.

- Worked with Angela Ghent at CoMission headquarters to integrate the CoMission Alumni Network (CAN) into the Prayer Committee's prayer strategy. Members received *The Chariot* newsletter each quarter, with its significant prayer needs.

- Extended conditional permission upon request for other missions organizations to modify/use the contents of the "Prayer Manual and Journal" in prayer training efforts.

- In 1996 presented to the CoMission leadership a prayer training strategy and formal document outlining prayer training recommendations, for the PTIs as well as CoMissioners in-country.

- Spent 1997 strengthening and establishing the committee's work.

- Sponsored a very well attended "Heal Your Land" prayer conference with the help of Michael and Elizabeth Darby and the Rostov Pastor's Association in Rostov-on-Don, Russia (October 24-26, 1997). Highlights: 175 attendees from more than twenty-three churches, representing nine denominations and six organizations. A city-wide Pastors' Association Prayer Committee was formed with two representatives from each church/para-ministry in the association, representing attainment of a Prayer Committee goal to see a prayer movement raised up among nationals as a model for other cities in the former USSR.

EACH FACE
WINS MANY

Samara, 1998:

"I know that you don't get to meet a lot of Russians whose lives have been impacted by CoMission teams. Thank you for all that you have done for them and for us," shared Taisia, her words filled with emotion and intensity, bringing tears to my eyes. She was a small-group discussion leader who had attended our original convocation in Samara.

For almost five years, Taisia used the "Foundations of Christian Ethics" curriculum in her school. She teaches at a school for troubled kids, the youth who often get thrown out of the regular public schools.

Ron, the CoMission team supervisor, and I visited Taisia and her husband. Our enjoyable and relaxed visit ended, and we began to say our goodbyes. Just as we prepared to put on our coats, Taisia grasped my arm and asked if she could share something with us.

She turned to Ron and I and thanked us profusely, but what she said next was unexpected. "Please know that you have not only been a part of changing my life for Christ, but that when you look at my face, it represents many more people that have come to Christ through my life."

How many more? I wondered. How many others who now know about Christ in her school, neighborhood and family are represented in her smiling face?

We will never know fully the many impacted for Christ through Taisia's life. Far beyond what we can see, the CoMission is reaping eternal fruit.

PRINCIPLE
TWELVE

ASK FOR PLEDGES OF PERSONAL PURITY.

At each Primary Training Institute we asked each CoMissionar to come forward and shake the hand of one of the Executive Committee members and say, "Before God I commit to you that I will be sexually pure this year." The same pledge was made by each of the members of the Committee. We also did not accept any applicant who had had extramarital or premarital sex in the six months prior to their application. This was a crucial step in the preparation, as CoMissioners of both sexes found themselves propositioned regularly during their time of ministry.

DR. J. B. CROUSE, JR., a veteran missionary, in 1992 became president of OMS International. OMS celebrated its 100th anniversary in 2001. During his tenure as president, OMS has expanded its worldwide ministry from fourteen to thirty-three countries. OMS works in the areas of evangelism, church planting, theological training and missions outreach. Worldwide, OMS International represents 5,572 churches, 1.2 million believers, and twenty-nine seminaries and Bible schools. Dr. Crouse is married to Dr. Elizabeth "Bette" Shipps Crouse. She serves as assistant to the president. Bette served on the Prayer Committee and the Training Committee of the CoMission. They have three sons who grew up in Korea. Now married, they live with their families in the US. Dr. Crouse served the CoMission as chairman of the International Sending Countries Committee.

THE CoMISSION'S IMPACT ON INTERNATIONAL MISSIONS

International Sending Countries Committee

Dr. J. B. Crouse, Jr., chairman

IT WAS NOVEMBER 1991 and my first trip to Russia when the Lord spoke to me through Psalm 60:

> "You have caused this nation to tremble and fear. You have torn it apart. Lord, heal it now for it is shaken to its depths. You have been very hard on us and made us reel beneath your blows. But you have given us a banner to rally to. All who love truth will rally to it. Then you can deliver your beloved people. Use your strong right arm to rescue us. God has promised to help us. He has vowed it by His holiness" (Psalm 60:2–6a, TLB).

I believe this was God's promise for Russia and her people. For my wife, Bette, and me, that first trip to Russia was what I like to call a "divine interruption." We were in the process of moving from South Korea, where we had served for thirty-four years, back to our ministry's International Headquarters in the United States. We had just been elected as the leadership team for OMS.

But the call had come through Paul Eshleman to come to Russia and see what God was doing. People were needed to follow up the great harvest resulting from the school convocations, which showed the *JESUS* film and taught morals and ethics from a biblical perspective. Bette and I went, in part, to discover if there was some way that OMS could be involved.

DIVINE INTERRUPTION, LASTING FRIENDSHIP

In November we flew to Russia and joined with about fifty people who would serve at the convocation in Pushkin, about twenty-five miles from St. Petersburg. It was there that God did a tremendous work in our hearts—my heart, my wife's heart, and each member of that team. It was there, too, that I met Dr. Bruce Wilkinson for the first time. Climbing the snow-covered, outside stairs together on the dome of St. Peter's Cathedral in St. Petersburg does contribute to a memorable event. Immediately we struck up a wonderful friendship.

Drs. J.B. and Betty Crouse enjoy an evening in Moscow before an Executive Committee meeting.

I thank God for those divine interruptions that take place in our lives. Before the convocation team left Russia, God had bound our hearts together. Every morning from seven to eight o'clock, we met for prayer and a devotional time together. That week changed our perspectives and priorities. Our horizons expanded. To be in Russia, meeting those once called our "enemies" and to feel their love and openness, to see the response to the *JESUS* film and watch as our own personal testimonies made an impact—it all defied description. A special personal joy: Bette and I had the privilege of leading our interpreter, Elena Vosdehyeva, to the Lord Jesus Christ.

The weeklong experience was inspiring, challenging and overwhelming. Our concern was deep and the burden almost crushing. How could we reach the former Soviet Union with the gospel of Jesus Christ? The task would be bigger than any one organization could do alone, we all agreed.

So we began to ask God, "What can we do?" We looked for a new paradigm, a new approach. That new paradigm was the CoMission, which Bruce Wilkinson was helping to develop and lead.

As we talked in Russia, Bruce said, "J. B., you are the new president of OMS International. You ought to go back and recruit 100 new missionaries, or just send 100 of your current missionaries to Russia."

I laughed like Abraham and Sarah,[1] because we at OMS had never recruited 100 missionaries at one time. I knew all the needs in the other countries where OMS was working. I knew it would be very difficult for us as an organization to make such radical change quickly. It would require us to restructure our mode of operation and absorb ourselves in the mission of the CoMission.

For me, and maybe for some of you, it's often easy to get excited, to make commitments and decisions for the Lord at a conference or a church service, and then return to the routine of things, forgetting all about the things what you promised God you would do. After we returned to Korea, my desk was piled high, and I was involved in a lot of ministry. However, the Holy Spirit did not let me get away from the burden, the commitment and all we had experienced in Russia.

COMMISSION VERSUS COMMON SENSE

Through my devotions one morning, the Lord said I should send Bruce Wilkinson a fax. I said, "Lord, Bruce is a great leader, a great Bible teacher. I'm a missionary out in Korea. Who am I to send him a fax?" But the urge was so strong that after about three days I sent it.

It means a great deal to me, and I think it has a very powerful message for us even today. Here's what it said:

> It is easier to serve God without a vision, easier to work for God without a call, because then you are not bothered by what God requires. Common sense is your guide, veneered over with Christian sentiment. But if once you receive a commission from Jesus Christ, the memory of what God wants will always come like a goad, and you will no longer be able to work for Him on the common sense basis.

That's from Oswald Chambers. A powerful message. I didn't know that Bruce was struggling regarding what to do in response to this vast new open door. It was this little fax—this word from the Lord through Oswald Chambers—that the Lord used to give Bruce the inspiration and courage to send the letters out inviting the first twenty-five leaders to come and be involved in the CoMission.

I believe, if we are honest, that the reason we haven't won the world for Jesus Christ is because we have attempted it from the common-sense viewpoint. Not many of us have been willing to trust God totally, to think big, to do things differently, and take on tasks that are far bigger than we can humanly accomplish. We must believe in who the Lord Jesus Christ is, let Him break the loaves and fishes and perform the miracles. He did that long ago with the disciples, and we must trust Him to do it in our lifetime.

No one dreamed that eighty-two organizations could work together under the umbrella of the CoMission or that they would take down their own organizational "flags" and work as one, in unity representing the body of Christ. Yet they did, and such unity, I believe, is what Jesus had in mind when He gave the Great Commission.

Commissioning service in August 1993 for hundreds of teachers headed to Russia.

What God did through the united effort of the CoMission between 1992 and 1997 was unbelievable. It was historic. It was stretching. It was exciting. It was empowering. It was unifying. It was one of the most sweeping and far-reaching movements in the history of Christian evangelism and discipleship. We shouldn't really be surprised that when God opened the door to the former Soviet Union, He also had in mind a plan to mobilize a great task force to bring the light of the gospel once again to shine in that great land. And so He caused the CoMission to be born. The chariot of Elijah[2] came by, our coats were caught in the spokes of the wheel, and God swept us along. The chariot of Elijah continues to get people's coats caught up in the spokes and carry them to the life-changing ministry of sharing Christ in the former Soviet Union. Yes, as Terry Taylor said, "The CoMission was the supernatural fingerprint of the Holy Spirit." God prepares nations and individuals for His use.

IMPACT ON AN ORGANIZATION AND A MAN

Besides its Soviet impact, the CoMission greatly impacted our mission, OMS International, and me personally in several ways:

- First of all, one of the most important things that I think the CoMission represented was an opportunity as Christian leaders and Christian mission organizations to challenge lay people to go and be personally involved in the Great Commission. As far as OMS is concerned, we traditionally had needed and sought people who were theologically trained: doctors, nurses, educators…people with a lot of training. But the uniqueness of the CoMission, I believe, was that for the first time we had an opportunity to go to the body of Christ and say, "If you love Jesus Christ and you are committed to Him, and you want the thrilling experience of sharing Jesus Christ in a foreign country, we can use you."

- The strategy of the CoMission was outstanding, as was the training to accomplish it. I believe the training was some of the most excellent that I have seen in terms of preparing people to serve cross-culturally. People were prepared spiritually, trained well and equipped to be effective communicators of the gospel of Jesus Christ. Think about taking men and women from all walks of life, from age twenty to eighty-two, and sending them to go and live in the former Soviet Union. It is amazing that ninety-seven percent completed an effective and fruitful year of ministry in this difficult environment, amidst much spiritual warfare, and that thirty-five percent of them signed up for a second year. This is tremendous.

- The CoMission brought new life to OMS International. It helped us to be able to go to the church and our constituency with a new paradigm, a new opportunity for men and women to think in a whole different way about being involved in the Great Commission. We were not just asking for their prayers, not just asking for their money or other kinds of support. We were able to talk to men and women, young and old alike, and say, "God needs you. You can make a difference. We need you to help us fulfill this great vision of seeing the former Soviet Union won for Jesus Christ." Another tremendous aspect was the opportunity the CoMission gave the teams to go into the public school system in the Soviet Union. What better way to reach a nation?

The strategy, the training, the opportunity to use lay people and the opportunity to work together in partnership were only some of the history-making things about the CoMission.

What did we do well and right? First of all, the unity of the CoMission was outstanding. It exemplified unity in the body of Christ. It was the first time I know of that we as organizations—Campus Crusade, Navigators, OMS, Walk Thru the Bible and the others that were part of the CoMission—were willing to take down our organizational flags and run only the flag of Jesus Christ up the flagpole, giving Him the glory and honor. The Lordship of Christ, the shared vision, the unified strategy, strong prayer coverage, the outstanding training program, exemplifying the body of Christ, the positive model of team work, not touching the glory for ourselves, good supervision, accountability and biblical foundations—all these, I believe, helped make the CoMission outstanding.

You recall that Bruce had challenged OMS to send 100 missionaries to Russia. Frankly, I didn't think that was possible. I'm delighted to share with you that God not only helped us to send 100, but nearly 250. We're still excited about that. The caliber of people whom God helped us recruit was outstanding. OMS International alone recruited more than thirty-five career missionaries out of the CoMissioners who went to Russia.

EYES OPENED TO MISSIONS

You see, it began a process. It opened a lot of people's eyes to what being a missionary is and what missions is all about. Many were so excited, burdened, challenged and thrilled with being a vessel for the Holy Spirit to flow through that they said, "Hey, this is good. We'd like to do it the rest of our lives."

We're looking for missionaries in OMS. We saw the CoMission as an outstanding model ministry, and an opportunity to draw many into a Great Commission lifestyle. How rewarding to see them awakened to the joy of being involved in missions!

Dr. J.B. Crouse preaching in Central Baptist Church.

Another very special thing about the CoMission was that it opened up a whole new world of relationships for me as I served on the Executive Committee. It was a great honor to have the opportunity of working with these leaders, gaining a better understanding of their ministries and working together in a new way. And the effects have not ended. The CoMission experience has helped us to cross denominational and organizational barriers. It helped us to work as one with the body of Christ and in the churches across the United States like we never had before.

In the eyes of those observing the ministry of the CoMission, one thing seemed to stand out above all else: the body of Christ working together and no one taking the credit. The glory was for Jesus. God gave us unity. It did not always come easily. It cost a lot. The devil fought and caused many difficult challenges. But, through repentance, confession, humility and the desire to be a part of what God wanted to do more than what we wanted, God has kept us together as an Executive Committee even beyond the five years of the CoMission ministry.

My wife, Bette, served on both the Training and Materials Committee and the Prayer Committee. Her philosophy and methods of teaching were powerfully impacted by this treasured and meaningful involvement. She relates that in the Training and Materials Committee meetings, Christ-centered leaders valued and stressed the need for unity in developing strategies and making decisions. The Prayer Committee was a combination both of experiencing times of the overflow of springs of living water, as our heavenly Father's presence was so real, and yet also of other times of great spiritual warfare related to our prayer times. Representing these two committees, Bette had the awesome privilege of leading devotional times for the CoMissioners during their preparatory training and teaching on prayer and spiritual journaling. The magnificent lessons on prayer written by Mary Lance Sisk, chairman of the Prayer Committee, were included in a notebook, given to each CoMissioner, along with lessons on journaling written by Bette. The Prayer Committee organized prayer coverage for each training session. A requirement that Bette felt strongly about, was for each CoMissioner to have a minimum of twelve daily intercessors.

The richness of fellowship and prayer times is indelibly etched on Bette's heart. Countless e-mails, letters and conversations affirmed the value of the devotional times, training and journaling—as well as the actual prayer for the teams. So strongly did this affect personal spiritual growth and ministry, that Bette urged a stronger emphasis on such training within OMS, and continues to use the Prayer and Journaling Manual in teaching OMS missionary candidates. We now require each of our missionaries to have a commitment from twelve daily intercessors. The effectiveness of this was felt so keenly by one OMS missionary family in Japan that they gathered prayer coverage twenty-four hours a day, 365 days a year—twelve hours of coverage in Japan and twelve hours in the USA. The CoMission definitely continues to have a vital influence on OMS International.

"God Is in This!"

As stories about the CoMission's impact reached those of us on the Executive Committee, they held a common thread: "God is in this! There's just no other way to explain it."

This included the stories of what the Lord was doing through the teams, but it also showed clearly in how He provided for them to go. At the first training cycle, a young CoMissioner told of feeling doubtful that she could raise the required funds for the year of service.

"By the time I got my acceptance," she began, "I had already committed myself to counsel at a youth camp. That meant I would have only four weeks to raise my support. I'd have to raise $5,000 each week. But I decided that if God was really in this, He could do it. So I did what they told me in the training. I sent out letters to everyone I knew and started making phone calls. All the money came in and I had $1,000 more than I needed."

The next story echoed that. Two sisters from the same family wanted to go. They both knew the same people. Between them they would have to raise more than $40,000. But they also sent out their letters, which yielded even more than they had needed.

Tom, one of the team leaders, told of a totally different situation: "We didn't think we were going to make the training this time. We thought we'd probably have to wait for the next group going over and join them.

"A close friend of ours came by the house to say hello before he returned to Hong Kong. We told him about our desire to go with the CoMission. As he was leaving, he asked me to give him my last promotional video. I was really reluctant, but he pressed, so I gave it to him. A few days later, he called from Hong Kong and asked if we had our bags packed. I told him no, because we still needed about $8,000. He said we'd better start packing, because he had shown the video to some of his friends in Hong Kong and they were putting the $8,000 in the mail to us. It's just a miracle of God."

"So was our situation," another couple broke in. "We knew we couldn't go on the CoMission unless we sold our home. We couldn't afford to make the house payments while we were gone. The training here started on a Sunday, so we knew that we had to have it sold by the Friday before we left. On Friday afternoon a couple who had looked at the house earlier called to say that they would buy it if we could guarantee that they would get the financing from the bank."

"We called the bank," the husband continued, "and asked to speak to the loan officer. Both the head loan officer and the assistant loan officer had taken an early weekend. I asked for their home phone numbers. The head loan officer didn't answer, but I finally reached the assistant loan officer on her car phone. She was stopped at a red light.

"When we told her our problem, she said she would like to help us, but the head loan officer really had to give the final approval. We were just about to hang up when she said, 'Wait a minute. He just pulled up beside me here at the light.' They pulled the cars over to the side of the road. He approved the loan over the phone, and here we are. God did it!"

INTENSE SPIRITUAL HUNGER

As the CoMission teams began serving, incredible reports began to pour in. The response continued to echo that seen during the teachers' convocations. Those three-day trainings were continuing across Russia, including cities in Siberia.

In Magadan, a city about four hours' flight from Alaska, the convocation team saw pictures depicting remains from some of the most brutal prison camps of the Stalin era, which had once been located across Russia. In one camp hundreds of Christian pastors had been brutally killed for their faith. Almost everyone they met was a descendant of someone who had been in a camp or had been one of the guards of a camp. Their memories indicated the crucial need for reconciliation, for a new start. The curriculum's lesson on forgiveness seemed too good to be true to many. All the lessons in the course taught the benefit to society of this moral foundational truth: When people practice forgiveness, the cycle of revenge is broken.

One of the most exciting reports came from Blagoveshchensk, down on the border with China. At the end of the convocation, the mayor of the city came to speak to the group of sixty Americans who had been conducting the sessions.

"I would like to make a request of you," he began. "We would like you to leave a picture of yourself, and any memento of your family with us. We would like to start a display in our museum in your honor. You see, the name of our city, Blagoveshchensk, means 'the gospel.' And we would like to honor you who brought the gospel back to us after fifty years."

It was into settings like these of such intense spiritual hunger that the CoMission teams went. The impact was easy to see. In Vladimir, for example, Berry and Lois Johnson and Bob and Sally Feldman led the CoMission teams. In School 9, eighth-grade students sat two to a table, a familiar sight to the CoMission teams. The Russians had wasted no money on new architectural ideas. It seemed that every school everywhere had been built from the same plans, and remained unchanged through the years. But one thing was missing that would formerly have been essential: The picture of Lenin had been taken down. With no money to buy new pictures, a poster had taken its place.

Paul Eshleman tells about visiting that classroom on the day they began studying the curriculum. Their lesson: "The Uniqueness of Jesus." Lubov, the teacher, had become a Christian about two and a half months before—and was nervous about teaching in front of the American visitors. "She feels that she knows so little," Sally Feldman explained privately to them.

Lubov began the lesson by saying, "All of us are unique people, different in many ways." They then went through a little exercise to see how they were unique, underlining the point that God had created each of us individually.

She then switched to the spiritual study. "Among all the leaders of the world, Jesus stands out as especially unique. He was unique in His birth, His teaching, His miracles, His death and His resurrection. We all have seen the film about His life, but now we will read about Him out of the book of the Christian faith, the Bible.

"Today, I will give each of you a portion of the Bible called the New Testament. It is the part that tells the truth about what Jesus said and did. It is divided into books that were written by people who lived at the time of Jesus. Each book is divided into chapters, and each chapter is divided into verses. These verses have numbers by them so you can find very good quotes by Jesus very easily.

"Please turn to the Book of St. Luke. You can find the page in the table of contents. Now turn to chapter two. We will read verses one through eleven about the uniqueness of the birth of Jesus." One of the young men near the front of the room signaled that he had found the passage. She called on him, and he stood by his desk and read the passage aloud.

"Now we need to know about the forgiveness of Jesus," she said, calling on one of the other students to read the story of the prodigal son. There was no coercion on her part, but her teaching on the uniqueness of Jesus was as fine as any that the Executive Committee members present had ever heard. And the students were extremely interested.

At that point in time, the team in Vladimir had opened the ministry in 117 schools. More than 7,000 students and 1,000 teachers had seen the film. They had scores of teachers in discipleship groups and forty-two schools were currently teaching the Christian ethics and morality course.

At School 10 in Vladimir, CoMissioner Joy Wease had explained to an English class for eight and nine-year-olds why the Bible is a reliable help to answer the most important questions of life. They were studying bilingual New Testaments that Joy had provided for them. Four teachers from other schools had come to observe how the course could be included as part of the English curriculum.

The class had written essays in English on why the Bible is important. This is what some of the students wrote:

After the great October Revolution, some cathedrals and churches were destroyed. Communists made a big historical mistake. They betrayed God. But He forgave them. And I think the best thing in the world and in the life is to forgive other people. As for me, I think that Bible must be important for all people, because in first place, Bible made our culture rich. In the second place, Bible teaches us be kind, do good deeds, forgive other people.

—ALEXI

I am fond of the Bible, and I can say that it is very important for our life. In the Bible we learn a lot of rules. We read about the creation of the world. We know more about Jesus and His life. We read there: Don't steal, since that is atheism. Don't be mean to friends and other people. Don't say anything false, and don't go on wrong track. Always love and remember our God.

—N. STEPANOVA

The Bible is important. Why? Because in the Bible we read God's laws.

God teaches us to be kind, good and to love people. When I read the Bible, I think what good things I do on this day, week, month, year. And I want to do more good things.

If people will love God, and if they read the Bible, killers will not kill and thieves will not steal. When all people love God, there will not be wars and it will be peace on the earth. There will be nice gardens, forests and fields. There will be many flowers in the streets. Rivers, lakes, seas and oceans will be clear, and there will be fish in the water. People will be happy to see other people. And all people will treat animals and birds well. And will be good in the world when all people read the Bible and love God.

—SASHA

THE TRUTH LIVED OUT

Even as teachers began to use the Christian ethics and morality curriculum, it was not uncommon for CoMissioners to hear them say, with underlying regret: "It's too late for me after forty years of communism, but I want the children to know." Yet as these people with little hope began to interact with the CoMissioners day after day, they began to understand that God was offering them a second chance.

At School 25, a teacher who had married a Muslim Tatar man told of finding Christ and leading her daughters and grandchildren to Christ. All were then baptized. When asked what made her decide to become a believer, her answer was simple: "Bob and Sally Feldman."

"All of our lives," she explained, "we have heard propaganda. We decided that Christianity was just more propaganda. But when I saw the lives of Bob and Sally, and how they showed the love of Jesus, I decided to believe."

At first one might wonder about that answer. One could think that she should believe because of the truth of the Bible. But increasingly in Russia we saw that the truth of God needs to be expressed through people's lives.

And not just in Russia. His plan indicates that each of us should reflect what God is like when others look at us. If we are filled with and controlled by His Holy Spirit, other people can see in our lives the character of Jesus, His love, joy, peace, patience and self-control. And they will be drawn to Him.

As the teachers of Vladimir saw Jesus in the lives of Bob and Sally, they were drawn to Him. Above and beyond all the teaching that the CoMission teams were doing, they were living demonstrations of how a person looked and acted as a true believer in Jesus.

THE CONTINUED IMPACT

In closing let me share that on one of our visits to Russia I made two observations that were very exciting to me. First of all, as we went to cities and saw the CoMissioners and met those nationals who had been won to Christ, we could see very clearly that the strategy, goals and ministry of the CoMission were being transferred from the CoMissioners to the nationals—and that, of course, was our ultimate goal.

Participants came from many churches and organizations, but once they put on their sweat shirts, they became CoMissioners.

The second thing that excited me was that as we talked with the CoMissioners and nationals who had been won to Christ—partners in Christ—they desired to see churches planted. That was the vision the Executive Committee had from the very beginning.

The CoMission opened many new opportunities for OMS. Not only did we have the joy and privilege of being a vital part of the CoMission, but God used it to open up a new country of ministry for us. OMS is a church-planting mission, and we now have twenty-four missionaries working in Russia. We believe in training, and we place a high priority on theological education. The CoMission opened up the door and gave us the opportunity to establish the Moscow Evangelical Christian Seminary. It is one of the premier seminaries in Russia today. God gave us excellent Russian leadership with Dr. Alexei Bychkov as the president, Dr. Vitali Koulikov, Dr. Sasha Tsoutserov and other godly men and women on the faculty. God provided a beautiful building with excellent facilities. We celebrated our 10th anniversary with five graduates, making a total of seventy graduates thus far. We are continuing to plant churches and seeing them thrive under Russian leadership.

The CoMission deeply impacted me personally. It has contributed greatly to our organization. It has also meant much to many men and women in America who had an opportunity they never thought they would have to go and witness for Jesus Christ. I thank God for the CoMission. From recruitment to human resources, in finances, prayer and training, throughout our international ministries and on to the President's Leadership team, each facet of OMS ministry was impacted positively by the CoMission experience.

The CoMission was a watershed in the history of Christian missions. It brought a new level of commitment by the body of Christ to do together what none could do alone: to carry out the Great Commission. It was God's divine and dramatic plan for taking the gospel to the former Soviet Union.

The results of the CoMission were indescribable. This movement of God left an indelible mark on churches, mission organizations, missionaries, educators and lay people. It forever changed the way we think about doing missions. The CoMission brought new life to OMS International. It made it possible for us to broaden our outreach and involvement with the evangelical world.

On a personal level, as the president of OMS International, I learned many valuable lessons from the CoMission experience. Seeing God do the miraculous forever changed my life. Indeed, as the chariot of Elijah came by, our coats were caught up in the spokes of the wheels. I pray we will never lose sight of the vision God has for us, and that we will never fail to have faith to believe Him for the miracles He wants to perform in reaching the nations with the gospel of Jesus Christ. May we never work for God on the common sense basis.

NOTES:

1. Genesis 17 and 18.
2. 2 Kings 2.

RUSSIAN TEACHERS RISE UP AS LEADERS

Kurgan, Spring of 1995:

"Please send another team to answer our questions about Jesus," the teachers in Kurgan begged. *For nearly two years, they waited patiently for someone to come back to answer their questions following the initial convocation. But none of them sat around idly waiting for our return.*

When our convocation team left, the teachers realized that there was no one to answer their questions, so they decided to work together and learn from each other. It didn't take long before several Bible studies were established and growing. Teachers met weekly to study the Word and to have fellowship.

Eventually they rewrote the curriculum, adding both kindergarten and college levels so that all ages would have the opportunity to learn Christian morals and ethics through the life of Christ. In their enthusiasm they started a television program presenting some of the lessons and concluding with a question and answer session with students. This was interspersed with scenes of the JESUS film and aired weekly on a local TV station.

The eagerness of this core group grew as the people started seeing astonishing changes in the lives of their colleagues, friends and family. Their excitement did not subside over time. Instead, they consistently brainstormed novel ways to reach others.

When our follow-up team finally arrived, these teachers were well rooted and equipped for dramatic growth in their ministries. They had grown and developed the curriculum far beyond our initial hopes. The visiting team helped provide insights and experiences that allowed these teachers to deepen their own knowledge and expand their ministry in Kurgan.

We affectionately named them the "Kurgan champions."

Many of them continued to grow as leaders and attended the Leadership Development Conference in Kiev, Ukraine. During the Conference, they soaked up every word and felt challenged by the teaching. They met together with teachers from other cities to brainstorm late into the night.

By the end of the conference their progress was astounding. They had visions of writing new curriculum lessons and training teachers in other schools. Their vision and commitment swept beyond Kurgan, to see how God could use them to help reach more of their country.

One of the teachers exclaimed, "Every teacher who has had training has the ability to reach out to other teachers who have not had such help. That is our responsibility now." Our dream became their vision, with Russians passionately motivated to help other Russians know Christ.

PRINCIPLES THIRTEEN AND FOURTEEN

WORK WITH LEADERS.

Because the initial effort was centered in the educational system, we worked with the leaders in Moscow on a continuing basis. By getting endorsements from the very top officials of the school system, we were able to see doors opened to 65,000 schools and 278 teacher-training colleges. In each city where CoMission teams were located, they talked to local Protestant and Orthodox pastors to inform them of why they were there. Many of the teams received criticism from these religious leaders because they were still operating under the old Soviet mindset of keeping anyone away who might be a threat to their power.

ENTRUST THE MINISTRY TO LAYMEN AND LAYWOMEN.

Because we believed it important to get people living and working in the former Soviet Union as quickly as possible, we needed to rely primarily on laymen and laywomen who could leave their jobs or schooling for a year to serve. The normal path of recruiting career missionaries, sending them to seminary, language school and support training would take too long. This level of workers would be needed in the future, but now it was important to get people who could go quickly and begin the process—even if it meant they weren't as knowledgeable and had to work through interpreters.

JOHN E. KYLE served for thirty-seven years with Wycliffe Bible Translators in the US and the Philippines. He served as the founding director of Mission to the World of the Presbyterian Church in America (PCA) for nine years. He then served for ten years as the vice-president, mission director and Urbana Convention director for InterVarsity Christian Fellowship. For the past seven years, he has been the senior vice-president of the Evangelical Fellowship of Mission Agencies (EFMA). John and his wife, Lois, have four children and ten grandchildren.

CHAPTER TEN

MOBILIZING MISSIONARIES— PRESERVING THE FRUIT

Mobilization Committee and Church Relations Committee

John Kyle, chairman

THE WAY THE LORD CALLED ME to serve on the CoMission Executive Committee was amazing, and transpired with unusual rapidity. I had heard early in 1992 through Paul McKaughan, president of the Evangelical Fellowship of Mission Agencies, that a new ministry called the CoMission was being formed. During the earlier collapse of communism in Eastern Europe, Paul had deplored the way mission agencies from the West had entered those nations in a helter-skelter manner, often doing more harm than good. Therefore, Paul was very interested in the orderly strategy of forming partnerships among Western institutions concerned for world missions to work together under the CoMission.

Paul was invited to an Executive Committee meeting of the CoMission that was held in Atlanta, after which he met with me. He told me that the leaders of the CoMission were interested in expanding, but were not sure how best to go about bringing denominations into the effort, since they basically represented parachurch organizations. Because I was the director of Mission to The World, Paul suggested to them that they invite me to their next recruiting meeting to learn about the CoMission, since I was known among denominations and parachurch organizations for my emphasis on the importance of partnering in missions.

Thus, on June 24, 1992, I, with a large number of other guests from mission agencies, Bible colleges and large churches, responded to the invitation of the CoMission Executive Committee to come to Atlanta and hear what God was planning to do in the former USSR.

At that Atlanta meeting, the CoMission leadership presented the strategy of the CoMission, including their expectations. Then Bruce Wilkinson, chairman of the Executive Committee, in his warm but forward manner, called upon us guests for our decision: Would we be interested in joining the CoMission as sending agencies? When my turn came, I enthusiastically answered that our mission agency would become a sending agency of the CoMission and that I would clear it with our leadership.

The man next to me represented a large denominational group that had many years of experience in sending members overseas as missionaries. He shared that he thought the CoMission concept was excellent, but he doubted that their mission agency leader or their president would agree to join the CoMission.

Bruce Wilkinson turned to me and asked if I knew the leaders our friend mentioned. I answered that I knew them well. Bruce asked, "Would you write those leaders and encourage them to join the CoMission?" I answered I would be glad to do so! Happily, that agency agreed to join the CoMission, and they eventually sent dozens of short-term, one-year CoMissioners to serve as missionaries in the former USSR.

During the Atlanta meeting, the leaders discussed the fact that church-planting operations would eventually evolve out of the CoMissioners' Bible study groups. It became evident that some of those present were much involved in church planting, while others were not and didn't fully understand its importance. Since my mission agency, Mission to the World, was deeply involved in church planting, I sought to bring understanding to those working with parachurch organizations.

Afterwards, Joe Stowell, president of Moody Bible Institute, suggested that I bring Mission to the World into the CoMission as a sending agency. At the same time, he asked me to become a member of the Executive Committee. I was asked to serve as Chairman of the Church Relations Committee which would handle the church-planting aspect of the CoMission operation.

A Scripture portion on the heading of the first quarter, 1994 CoMission newsletter best expressed the way the CoMission operated: "Be devoted to one another in brotherly love; give preference to one another in honor, not lagging behind in diligence, fervent in spirit, serving the Lord, rejoicing in hope, persevering in tribulation, devoted in prayer" (Romans 12:10–12).

I saw this myself as I chaired two committees: Mobilization and Church Relations. Twelve committees supported the strategy of the CoMission. In my opinion, without these committees functioning well and in harmony, the CoMission operation could not have succeeded.

THE MOBILIZATION COMMITTEE

The first committee I chaired focused on mobilizing organizations to be involved and volunteers to go as CoMissioners. The success of the CoMission depended on the recruiting of quality people, as illustrated in what follows.

It was a cold afternoon in Odessa, Ukraine, on November 22, 1996, when five members of the CoMission Executive Committee visited Public School #15, an elementary school, and headed for a third-grade classroom. An attractive CoMissioner, a schoolteacher from Texas, accompanied us.

The class, composed of about thirty Ukrainian children, was taught by a most gifted lady who expertly moved among the children and encouraged them in their learning. As she began to teach the children the CoMission Christian morals and ethics curriculum, you could sense the expectancy and excitement of the children. When asked questions concerning the lesson, their response was immediate. They properly raised their hands and, when called upon, stood immediately to their feet and answered the question. Their teacher taught them the Bible, and then they recited Scriptures they had memorized to undergird their learning process.

As the class concluded, the children joined their teacher in a circle in the front of the classroom, holding hands. First they shared requests and prayed together. Then we, their guests, were asked to join the circle and, through our interpreters, share our prayer requests. One of our members requested prayer for Jennifer, his daughter, who had an injured foot. After a time of prayer, the teacher dismissed the children for the rest of the day. One little girl came up to Jennifer's father and told him she would continue to pray for Jennifer!

Afterwards we met with the teacher and learned that after she became a Christian, she led her parents, husband and daughter to Christ. She was currently teaching other teachers in her school how to teach the CoMission biblical curriculum. It was wonderful to observe the loving Christian friendship between this wonderfully committed Ukrainian teacher and the CoMissioner teacher from Texas, her mentor teacher.

The key to the success of this elementary school's third-grade teacher in Public School #15 in Odessa was the quiet but efficient schoolteacher from Texas who had mentored her in teaching the CoMission's biblical curriculum. This CoMissioner had been carefully recruited, joining an eventual total of over 1,500 men and women recruited by partnering agencies of the CoMission to serve one year overseas, seeking to reach the well-educated people of the former Soviet Union for Jesus Christ.

LONG-TERM SERVANTS

Eventually, many decided to stay on and serve for another year or more. In fact, even as I write, a woman from Florida in her seventies, who went out on an original team in the early 1990s, is still serving the people of Odessa by running a much-needed orphanage. Also, a dentist from Maryland continues to serve the people there, as well as a former team leader, a retired US Army lieutenant colonel and his wife, who spend most of the year in Odessa. The concept of the CoMission among lay people caught fire. Although the Reformation brought forth the belief of the priesthood of all believers, the CoMission actually freed up a massive explosion of the laity to serve. As far as I know, the CoMission was the largest people-lift of lay people proceeding to a needy and open mission field in the history of world missions.

The recruiting of such CoMissioners to serve for one year in the former Soviet Union was not done in a random manner, but was well organized. During an Executive Committee meeting on August 17, 1993, it became apparent to Paul Kienel that our chairman, Dr. Bruce Wilkinson, was overloaded. With too many responsibilities, his health was suffering. Paul volunteered to assume some of Bruce's responsibilities. I found myself also concerned, and volunteered to chair the Mobilization Committee that Bruce had organized and chaired along with the help of his executive director, Matt Martin of the Navigators. I could see an immediate look of relief sweep across Bruce's face. He jumped to his feet, ran around the conference table and kissed each of us on the forehead. This he proclaimed the "Ritual of the Blessing of the Forehead." It was an amazing moment in the life of the CoMission. I believe that this released Bruce to continue to develop videos, which were being used in teaching new Christians reached by CoMissioners. Bruce and Matt had very capably organized the Mobilization Committee. They were doing a wonderful job of working with all of the agencies and churches who had volunteered people to assist in the mobilization of CoMissioners for a one-year term of service in the former USSR.

For my part, I knew that I had plenty on my platter chairing the Church Relations Committee while also serving as the executive director, CEO, and COO of Mission to the World with its 500 career missionaries serving on many fields across the globe. I had a burden for recruitment of missionaries for overseas service, having recruited with Wycliffe Bible Translators, and after that for Mission to the World. My responsibility as missions director of InterVarsity Christian Fellowship for ten years, directing Urbana Conventions, grew out of my burden for the recruitment of potential overseas missionaries. So here was my opportunity not only to relieve Bruce

Wilkinson of an added responsibility, but also to be involved in a burden that the Lord had placed upon me many years before.

Early in the CoMission, a fifty-page Mobilization Manual was developed that covered such items as prayer, recruiters, philosophy, principles, presentations, follow-up, CoMission strategy, convocations, answers to questions often asked, materials and order forms, as well as the first years of the CoMission history. The mobilization strategy was set up in September 1993. When I became chairman of the Mobilization Committee, I clearly saw the need to divide the enormous task for implementation and accountability.

This excerpt from the strategy document outlines the challenges and objectives of our committee:

■ **The mobilization of the laity.**

The mobilization of hundreds of lay people during the next five years is essential to accomplishing the CoMission strategy. One of the primary challenges we face in enlisting people as CoMission team members involves adequately motivating interested individuals regarding the ministry opportunities with the CoMission. Some of the avenues utilized to fulfill these challenging goals are public relations, national publicity, recruitment trips and mailings, development of communications tools such as brochures and videos, and the solicitation of church involvement through an annual pastors conference. This also includes personal interaction with potential candidates, paperwork involved with the recruitment process and the coordination required to avoid duplication of efforts in mobilizing the needed staffing for the CoMission teams.

■ **Coordinating the mobilization efforts of all CoMission members.**

Although each sending organization is designating individuals who will implement mobilization for their own agencies, further coordination is needed to maximize the recruitment efforts of all CoMission members. Through the international headquar-

ters of the CoMission, efforts will be made to find, recruit and network possible team members with the sending organizations of their choice.

- **Fielding of all CoMission inquiries.**

  All inquiries from CoMission publicity are directed to the CoMission international headquarters, including individuals who want to sign up as prayer partners, churches who would like to learn about the vision of the CoMission, missions organizations that would like to be involved and Christian and secular news agencies requesting press releases.

In summary, the Mobilization Committee worked to:

1. Establish recruiting guidelines and policies.
2. Develop varied recruitment strategies for participating organizations to utilize.
3. Coordinate the sending organizations' representatives at the Association of Christian Schools International teachers conventions and other major events.
4. Develop a "Mobilization Manual."
5. Coordinate overall mobilization efforts to provide an optimum environment of recruitment.

Basically, the committee was made up of mission-sending agency people who were assigned to recruit CoMissioners for their teams. These teams being sent to cities across the former USSR came from the overseas divisions of many organizations. Other members of the CoMission who were concerned for mobilization included local churches and individuals.

Soon after I became the Mobilization Chairman, Matt Martin, our capable executive director, was drafted to serve in another vital ministry of the Navigators and tendered his resignation. Fortunately King Crow, chief of staff of the CoMission, although already overloaded with responsibility, volunteered to also become our executive director, which gave keen emphasis to the work of mobilization.

The more than thirty people who were on the Mobilization Committee met at least twice a year to find out what strategies were work-

Prayer of dedication at commissioning service prior to departure for Russia.

ing or how we needed to reevaluate our procedures. We also produced new literature or videos for use by those assigned by their agencies to recruit CoMissioners. Our meetings were like "popcorn" settings, with excellent reports, sharing of experiences, setting goals and, in general, a great sense of cooperation. I always left those meetings amazed at the versatility of those involved, as well as their dedication to the task of all-out mobilization of CoMissioners. It was evidenced by the fact that over a five-year period, from 1992–1997, more than 1,500 CoMissioners were recruited, carefully trained and fielded overseas in difficult fields of service.

Strategies of a Maturing CoMission

Various strategies were added as the CoMission grew in maturity, including an important special conference held by the newly organized CoMission Alumni Network at one of the summer meetings. This drew many of the CoMissioner alumni who had already served a year overseas. Their enthusiasm was tremendous, and they desired to assist in recruitment for the remainder of the CoMission's existence. Angela Ghent, a former CoMissioner in Apatity, Russia, became the southeastern coordinator of the CoMission Alumni Network.

CoMission headquarters, under King Crow's leadership, had multiple functions, including setting up and monitoring a mobilization system. King and his staff went all out in organizing informational events for the CoMission for pastors and mission-minded lay people in major US cities.

The major events for recruitment were the Pastor and Christian Leaders Conferences, organized by Paul Kienel in major cities across the USA. Several hundred people attended each time. Bruce Wilkinson explained the CoMission operation at each of these meetings. We always had a major speaker, a report from each committee and testimonies from overseas staff and former CoMissioners. On the last evening, time was given for recruitment of potential CoMissioners. Rooms were provided for breakout sessions where guests could interact with the sending agencies of their choice. In those sessions the agency's representative would tell of their agency's CoMission ministry in their city or cities in the former Soviet Union. The guests were given an opportunity to respond for service or be placed on a mailing and phone list. These events were highly profitable in sharing the CoMission story with pastors and lay people in major cities. They provided an excellent opportunity for the recruitment of CoMissioners.

During the CoMission's existence from 1992–1997, the Urbana '93 Student World Missions Convention took place at the University of Illinois at Champaign/Urbana, Illinois. I was able to get permission for a special booth for the CoMission. Our sending agencies did an excellent job of manning the booth and meeting with college students and young college graduates.

We also requested that Executive Committee members be alert to opportunities to recruit for the CoMission. While attending a mission conference at a large church in Montgomery, Alabama, word got out that I was on the Executive Committee of the CoMission. Over thirty adults gathered for a two-hour presentation followed by an excellent question and answer session. Then a wonderful radio host of a local radio station interviewed me concerning the CoMission. These types of opportunities were multiplied across the United States and Canada.

The Executive Committee requested that J.B. Crouse of OMS International head an International CoMission Committee. J. B., with the help of his executive director, Roy Kane, began to tell the story of the CoMission in Australia, South Africa, Singapore and South Korea. A CoMission sending country committee was set up in South Korea and Singapore.

I recall a meeting of CoMission members in 1993, when forty-two organizations, representing mission agencies, Christian colleges and churches pledged to recruit certain numbers of CoMissioners. At one point Moody Bible Institute (MBI) had Bruce Wilkinson as a special preacher speaker for several days. The Lord used him in a very significant way to begin a movement on the campus called the Moody 100, indicating that 100 students would go to the former USSR and serve as CoMissioners on a team. Dr. Joseph Stowell, MBI's president and a member of the CoMission Executive Committee, was thrilled that his students would be involved. I had the privilege of meeting one of the Moody 100 named Kevin True, a twenty-one-year-old student, when he was commissioned to go overseas. He was an outstanding young man!

One of my responsibilities was also to recruit sending agencies and bring them into the CoMission as partners. These agencies would agree to recruit at least one team of ten to go for a year to serve in a city chosen or assigned to the sending agency. Eleven such agencies contributed to sending 1,500 CoMissioners during the five years of the CoMission operation.

It was a privilege to serve as the chairman of the CoMission Mobilization Committee. During my time as chairman, we met five times to develop strategy and receive reports of CoMission members. I still remember when Thomas Home, at the age of eighty-one, was commissioned as a CoMissioner to serve in the former USSR. He brought with him forty-three years of educational experience, and said, "This is what God has prepared me to do all of my life." It was very rewarding to work alongside Christians who had a burden to take the gospel of Jesus Christ to a group of people who had been systematically "sealed off" from the rest of the world by atheistic communism for seventy years.

THE CHURCH RELATIONS COMMITTEE

The following excerpts from an official document aptly describe the ministry of the CoMission Church Relations Committee during its service from January 1993 through January 1997:

> "***The training of emerging leadership.*** *Although it is not the purpose of the CoMission to plant churches directly, many of the ministries involved with the CoMission will be utilizing some of their long-term staff to work with the existing churches in the former Soviet Union to meet the opportunities for growth that will result from the interest in the CoMission Bible studies. As leaders are identified in the Video Bible Classes, training opportunities will be provided for them to discover how they could be involved in existing local churches, as well as how they might be able to start new churches.*
>
> ***Conserving the fruit.*** *The leadership of the CoMission shares a deep burden that all individuals touched through the CoMission Video Bible Classes be encouraged to identify with a Bible-teaching local church. There is also great concern that as much as possible be done to work in coordination with the existing churches and their leadership. Although every effort will be made to work with the existing churches to provide training for their leadership in church planting, there is a strong possibility that many new churches will need to be established to provide worship opportunities for all of those who are sitting under the teaching of the Scriptures every*

week. Although the Video Bible Classes will provide a foundational
level of training and application of the Bible, it is hoped that every
individual will choose to identify with a local church body."

Another set of guidelines, which gave direction to the committee, was as follows:

1. Develop recommended strategy for leadership training and development.
2. Determine appropriate guidelines and standards for church-planting activities.
3. Solicit input regarding specific methods to integrate committed Christian nationals in CoMission activities.
4. Establish policies and procedures of cooperation with the local and national church.
5. Coordinate and track each sending organization's particular church-planting plans.

I was very fortunate to obtain Jim Young of Mission to the World as my executive director for the Church Relations Committee. He had already been in charge of recruiting and overseeing the two teams of ten CoMissioners each who went to Odessa, Ukraine. There they followed up on the 500-plus public school teachers and administrators who had attended the convocation held in Odessa.

WALKING A TIGHTROPE

The Church Relations Committee's work was difficult. In December 1992 eight members of the Executive Committee of the CoMission signed a Protocol of Intention with the Minister of Education of the Russian Federation, which allowed us to teach a Bible-related curriculum to the public school teachers. They in turn would teach the curriculum to their students, thereby assisting the new government in establishing a new moral and ethical standard, based on the Bible, in the Russian society.

The problem was that such a protocol did not make any allowance for the planting of churches in order to preserve the fruit of nationals who became Christians. Therefore the Church Relations Committee continued to "walk on eggs," so to speak, for two years until January 1994, when the Ministry of Education of the Russian Federation suspended the protocol. At that point, we could be more specific as to how to go about preserving the fruit of the CoMission ministry.

Twelve active members of the Church Relations Committee represented eight member organizations of the CoMission. A great need emerged for more deliberate action on our part as a committee, as CoMission teams in various cities began to see the need of moving new national Christians from Bible studies into churches. The following account of our experience as a CoMission Executive Committee in Odessa, Ukraine, very well illustrates that need.

> We gathered together in Odessa, Ukraine, on November 21–23, 1996 to meet some of the Ukrainians who had accepted Christ as their Savior through the CoMissioners' small group Bible Studies. It was quickly evident that these new believers were rapidly growing in their faith in Jesus Christ. One man was particularly quick to answer questions following his testimony. He then asked why some of them could not start a church and begin to worship in a more formal manner. This was discussed, and they were encouraged to start a church. Fortunately, Mission to the World, sponsor of the Odessa CoMissioners, had already sent one of their experienced church planters to Odessa. He began training sessions to encourage converts and to assist them in founding churches.
>
> That evening the CoMission Executive Committee hosted a dinner to honor the new Ukrainian believers in Christ. At its conclusion Bruce Wilkinson spoke and encouraged them in their new faith in Christ. All of them were then invited to the front of the gathering and asked to kneel, after which the Executive Committee members laid hands on them and prayed for them. It was a most meaningful experience.

CHURCH PLANTERS AND NEW CONVERTS

It had always been the intention of the CoMission to eventually see churches planted in the former USSR, but how the timing would develop was unknown. We had intentionally recruited mission-sending agencies as partners or members of the CoMission because they offered two resources. First, they were capable of recruiting CoMissioners to go in teams of ten to teach the biblical curriculum to public school teachers. Secondly, they were equipped, for the most part, to eventually recruit church planters to proceed to the city where CoMissioners had served and help the converts begin their church.

This fit with the policy of Mission to the World, where I served at that time. We sent two teams of CoMissioners to Odessa. At the same time, we began to recruit seasoned church planters from our other fields, as well as new career missionaries, to go and assist the new national Christians to plant churches. Two sending agencies, Campus Crusade for Christ and the Navigators, did not historically see themselves as directly planting churches. They decided that they could request one of the other sending agencies—such as the Christian and Missionary Alliance, OMS International, Mission to the World or another CoMission sending agency of their choice—to send them trained church planters to assist the national Christian converts in planting churches.

We discovered that new converts coming out of communist atheism often did not feel comfortable in the existing traditional Orthodox Church, nor in the old line Pentecostal or Baptist denomination churches that the communists had formerly persecuted, but allowed to exist in small numbers. The cultural impact of so many years of harassment of such churches caused some hesitancy on their part, in those early days of freedom, to reach out into this new arena. New believers came from a very different lifestyle and belief system, making it hard for them to step into the existing churches. In order, therefore, to preserve the fruit of new Christians brought to faith through the CoMissioners' activities, such as Bible studies, we saw a need to plant new churches.

Myles Lorenzen of WorldTeam, a very active member of the Church Relations Committee, was also involved in the training curriculum and the actual training of CoMissioners. We requested that he put together a church-planting training module, which he produced and named the "Home Fellowship Training Module." He took it overseas to three cities where CoMission sending agencies were serving and presented it to their staff and national Christians. He also held two training sessions of five days each and presented the material, alongside the regular CoMissioner training sessions, for people from the sending agencies who were interested in church planting following the initial Bible studies.

At about the time the CoMission was formed, the Alliance was organized by a group of mission agencies interested in church planting in former communist countries. The original purpose of the Alliance was to begin a church saturation movement throughout Eastern Europe following the fall of communism in that region of the world. I encouraged Carl Wilhelm, our Mission to the World regional director for Europe, to join the Executive Committee of the Alliance, which he did, and became chairman of their Executive Committee. There were

John and Lois Kyle in 1996 in St. Petersburg, Russia.

some problems relating to how the CoMission and the Alliance operated, with some apparent overlap on the overseas fields, which required interaction between the two. In September 1993, representatives of both came to a consensus of how we could cooperate in the area of church planting, as well as encourage and assist each other in our ministries.

Eventually, each sending agency of the CoMission was requested to establish a church-planting strategy to be reviewed by the Church Relations Committee. This helped strengthen the CoMission Executive Committee's desire to see churches established as an outgrowth of the Bible studies created for new believers and seekers by the CoMissioners. Some excellent plans were formulated by the sending agencies.

Chairing the Church Relations Committee had its challenges. It was difficult to come to a clear-cut decision about when a church plant would begin out of the CoMissioners' ministry in a given city. The early protocol with the Ministry of Education of the Russian Federation caused some members of the CoMission to proceed more cautiously, to be sure the intent of that agreement was kept. It would have been much easier if the committee had been named the "Church-Planting Committee" from its inception.

However, we knew from the beginning of the CoMission that the purpose of the Church Relations Committee was to see that every effort was made to ensure that the fruit of the CoMissioners' outreach and Bible studies would be preserved. Bible studies tend to come and go, but generally, a church is long term and more permanent in nature. Also, a church traditionally carries with it marks concerning the propagation of the gospel, discipleship and the sacraments. It is rewarding to know that out of the CoMissioners' outstanding ministry, many churches, Bible schools and seminaries exist today across the former Soviet Union.

To God be the glory, great things He has done!

LASTING RELATIONSHIPS

Nogorov, 2002:

Eleven years had passed between the first convocations in the city of Novgorod and my return. In that time much had changed, but much also remained the same.

Novgorod, with its beautiful skyline sprinkled with spires and steeples of churches and cathedrals, remained at the center of Russian Orthodoxy in the northwest region. At the same time, tremendous changes were taking place as industries were revitalized and growing.

What remained uncertain to me was the reception we would receive from those we had met long ago. Would their welcome be as warm and friendly as at our first arrival, or had their opinions of us changed over the years?

As we arrived, the uncertainty evaporated among the hugs and smiles of our welcoming hosts. Nadia was one of the teachers who had attended those first convocations, and at the mention of our return, she became so excited she could not wait to welcome us.

There were no buses running from Nadia's home to the train station. In her zeal to meet us, she decided to bicycle through unlit streets at 3:30 A.M. so she could be there to greet us with proper enthusiasm. Pedaling through the winding streets, she arrived at the station before 5:00 A.M. Yet, to her dismay, we didn't arrive. Unknown to Nadia, our train from Moscow was not arriving until the following day.

Even in her disappointment of having missed us, she later shared with me that it was worth it, because she knew we were returning and that had been satisfaction enough. Nadia's enthusiastic response to our return confirmed that eleven years did not diminish relationships grounded in the Lord.

PRINCIPLE
FIFTEEN

EXPRESS LOVE IN TANGIBLE WAYS.

Through our Development Committee, we were able to bring more than 18 million dollars in various kinds of aid to the communities where we worked. These tangible expressions of Christian compassion opened doors that had been initially closed by local officials opposed to the core purpose of the CoMission. This effort also illustrated the incarnational nature of the CoMission's purpose in "living Christ" before them. In a society where people often professed one thing and lived another, this was extremely important.

DR. RALPH E. PLUMB has spent thirty years involved in the "ministry of compassion" to the poor and homeless. He has traveled more than 2 million miles in ninety countries and has developed or managed a diverse range of humanitarian programs, including primary health in Cape Town, South Africa; vocational training for widows in Tegucigalpa, Honduras; emergency assistance to homeless street children in Saigon, Vietnam; and transitional housing for women in Southern California. From 1978–1989 he held key program director positions for both World Vision US and World Vision International. From 1990–2000 he served as president/CEO of International Aid, a $90 million (annual) Christian relief agency based in Michigan, and collaterally as president of AERDO, the Association of Evangelical Relief and Development Organizations. He is currently president/ CEO of the highly respected 113-year-old Union Rescue Mission in Los Angeles, the largest such mission of its kind in the United States. He, his wife, Ann, and their family live in the Los Angeles area.

CHAPTER ELEVEN

THE MINISTRY
OF COMPASSION
TO RUSSIA

Relief and Development Committee

Dr. Ralph E. Plumb, chairman

THE VISION WAS forming. Word had spread of the historic meeting in January 1992 that brought together a group of Christian leaders from a wide range of evangelical ministries across the US. In La Habra, California, they had met and prayed about what to do with the enormous door of opportunity which had suddenly opened in the former Soviet Union.

A second meeting, by invitation, was held at the Moody Bible Institute in Chicago in February 1992. As the (then) president/CEO of International Aid, Inc., based in western Michigan, I planned to attend, taking the short, three-hour drive around Lake Michigan because I felt a tugging at my heart to participate in this formative gathering. Yes, I had heard that this vital mission thrust would focus on laying a foundation for Christian education in the Russian public school system—a door amazingly and divinely opened to us by a loving God. But I also knew that I had been given the spiritual gift of mercy and was tremendously aware of the benefit that the ministry of compassion could have in the Russian context, and in particular in and through this emerging ministry thrust.

I sat in the back row. Dozens of godly men and women had come with disparate but equally passionate commitments to serve Russia. I admired the moderating skill and group dynamic of Bruce Wilkinson as he led us in prayer, then outlined the purpose and vision of this gathering. He then went to the chalkboard to capture nuggets of truth and revelation, sometimes sitting down to let the Spirit clear the air. Again, he led us in prayer; fielded questions, objections and counter-proposals; then led us in prayer a third time.

I said nothing. I listened and prayed silently: "Oh, Lord, You know my passion and my gifting. Please show me if there is any role for me in this significant ministry to the people You love so dearly in Russia."

One year passed. I was kept up to date by mailings and occasional personal contact regarding this unique consortium of organizations now called the CoMission. Each significant organization that joined brought to the collective task resources, manpower and professional expertise. As I later learned, the original Executive Committee of seven (Bruce Wilkinson, Paul Eshleman, Paul Kienel, Peter Deyneka, Joe Stowell, Terry Taylor and Paul Johnson) had been praying about adding five new members to their team.

First, the underpinning of prayer that so vitally bathed this entire effort was assigned to one of our nation's most dynamic intercessory prayer leaders, Mary Lance Sisk. She accepted their invitation to join the Executive Committee. Second, the discovery that the entire system of Russian Pioneer Palaces—the central facilities for the communist youth leagues—was also available to be used by the CoMission prompted an invitation to Margaret Bridges to join the Executive Committee. This gifted Christian educator, working with leaders in Russia's Ministry of Education, played a pivotal role in the transformation of a number of these facilities into Christian Cultural Exchange Centers. John Kyle, president of Mission to the World, was selected to head up the CoMission's Mobilization Committee. J. B. Crouse, president of OMS International, accepted the CoMission's invitation to serve as chairman of the International Sending Countries Committee.

And then, finally, as the CoMission leadership encountered obstacles in accessing certain geographic regions for holding convocations, and/or discovered a Russian school district with a particularly reticent administrator, they made a commitment to pursue targeted humanitarian assistance. The objective was to build stronger relations with local officials. This resulted in my being asked to serve as the fifth and final new member of the CoMission Executive Committee. Beyond the obvious value of this practical function, the ministry of compassion is really at the heart of God. Throughout salvation history, He has reached out to humankind with love, mercy and compassion. CoMission would now function as the loving extension of Jesus' hands.

By 1993 the CoMission had grown from being a movement to a model. Its chairman, Dr. Bruce Wilkinson, was blessed with a very capable executive administrator, King Crow, who had first initiated contact with me as he investigated the relief world. In addition to leading the growing agency International Aid, Inc., I also served as president of AERDO, the Association of Evangelical Relief and Development Organizations. This association consists of about forty Christian relief and development organizations, many of whom had ministry and physical presence in the various republics of the former Soviet Union. But just as some missionary-sending agencies and Christian education ministries chose not to join or participate in the CoMission, so, too, not all relief and development agencies wanted a tacit association with this distinctly "visible presence" in Russia.

In April 1993 the Executive Committee approved the establishment of a permanent standing committee to respond to tangible human need originating from CoMission field teams. We named it the Relief and Development Committee. After my installation with prayer and the laying on of hands, the challenge began in earnest. The first reality I needed to deal with was that, by this point, both the CoMission organizational and funding structures had each been pretty well defined. This meant that there was no opportunity to add even a modest dollar allocation for CoMission volunteers to raise for relief work during their deputation cycle. This step would have created the necessary funding pool for regional relief efforts. In addition, each of the CoMission member agencies were already quite stretched with the demands of dollars and people they had committed to the larger CoMission effort.

At our first Relief and Development (R & D) Committee in Orlando, Florida, about twenty participants joined their shoulders to this task. Excellent ministries such as MAP International, Mission Aviation Fellowship, Compassion International, CAMA Services (Christian and Missionary Alliance), Food for the Hungry, Missionary Expediters and others prayed and developed strategy together.

By this time Dennis Steussi of MAF was serving as our committee's capable executive administrator. Of course, we first set about defining our mission and purpose. After achieving this, we structured our volunteer consortia to be as responsive as possible to serve in the short, three-year window that remained of the original five-year mandate of the CoMission.

OUR MISSION:
EXTENDING THE KINGDOM OF GOD THROUGH
MINISTRIES OF MERCY AND COMPASSION.

From the beginning of our involvement with CoMission, the Relief and Development Committee provided physical resources to enhance the central mission of the CoMission: helping bring the light of the gospel to people in greater Russia, a people whom God loves very much. We sought out opportunities to link a "cup of cold water" given in Jesus' name with the good news of salvation. Without exception, we repeatedly found that these tangible expressions of Christian compassion opened doors that had been closed by officials initially opposed to the core purpose of the CoMission. It also kept other doors open when secular Russian officials mounted opposition or some local religious leaders took offense to the evangelism and church planting that bore fruit during the involvement of a CoMission team in a particular district.

MATCHING REQUESTS WITH RESOURCES

As a committee, our purpose was to establish a communication exchange matching humanitarian requests from CoMission field sites to US-based resource agencies and churches. The information matrix that was best suited for this task flowed to and from the local church in the US. It looked something like this:

Churches ⟶ Field Teams ⟶ Sending Agencies ⟶
R and D Committee ⟶ Churches.

The local church gifted the ministry of CoMission with called and committed individuals volunteering for a one-year field assignment. Assigned to a field team, these individuals came under the authority and umbrella of one sending agency. While on a field assignment, nearly everyone discovered daunting human need and saw the tremendous opportunity to engage the ministry of compassion. This resulted in requests for humanitarian assistance generated by either the individual or the sending agency and forwarded to the Relief & Development Committee of the CoMission. These requests for goods and services were then sourced among the relief agencies participating in the R and D Committee or to their partner affiliates. Since we could not tap into any existing CoMission funding, the money needed to secure and ship relief goods or to provide various humanitarian services was funded either unilaterally by the participating relief agency or, more often, by the sending church from which the volunteer originally came.

Obviously our committee needed to prepare all of the appropriate communication tools, such as creating a Project Information Form and delineating the proper procedures for channeling requests by e-mail, fax, or other means. Within a short time, we were receiving numerous requests for humanitarian assistance such as medical supplies and equipment. We also coordinated inquiries for micro-enterprise and other development training. And we fielded an increasing number of inquiries about sending professionals for short-term assignments as tradesmen, physical therapists, health professionals and others. God was indeed blessing our modest but sincere effort.

THE MINISTRY OF COMPASSION
A BIBLICAL FOUNDATION

Redemptive history overflows with expressions of God's mercy chronicled in Scripture and in the writings of the church over the centuries, such as this verse: "The Lord is full of compassion and mercy" (James. 5:11c, NIV). Mercy is one of the distinct attributes of God's nature and an integral part of God's relationship with His creation. Throughout history God has reached out compassionately to humankind. We are called to be Christ-like. Thus, mercy is an important expression of the character of God, which He desires to see manifest in His people, in the community of believers. The tangible outpouring of God's mercy expresses itself through the ministry of compassion.

Therefore, mercy/compassion represents one of the most important themes in the mission of the church. It is vitally important that the church remain committed to the ministry of compassion. Yet, over time, works of compassion in the mission of the church have varied in theological commitment and practical intensity. Today visible trends and empirical evidence show that the ministry of compassion has again become a strategic tool in the growth and health of the church. It is not the intention of this short chapter to outline this biblical principle, but suffice it to say this was absolutely true in the church in Russia during the CoMission years of 1992–1997.

The English words in Scripture translated as mercy or (compassion) come from three different Greek words: *eleos, oiktirmos* and *splanchna*.[1] These form our biblical foundation for the ministry of compassion.

Eleos—*concern for the welfare of others*

Eleos and its derivatives can be found in Greek literature from Homer onwards. It is found in the Septuagint (LXX) nearly 400 times and in the New Testament seventy-eight times. It is "the emotion raised by contact with an affliction which comes undeservedly on someone else."[2] *Eleos* is always concerned for the welfare of others and is expressed with "the elements of both awe and mercy."[3] The verb *eleō* means to have or show compassion, be sorry for, or to be merciful. Quite often the mercy of *eleos* plays an important role in the administration of justice. In fact, the Old Testament and other Jewish usage of the word (*hhesed,* translated as *eleos* in the LXX) emphasized the attitude that arises out of a mutual relationship. Its predominant use in the New Testament/Greek context, especially the Pauline writings and the Synoptic Gospels, is expressed clearly as the foundational expression of the love of God toward humankind. It is God's mercy, which precedes ours. *Eleos* is the basis upon which we are to follow God's pattern. When the word is used in the human context, it emphasizes "the divinely required attitude of man to man . . . (and the) sense of the kindness we owe one another."[4]

Oiktirmos—*both feeling and action*

Oiktirmos and its derivatives have been found since the writings of Gorgias in the 5th century B.C. There are eighty references in the Septuagint, and in the New Testament it can be found in noun, verb and adjective forms. The important distinction in this word usage is ". . . the sense both of mere feeling and of active merciful action . . . . God's mercies are the presupposition—the grounds of the 'therefore'—for the Christian life. . . . Jesus calls for merciful behavior, putting God's merciful attitude as the measure of human action."[5] The distinctive of this word is the linkage of both the feeling and action of mercy. It is sympathy that is ready to help. Our human *oiktirmos* is grounded in divine *eleos,* which forms the basis of our mandate for the ministry of compassion.

Splanchna—*from the inward parts*

The third word, *splanchna,* and its derivatives predominantly focus on emotive words from the inward parts—the entrails, the heart. It represents the strong, compassionate emotion ". . . at the sight of crying human need and characterizes the messianic compassion of Jesus . . . ."[6] We see this powerful mercy in Jesus' response to the leper (Mark 1:41); to the people like sheep without a shepherd (Mark 6:34); to the sight of the harassed and exhausted crowd (Matthew 9:36); to the blind men who sought Jesus out (Mt. 20:34); and to the widow mourning her only son (Luke 7:13). This *splanchna* is also found in the list of Christian virtues in Ephesians 4. It is ". . . the heart as the source of action that helps and relieves need."[7] Compassion is grounded in God's example and clearly involves both emotive and active expression. The importance of this word is that it represents one of the distinctive marks in the life of the Christian community. And it was our strong commitment to this biblical foundation amongst those participating in the Relief and Development Committee that undergirded our service to the larger objectives of the CoMission.

COMPASSION IN THE RUSSIAN CONTEXT

The recorded lists of God's provision to the people across the eleven time zones of greater Russia accumulated quickly:

- wheelchairs for Vladimir and Odessa
- clothing for Orenburg and Rivne
- medicines for Novosobirsk and Orlyonok
- burn treatments for Volgograd
- tuberculosis medicines for Novgorod and Samara
- vitamins for Ivanova and Arkhangensk
- orphan care items for Magadan and Moscow
- food for Krasnodar and Sumy
- hygiene kits for Blagoveschenk and Vologda
- emergency supplies for refugees in Chechnya

When all was said and done, the valiant efforts of a small group of under-funded co-laborers in the Relief and Development Committee provided more than $18 million in medical and relief products to more than sixty partners in twelve separate republics of the former Soviet Union. Again, this occurred in the last three years of the CoMission's five-year commitment. It was a drop in the bucket in terms of the overall human need that CoMissioners saw and experienced. But the ministry value that it represented is hard to calculate in human terms. This three-year ministry of compassion was a strong testimony of God's faithfulness, and was warmly received and graciously appreciated by the wonderful people of Russia. Here are just a few program highlights to illustrate the diversity of the effort:

- CoMission sent $894,000 in emergency relief supplies to war-torn Chechnya in March 1995.

- The Wesleyan CoMission team in Vladimir received and distributed $70,000 in medical equipment and supplies to be used in four locations: the student clinic, the maternity hospital, the hospital serving railroad employees and the orphanage at Suzdahl.

- CoMission provided cash funding to purchase eyeglasses and pay for eye exams for 200 children in the Vladimir region.

- Forty-five hospital beds were sent to the Ukrainian Center for Christian Cooperation.

- CoMission brought a Ukrainian orphan to the US for medical treatment. British Air provided two free, round-trip tickets for the boy and his translator. US Air pilots donated buddy passes to fly them to Charlotte, North Carolina. A plastic surgery group and an orthopedic surgeon donated their services. The hospital and prosthetist also donated their services. A local host family gave $1,000 toward expenses incurred during the visit of the boy and translator.

- The Mission Society for the United Methodists sent a relief and medical container to the far reaches of Eastern Russia, contents shared with the Navigator teams in the region.

- A large quantity of vitamins and hygiene items, such as

toothpaste, were hand delivered to an orphanage in Novgorod by a soccer team with the Missionary Athletes International ministry.

■ Joni and Friends donated a motorized wheelchair, and Serve International sent an ultrasound machine.

These and many other individuals and agencies responded to the call of God to participate in this ministry of compassion—because that is what Jesus had whispered in their hearts to do.

Dr. Ralph Plumb presents humanitarian gifts to Russian educators.

TESTIMONIES OF GOD'S FAITHFULNESS

More important than a list of projects or dollars is the personal testimonies from individuals who were on the front lines of this ministry of compassion in Russia during the CoMission years. I offer just three that illustrate the incarnational nature of this important element of the CoMission's mission and purpose.

Words could never express our gratitude for the ministry you provided to us out in the field. We could never begin to put together the extensive medical supplies you provided all under one roof. Just as so much of our shopping here in America has become warehouse-style shopping, you provided us missionaries with a one-stop shopping capability. Not only needful items for our personal use, but items for use of those in the community we serve. In the burn center, most of the patients happen to be children from rural villages. There is a high rate of burns occurring to children because of the poor heating and cooking conditions in the homes. We were able to purchase mattresses from you for about the cost of a meal at McDonald's, and now these patients are resting comfortably on vinyl mattresses, which are easy to clean. When I think about the money the Lord has entrusted me with, I could not think of a more cost effective way to spend my money.

—Robert Medema, Volgograd

Last Monday, we were meeting with the director of the orphanage, reviewing our first two weeks of ministry there. The meeting was interrupted by one of the assistants who worked there. An Italian couple had just come with the final paperwork in hand to pick up their soon-to-be-adopted eight-year-old daughter. The director invited the excited couple into the office where Paul and I were and asked us to stay. The room was charged with emotion as Svetlana came into the room wearing what I'm sure were the best clothes she had. Svetlana's new mother began showering her with gifts— more toys and dolls than this young girl had probably ever owned in her entire life. The mother started replacing her new daughter's clothes and shoes with those taken from several of the many shopping bags she had carried into the room. It was hard not to notice that the feelings of the orphanage director were offended as the new mother quickly returned to the assistant all of the items that the orphanage had provided for the little girl. Soon Svetlana had nothing left that had been given to her by the orphanage.

In accordance with Russian traditional custom, we then had tea, which, of course, included more food than you should eat for the entire day. As the prearranged time approached for the new parents and Svetlana to leave (they were waiting for the driver to return), the orphanage director asked to speak directly to Svetlana. The orphanage director reminded Svetlana of the good times they had together at the orphanage, about how much they were going to miss her and about how much they all loved her. The director told Svetlana, "I want to give you a present to take to your new home…something to remind you of your native country…something to remind you of your native language…something to remind you of what is really important in life."

The gift was The Illustrated Children's Bible recently provided to the orphanage by the CoMission. From the Russian field, we say thank you to the donors and supporters who have made a profound contribution to this land and its people.

—Ron Dawson, Vladimir

(Ron died suddenly in Moscow from a medical complication, but he did so in service to His Lord and the people of Russia whom he loved. His wife Barb now serves on the mission field in Croatia.)

I have news of a medical need of a woman who lives in a village outside Novgorod. Her varicose veins in her legs are so enlarged that she cannot carry things and can barely walk. Life in the village requires both. She has no running water and needs to carry it in each day, not to mention wood for her heat. She is only forty-five years old and is about 5'2," weighing 130 lbs. She knows of a doctor who has an American medicine called "trambar" that he charges lots of money for injections. Could you find some medicine by that name, or one that would relieve this woman's condition? Of course, there are many needs here, but I believe God lets us see specific ones so that He can receive the glory for meeting them.

—Leslie Johnson, Novgorod

On December 25, 1991, Soviet President Mikhail Gorbachev called US President George Bush, Sr., and said, "I have a Christmas present for you. The Soviet Union is no more." Beyond the political implications, by far the greatest gift—from God—was open access, for a divinely appointed time, to an eager nation of literate but spiritually starving people. In those tumultuous early days of the fall of the Soviet Union, the civil society of Russia imploded, chaos and corruption took hold of a rudderless government, and the deep void of ethics and morality found in the godless culture of post-communism was clearly evident. It was into this milieu that the CoMission was born in the heart of God, and then inspired in the hearts of His servants. I was humbled to play a small role in this historic movement of the Holy Spirit.

In my 1997 concluding report to the joint session of the CoMission and CoMission II leadership, I wrote these words:

> My dear co-laborers of the CoMission,
>
> What a privilege it is for me to affirm and celebrate the marvelous way in which God has worked in our lives together. It has been my great joy to see how the Lord has used each one of you to help bring the wonderful people of the former Soviet Union into His kingdom. It has been a highlight of my ministry these past years to have co-labored with you to extend the good news of the gospel to these dear ones. I can't say enough about the quality of leadership that each of you provided in making this one of the most significant efforts in recent missiological history! But before we take too much credit, I think we would all agree that it is by the Lord's grace and eternal timing that we have each been blessed to be used as His servants at this time and in this way.
>
> The Relief and Development Committee played a modest overall role in the CoMission, helping people to meet tangible physical need. Our goal was to link this ministry of compassion with the strong Christian witness of the CoMission. In every God-inspired human endeavor, there is a passing of leadership responsibility. I pray for those of you who will step forward now to lead this important outreach, that you may have abundant wisdom, great insight and God's continued blessing as you proceed in faith."

And as we each proceed in our journey of faith, I am confident that the ministry of compassion will continue to be an invaluable tool in the mission outreach of the church–because mercy is at the heart of God and His very nature. To Him be all glory and honor and praise.

NOTES:

1. Sources drawn upon for the presentation of the Greek words *eleos, oiktirmos* and *splanch-na* include:

Colin Brown, ed., 1976, *The New International Dictionary of New Testament Theology,* Vol. I-III. (Grand Rapids, MI: Zondervan Publishing House, 1976).

Gerhard Kittel and Gerhard Friedrich, eds., *Theological Dictionary of the New Testament, Vols. I, V, VI, VII.* (Grand Rapids, MI: Wm. B. Eerdmans Publishing Co., 1980)

2. Bultmann quoted in Brown 1976:594).

3. Kittel and Friedrich, 477.

4. Ibid., 482.

5. Brown, 598.

6. Ibid., 599.

7. Ibid., 600.

NITA'S
PRAYER

Bila Tserkva, Ukraine, 2004:

My Dear Lord,

I can't understand how this happened! Only a short while ago I claimed I "didn't do" missions. Now I'm sitting in a tiny flat in Bila Tserkva, Ukraine, snow on the ground, little or no hot water each day, problems and hardships at every turn. Yet, I am the most blessed of women! You have given me a ministry among these people and your Word and love to share with them.

You gave me favor with the directors of the orphanages, and I was able to cuddle the babies, visit the young people and eventually even teach the Bible! You made it possible to take four boys from the mentally disabled institution and put them in a home with foster parents to care for them and give them a rewarding life.

You even allowed two of these boys to work in the wheelchair center and learn the joys of service to others and gainful employment. You brought two handicapped men to manage the wheelchair center, and now you're expanding the ministry to many other cities, allowing more than 1,000 people (at last count) to be mobile.

You showed me the needs of the people: the lack of medicine that diabetics face, the need for education and therapy for stroke victims, the children denied necessary surgery and, most of all, the holes in all of their hearts that You want to fill with Yourself. You sent a nurse to begin a stroke rehabilitation program and a diabetic program and to help locate children we could send to Shriner's Hospital (and in-country hospitals) for surgery.

You have softened hearts in the United States to support this ministry with monetary donations, ministry teams, toy drives and $1,000,000 worth of medical equipment and supplies.

You nudged the mayor into leasing me 30 acres of land by the beautiful Ros River where together we will build a village with homes and gardens and shops, a wheelchair manufacturing plant, a school for the handicapped and a church. It will be a place where all will be welcomed in Your name and loved unconditionally.

You graciously provided a family of all ages in the staff and friends surrounding me. How generously You have protected and guided and comforted like a Father and a Husband and a Brother. You have faithfully supplied all my needs beyond anything I could ever have asked or imagined.

And all of this came about through a three-week convocation with the International School Project, teaching a course of morals and ethics to the teachers in Ukraine. This was followed by a one-year commitment with CoMission to teach the Bible. However, You opened my heart and gave me such a love for these people, that one year turned into a lifetime. I can only imagine what You might have planned in my future!

I'm forever grateful to You,
Nita Hanson

TEACHER COMMENTS

"I had never heard of God, Jesus Christ or the Bible. The model of Jesus as a leader was amazing. I also learned that what you share and what you teach comes from what you believe. So it is important what you believe."

—School Director, 1993 Convocation

"The materials are excellent, useful and necessary. The teaching staff and students of our school thank you very much. Some children had zero idea about God, and now they know of the foundations. They started reading the Bible and pondering the meaning of their lives regarding God and morality. Thank you."

—Natalya, 1999 school psychologist

"This is the first chance my students and I have to learn about the life of Jesus Christ. We study the materials with interest."

—Sergey, history instructor

"I heard about a life of Jesus from my colleagues. Teaching this course will bring many positive results to the general humanitarian education of our students. If it is possible, please send me a copy of "The Story of Jesus" in both English and Russian."

—Maksim, English language and literature teacher

"These materials are very good and clear to teach. They are well received by the students, as well as by the adults."

—Nikolay, history teacher

"These materials are very helpful for my work as a deputy director and teacher of the Russian language and literature. The purpose of the school curriculum is a deep study of the Russian culture, which is based upon the Christian traditions."

—Irina, deputy director

"We've been in need of these materials for long time. In schools there is nothing like them, not even a copy of the Bible. The curriculum is excellent. I have read them without pausing for breath. The tapes attracted the attention of students immediately. We'll keep applying them."

—Nina, math teacher

THE PRINCIPLES OF THE COMISSION

What is there to learn from the experience and the CoMission enterprise? Are there some principles that God showed to those involved that can be lessons for the future? We think so. Here are a few.

REALIZE THAT WORKING TOGETHER PLEASES GOD.

There are at least two reasons for this. No organization or denomination is gifted to do everything that needs to be done for the Lord in an area. The Scriptures say "One can chase a thousand, two can put 10,000 to flight." In areas where there are open doors for the gospel, the message will go out more quickly and with greater power when we cooperate.

Secondly, it is with the heart of God to work together. In John 17:20–23, the unity of believers is not an option in evangelism. It is the sign that God left to validate and show the deity of Jesus and is present-day evidence of God's love for mankind. Our love for one another is the evidence that we are followers of Jesus. Is it any wonder that our unity as believers is continually attacked? Could loving one another be our greatest God-given secret weapon for worldwide evangelism?

MAKE REPENTANCE CENTRAL TO ALL
ORGANIZATIONAL PLANNING.

The sins of pride, territorialism, credit taking and individualism are endemic in Christian leaders and we did not hold a meeting during the five years of the CoMission in which we did not repent of our sins. When new people joined the group who had not repented, problems and conflicts arose immediately. And, among some of us who had already repented, we found that some of the old habit patterns of wanting our *own* way, and *our* strategy, and *our* material came back and we had to repent again to keep the CoMission moving forward.

EXPECT OPPOSITION FROM YOUR OWN ORGANIZATION.

We were not prepared for this, but it happened—almost without exception. The leaders, board members, etc. from our own organizations thought that their CoMission participants were being taken advantage of or "used" for someone else's plan. How does the president of Navigators explain that the CoMission participants will be trained to share the Four Spiritual Laws published by Campus Crusade for Christ? And how do the Crusade workers explain that all CoMissioners will be using Navigator materials for follow-up?

GIVE THE CREDIT TO GOD.

Though this is the desire of all of us in ministry, we sometimes are guilty of stealing some of the glory for our organization or ourselves. Since none of us did the CoMission work alone, we all had trouble writing reports for our magazines and newsletters. If we took too much credit for ourselves, it would be a slap at the effort of the other members of the CoMission. So we just rejoiced in what God was doing—through so many different churches, backgrounds and confessions. And that is how the Lord has always intended that ministry should be reported. To God be the Glory! Great things He has done!!

DO THE WORK UNDER A NEUTRAL BANNER.

Wherever we were doing CoMission work, we took off our "agency hats" and put on "CoMission hats." This meant we did not take our organizations' "agendas" to the CoMission, but rather that we left them at the door to serve the whole of CoMission. This allowed us to operate in a spirit of unity and purpose.

EXPECT EVERY ORGANIZATION TO PAY ITS OWN WAY.

There was no central fund raising force for the CoMission. Every person involved paid his own way to every conference, committee meeting or task force—as well as a share of the ministry costs. If an organization wanted to provide literature, Bibles, videos, etc.—that organization paid for them. We had some organizations that were willing to join the CoMission if their material could be purchased or they could get funding. We had to decline their participation. We never spent funds that were not already raised. The CoMission ended without any deficits.

RESPECT THE UNIQUE GIFTING AND CALLING OF EACH ORGANIZATION.

We asked those people who were strong in a particular area of ministry to lead us and teach us in that area. This made our training and preparation very strong, since it was led by the best practitioners in the area. We centered our teaching and materials on the person and work of Christ—where there was little disagreement.

BE FLEXIBLE.

Throughout the time of the CoMission, conditions changed continually. Strategy changed as more needs were discovered. We listened continually to those on the field in order to make our policies and supervision relevant. We realized we needed to train people with both practical ministry skills and general principles. We trained in specific skills, but allowed adaptation on the field as needed. We learned the importance of having field supervisors regularly visit the team of laymen. Since the teams were there for only one year, we had to help them solve problems quickly if they were to be effective. And we needed to train each team in the essential tools and systems to be self-feeding and sustaining on the field.

DIVIDE THE TASK AND THE TERRITORIES.

In our practical ministry we genuinely attempted to count others more important than ourselves. One of the first questions occurred when five organizations all felt "led" to place their CoMission teams in Moscow. That would have created great duplication of effort there and left other major cities without a team. But the leaders, in the spirit of cooperation, offered to place their teams in cities most in need and began ministries in places that virtually no one had heard of—and could not spell or pronounce. They were places like Dnipropetrovsk, Chelyabinsk, and Nizhny Novgorod. Some places were high in radiation levels from nuclear accidents. One organization sent older CoMissioners past child bearing ages to go to these places of high radiation.

RESPOND TO OPEN DOORS QUICKLY.

Every organization already had more than enough to do when the new opportunities opened up in the former Soviet Union. All of us lacked the manpower needed, to say nothing of the leaders and finances that would be necessary. We believed that just as there are critical periods where individuals seem more open to the gospel, there are similar times that occur to cities, nations and peoples. We were finding an unprecedented spiritual curiosity in Russia. Whether it was true spiritual hunger or not would be discovered later. But while people were interested in hearing the message of Christ, someone should go and tell it and live it so that they could respond. This meant, for everyone, that we had to make decisions quickly and train people on the job. What other opportunities have we missed during the centuries because we were too slow to respond?

MOBILIZE PEOPLE TO PRAY.

The Prayer Committee rallied over 20,000 people to pray daily for the CoMission. Each CoMissioner recruited prayer teams. Weekly newsletters contained the latest reports of praise as well as the challenges being faced. We prayed for ourselves. We prayed for the Russians. We prayed for the Church. We prayed for the workers. We prayed for the new believers. We had prayer walks, prayer seminars and prayer days. There were so many obstacles in the CoMission effort, that without the hand of God involved, we had no way to recruit the workers, raise the resources and get permission for the ministry in every school. Every participant in the CoMission saw the miraculous hand of God at work continually.

ASK FOR PLEDGES OF PERSONAL PURITY.

At each Primary Training Institute we asked each CoMissionar to come forward and shake the hand of one of the Executive Committee members and say, "Before God I commit to you that I will be sexually pure this year." The same pledge was made by each of the members of the Committee. We also did not accept any applicant who had had extramarital or premarital sex in the six months prior to their application. This was a crucial step in the preparation, as CoMissioners of both sexes found themselves propositioned regularly during their time of ministry.

WORK WITH LEADERS.

Because the initial effort was centered in the educational system, we worked with the leaders in Moscow on a continuing basis. By getting endorsements from the very top officials of the school system, we were able to see doors opened to 65,000 schools and 278 teacher-training colleges. In each city where CoMission teams were located, they talked to local Protestant and Orthodox pastors to inform them of why they were there. Many of the teams received criticism from these religious leaders because they were still operating under the old Soviet mindset of keeping anyone away that might be a threat to their power.

ENTRUST THE MINISTRY TO LAYMEN AND LAYWOMEN.

Because we believed it important to get people living and working in the former Soviet Union as quickly as possible, we needed to rely primarily on laymen and laywomen who could leave their jobs or schooling for a year to serve. The normal path of recruiting career missionaries, sending them to seminary, language school and support training would take too long. This level of workers would be needed in the future, but now it was important to get people who could go quickly and begin the process—even if it meant they weren't as knowledgeable and had to work through interpreters.

EXPRESS LOVE IN TANGIBLE WAYS.

Through our Development Committee, we were able to bring more than 18 million dollars in various kinds of aid to the communities where we worked. These tangible expressions of Christian compassion opened doors that had been initially closed by local officials opposed to the core purpose of the CoMission. This effort also illustrated the incarnational nature of the CoMission's purpose in "living Christ" before them. In a society where people often professed one thing and lived another, this was extremely important.

CoMISSION MEMBER ORGANIZATIONS

(sending organizations are shown in bold)

1. A.C.M.C (Association of Church Missions Committee)
2. Alpha Care Therapy Services
3. American Tract Society
4. Association of Christian Schools International
5. Baptist General Conference
6. **BCM International**
7. B.E.E. International
8. Biola University
9. BMC International
10. BMC of USA
11. Boneem International
12. Bright Hope International
13. **Campus Crusade for Christ**
14. Campus Outreach Augusta
15. Cedarville College
16. Child Evangelism Fellowship
17. Chosen People Ministries
18. **The Christian and Missionary Alliance**
19. Christian Associates International
20. The Christian Bridge

21. Church Resources Ministries
22. Columbia International University
23. Community Bible Study
24. Daniel Iverson Center for Christian Studies
25. Educational Services International
26. **European Christian Missions**
27. Evangelical Covenant Church
28. Evangelical Free Church Mission
29. Evangelical Friends Mission
30. Evangelical Mennonite Church
31. Evangelical Methodist World Missions
32. Evangelism Explosion III International
33. Fellowship of Evangelical Bible Churches
34. Focus on the Family
35. Foreign Mission Board of the Southern Baptist Convention
36. Gospel Light Publications
37. **Gospel Missionary Union**
38. Grace College of the Bible (Nebraska)
39. Great Commission Ministries
40. HCJB World Radio
41. In Touch Ministries
42. Institute for East/West Christian Studies
43. Wheaton College
44. International Aid, Inc.
45. International Coalition for Christian Counseling
46. International Cooperating Ministries
47. International Teams
48. John Guest Evangelistic Team
49. Lancaster Bible College
50. Maranatha Ministries International
51. Mission Athletes International
52. Mission Aviation Fellowship

53. The Mission Society for United Methodists
54. Mission to the World
55. Mission to Unreached Peoples
56. Missionary Board of the Church of God (Anderson, Indiana)
57. Missions Fest Vancouver
58. Moody Bible Institute
59. Multnomah School of the Bible
60. Nashville Bible College
61. **The Navigators**
62. **OMS International**
63. Philadelphia College of the Bible
64. Prairie Bible Institute
65. Project C.A.R.E. (Coordination of All Resources for Evangelism)
66. Reimer Foundation
67. Ronald Blue and Company
68. Russian Ministries
69. Salt and Light
70. Sea-Tac Ministries
71. **SEND International**
72. Serve International
73. Slavic Gospel Association
74. Team Expansion
75. Transport for Christ
76. U.S. Center for World Missions
77. Walk Thru the Bible Ministries
78. **Wesleyan World Missions**
79. World Gospel Mission
80. World Help
81. World Partners
82. **Worldteam**

CONTRIBUTORS TO THE CoMISSION COMMITTEES

THE EXECUTIVE COMMITTEE (SEE CHAPTER 1)

Bruce Wilkinson, chairman

THE SENDING ORGANIZATIONS COMMITTEE (SEE CHAPTER 2)

Paul Eshleman, chairman

THE SCHOOL TEXTBOOK/CURRICULUM REDESIGN COMMITTEE (SEE CHAPTER 3)

Paul Kienel, chairman
Sharon Berry
Ellen Black
James Braley
Blair Cook
Jerry Franks
Gene Garrick
Ollie Gibbs
Loreen Itterman
Curt Mackey
Olga Polykovskaya
Vernie Schorr

THE ARRANGEMENTS COMMITTEE (SEE CHAPTER 4)

Paul Johnson, chairman

TRAINING AND MATERIALS COMMITTEE, LISTED BY AGENCY (SEE CHAPTER 5)

Terry Taylor, chairman

Navigators

Terry Taylor
Stacy Rhinehart
Andy Weeks
Ralph Ennis
John Hamilton
Dennis Stokes
Eddie Broussard
Bob Lovvorn
Cheryl Merideth
John Purvis
Bob Sheffield
Chuck Steen
Chuck Broughton
David Smith
Tim Frye

Campus Crusade for Christ International

Curt and Lois Mackey
Dick Katz
Bill Wolfe
Alan and Tina Nagel
Andria Wolfe Gynn
Jim and Juanita Wyatt
Hank and Maureen Hornstein
Rebecca Bramlett Goldstone
Tracy Jensen Mancino
Rex Johnson

OMS

Bette Crouse
David Dick
Christine Weddle
Darrell and Lynn Mischler

World Team

Myles Lorenzen

Walk Thru The Bible

John Hoover

Appalachian State University

Gerald and Mary Parker

Ukrainian Nationals

Nick and Maia Mikhaluk

Church Resources Ministries

Paul Ford

THE RUSSIAN FEDERATION (C.I.S.) LIAISON COMMITTEE
(SEE CHAPTER 6)

Peter Deyneka, Jr. , chairman

THE CHRISTIAN CULTURAL EXCHANGE COMMITTEE
(SEE CHAPTER 7)

Margaret Bridges, chairwoman

THE PRAYER COMMITTEE (SEE CHAPTER 8)

Mary Lance Sisk, chairwoman
Bette Crouse of OMS International, vice-chairwoman
Robert. V. Sisk of Leighton Ford Ministries, treasurer
Anne Crow of the CoMission international headquarters, coor-
    dinator of *Fast Fax Facts*

Jennifer Ennis of The Navigators, prayer liaison to The Equipping
   Network (TEN)
Annie Kienel of Association of Christian Schools International
Lois Kyle of Mission to the World, coordinator of Member Organi-
   zations and Churches
Milton Monell of Campus Crusade for Christ, coordinator of
   on-site prayer and liaison to both the European Prayer Link
   and to Dan Peterson, Campus Crusade for Christ Eurasia
Carol Moyer, coordinator of prayer for convocations
Paula Rinehart of The Navigators
Elaine Springer of Peter Deyneka Russian Ministries, coordina-
   tor of *The Chariot* newsletter.

***Prayer Committee members who went on to serve with the
Navigators on CoMission teams within the nation of Russia:***

Michael and Elizabeth Darby, in Rostov
Ruth Holmsten in Pushkin.

Others who served abbreviated terms:

Jim Moyer, who served a short term as the Prayer Committee's
   executive director
Mary Jean Vesper, who represented International Aid, Inc.

THE INTERNATIONAL SENDING COUNTRIES COMMITTEE
(SEE CHAPTER 9)

   J.B. Crouse, chairman

THE MOBILIZATION COMMITTEE (SEE CHAPTER 10)

   John Kyle, chairman
   King Crow, executive director
    his staff: Lisa Borden,
               Ivey Harrington,
               Mark Bullock
               Sabra Romero

Matt Martin
Jaan Heinmets
Fred Wevodau
Roy Kane
Jerry LaGambina, Campus Crusade for Christ
Fred Wevodau of the Navigators
Joe Moore
Terry Graham and Donna Mood, volunteers CoMission Mid-
    Atlantic Office
Tina Fiol, Mission to the World
Wayne Wright, Wesleyan World Missions
    and a host of others who served on the committee with great
    productiveness, faithfulness and enthusiasm. It was an incred-
    ible team effort! I felt honored to work with them.

THE CHURCH RELATIONS COMMITTEE (SEE CHAPTER 10)

John Kyle, chairman

Many contributed invaluable help, including but not restricted
to those noted here:

Jim Young, executive director
Myles Lorenzen
Bob Sheffield and Ruth Holmsten, the Navigators
Steve Miller and Myles Lorenzen, Worldteam
Fred Smith and Stuart Lightbody, Christian and Missionary Alliance
Paul Swager, Wesleyan World Missions
Sam Metcalf, Church Resources
Curt Mackey, Campus Crusade for Christ International
Bob Erny and Harold O. Brown, OMS International
Rich Correll, John Guest Evangelistic Team
Harold Peters, Gospel Missionary Union.

THE RELIEF AND DEVELOPMENT COMMITTEE (SEE CHAPTER 11)

Ralph Plumb, chairman

OVERVIEW OF THE CoMISSION STRATEGY

STRATEGIES CHANGED DURING the years of the life of the CoMission. On subsequent pages you will find overview charts which reflect that, coupled with notes that explain the elements and overall points of training, strategy and materials.

Note how the charts moved from complexity toward simplicity. The Primary Training Institute manuals, given to the CoMissioners only days before they left on assignment, contained enormous amounts of materials. The creativity of those on the Training and Materials Committee was amazing. Everyone profited from watching master trainers at work as they developed new approaches to train the CoMissioners.

CoMission Integrated Model-School Strategy

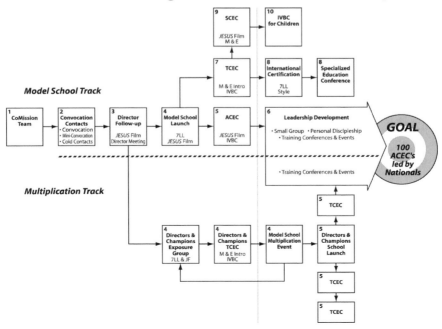

CoMission Strategy Flow Chart

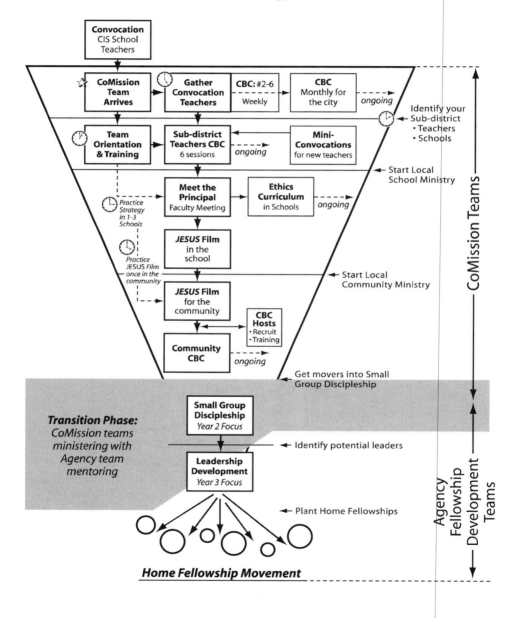

The Three Stages of CoMission Ministry

Payload

Goes into
Ministry Orbit

National Leaders Multiplying NCEC's

7 Processes [2]
$ 2 Tool Types
 – Bible only
 – Contextualized
   carryover tools

Stage III

Booster Rocket: 2 Stages

Crucial to
Payload
delivery, but
doesn't go
into orbit

Note: Stages 1 and 2 emphasize a priority focus of the ministry. Contact stage work should continue into the NCEC stage, however, as time permits.

NCEC Stage

7 Processes [2]
$ 4 Tool Types
 – Bible & printed
   materials
 – Video only
 – Video & printed
   materials
 – Audio & Other

Stage II

Contact Stage

7 Processes [2]
• Educational Track
 – TCEC's
 – CCE's
• Community Track
 – CCE's
 – Friendships
 – Other

Stage I

Payload — **Stage III: Multiplication** — Multiplication of NCEC's — Nationals Own & Lead Movements — Bible-focused Strategy — Growing National/Regional Network

Booster Rocket — **Stage II: NCEC** — Small Groups; Contact Stage Ongoing — CM Teams Enable Nationals — Networking Nationals & NCEC's

Stage I: Pre-NCEC — Contacts; Communicate Good News — CoMission (CM) Teams Initiate — Materials-focused Strategy — CM Teams Networking Together

---

Launching Pad

Guidance System Target: Movement of NCEC's Led by Nationals
Core Values & Philosophy of Ministry
Teams Trained & On Location

The CoMission Ministry

Training Graphic Organizer

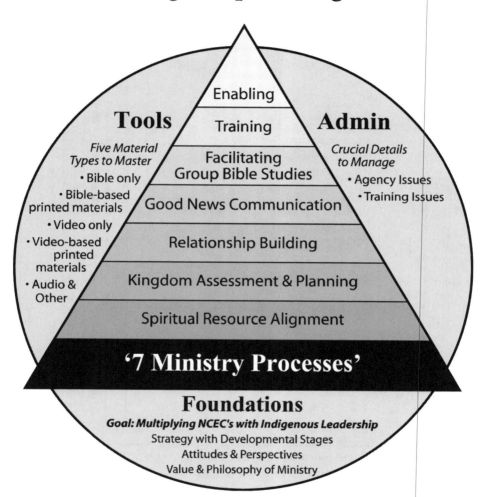

Enabling
Training

Tools

Admin

Five Material Types to Master
• Bible only
• Bible-based printed materials
• Video only
• Video-based printed materials
• Audio & Other

Facilitating Group Bible Studies

Crucial Details to Manage
• Agency Issues
• Training Issues

Good News Communication

Relationship Building

Kingdom Assessment & Planning

Spiritual Resource Alignment

'7 Ministry Processes'

Foundations

Goal: Multiplying NCEC's with Indigenous Leadership
Strategy with Developmental Stages
Attitudes & Perspectives
Value & Philosophy of Ministry

EXPLANATION: "7 MINISTRY PROCESSES"
Equipping People to Catch Fish, Not Just Fry Them

A process, not a mere program or procedure, is a series of related functions or actions which lead to a certain result. Ministry in the lives of people should be viewed as a process, rather than an isolated event. None of us comes to faith in Christ or experiences significant life changes apart from a number of interconnected, spiritual happenings. These are engineered by a sovereign God, even if unseen at the human level—hence, a process. Below are some basic ministry processes that are needed to build and sustain a movement. As with any process, these are transferable; that is, you can equip people to apply the same processes to others. They can and must be passed on to nationals if real multiplication is to occur.

I. The "Spiritual Resource Alignment" Process:

In this process, one assesses one's personal walk with God and makes proper adjustments so as to tie into God's blessing and power. Jesus promised that those who abide in Him will bear much fruit, and that their fruit will remain (John 15:5,16). We ABIDE by practicing:

A **Adoration.** Worship is the most important ministry that we can have as God's children, since it is directed to Him and for His glory. It is out of a consistent discipline of "attributing worth" to our heavenly Father, both individually and corporately, that our lives and ministries are refreshed, energized and brought into focus.

B **Biblical alignment.** Jesus urges us to allow His word to abide in us. Paul instructed the Colossians to "let the word of Christ richly dwell within you, with all wisdom, teaching and admonishing one another. . . ." There can be no growth or impact apart from becoming people of the Book–those who love it, trust it, study it, meditate on it, obey it.

I **Involvement with people.** Jesus gave us His great commandment to love others as He has loved us. Paul would urge the Galatians to exploit their great freedom in Christ by serving one another in love, thereby "walking by the Spirit" (Gal. 5:13-16).

D **Dependency in faith and prayer.** Without Jesus we can do nothing (John 15:4, 6). He promises answered prayer to those who abide in Him (John 15:7). A deep sense of our inadequacy in changing our lives should drive us all back to our Source in faith and prayer.

E **Expectancy in His Spirit.** Yet, through Christ and in the power of His Spirit, we can do all things. Jesus promises that we will be fruit bearers. We can count on God to keep His promises. As we minister in the Spirit, we can be optimistic, looking ahead to His victory.

II. The "Kingdom Assessment and Planning" Process:

This process of strategic ministry planning prayerfully takes into account what God is doing, the needs of people and how He wants us to be His instruments in meeting those needs. We "attempt great things for God and expect great things from God." It is a "ZAP" pray-and-plan process. This contrasts with mere "projection" planning, where one begins with point A (where we are now), moves on to point B (where we can see ourselves being in the near future), and on to the next logical point C, etc. Instead, we first start with God's kingdom vision, the "Z."

Z **"Z"—God's Kingdom Vision.** We begin by prayerfully drawing a circle around the "great things" God has led us to attempt for Him. It may be a whole city, or province, or nation turning to the Lord. Whatever, this "Z" is something bigger than we would ever undertake in utilizing mere "A to B to C to D..." planning. It is this "Z" that gets under our skin; that makes our blood churn. It motivates us and becomes God's calling for us.

A **Assessment.** Our "A" is where we begin, where we are now. We assess the resources at our disposal to press toward God's "Z." We soon realize that we can't carry out such a great vision alone. We need the whole body of Christ, working in partnership, involved in this vision. Mobilizing these brothers and sisters becomes an important element of our planning.

P **Planning.** We now lay out a strategic plan, the "P" of how to get from our "A" to God's "Z." Of necessity, this plan will have core ingredients of supernatural involvement: prayer, spiritual warfare and working in partnership with all of God's people. This plan, periodically and prayerfully reviewed, is God's blueprint for us as we move out in faith.

III. The "Relationship-Building" Process:

The ongoing process of building and maintaining meaningful relationships with people provides the basis of significant, mutual ministry. Solid relationships are key to successful teams, effective communication of the gospel, discipleship, leadership development, and especially the crossing of cultural barriers for ministry. The principles below give us TRACKS to grow on together:

T **Trust.** The ultimate goal in our relationships is to develop the kind of mutual trust that will enhance intimacy ("into-me-see"). Risking transparency yourself, along with an empathetic response to the open vulnerability of others, helps develop such trust. Prejudice and mistrust tend to dissipate as relationships mature.

R **Resolving conflict.** Solid relationships depend upon a commitment to keep short accounts; to actively manage the conflicts that normally arise in the course of life. Misunderstandings and hurts can easily become the acid rain of bitterness that destroys team or group unity and any hope of effective ministry.

A **Appreciating one another.** Every person is unique as an individual in God's image. Personal uniqueness is amplified when you factor in any cross-cultural differences. One sign of healthy, growing relationships is a growing appreciation of each person's unique gifts, personality, culture and contribution to a team or group. An eager willingness to learn from others is important, especially in cross-cultural settings where the relational learning curve is steep. It is easy to have unrealistic expectations, assuming that people of the host culture relate just as North Americans do. This often is not the case.

C **Camaraderie.** Having regular times of fun and/or adventure are important to growing relationships. Shared memories and laughter become an important bond, especially during times of stress. The press of much work often precludes such recreational opportunities. Wise teams will, however, make such times a priority.

K **Kindness.** A commitment to treat each other with respect and kindness should be a hallmark of Christian relationships. It is unrealistic to expect everyone on a ministry team to be "best of friends." It is a requirement, however, that their interactions be characterized by practical love.

S **Spiritual Unity.** The core quality that matures our relationships is that of our oneness in Christ. Regular times of prayer, worship, Bible study and sharing center around Him as our risen Head.

IV. The "Good News Communication" Process:

This four-phased process helps people come into a vital relationship with Jesus Christ and His people. Success in witnessing, then, is discerning where people are in the process and helping them move to the next phase. Serving as a "Good News BEAR-er" involves:

B **Bridge-building Phase.** In this, seek to creatively and caringly build both an awareness of and openness to the messenger and his message—the gospel. This is the **cultivation** phase of the process, helping get the ground ready to receive the good seed. It is important to realize that these phases are not linear. People will ebb and flow in interest and openness, so it is important to stay involved with them relationally. Cultivation never ends.

E **Explanation Phase.** Here, clearly communicate the truth of the gospel in such a way that a person understands it and its implications. This is the **sowing** phase, spreading the seed.

A **Appeal Phase.** Now seek to persuade the person to make a decision of faith in Christ alone for salvation. The gospel has been clarified, but a mere intellectual understanding isn't enough. A decision of the will is called for, and love demands that we urge just such a step on their part. This is the **harvest** phase, persuading people to trust Him and be converted.

R **Relationship Phase.** Assimilating the new convert into Christian community for growth and reproduction is essential. This is the **gathering** phase, encouraging a public identification with God and His people. No farmer worth his salt would harvest a crop and leave it laying in the field. It must be gathered and stored or immediately put to use to fulfill its intended purpose. Likewise, communicating the Good News is not complete until those who respond positively have been assimilated into the family.

V. The "Facilitating Group Bible Study" Process.

This helps a small group of people discover God's word to them in the Scriptures. As you START people doing this, remember some key rules, following the acronym of PAIRS:

P **Process over product** (especially at first). If you hook them on a good PROCESS, a good PRODUCT will come in time.

A **Answers** that are true, if not complete. It's okay not to have complete answers for all of the questions. Keep the approach simple! Simple is transferable; complicated will collapse of its own weight.

I Issues that are theirs. Ferret out and explore questions that are relevant to them in their situations and culture, even though they may not be consciously aware of them.

R Role of the leader = facilitator, NOT expert! Experts impress and intimidate, but rarely facilitate imitation. Your role is to help them discover more of the Word and each other. Your task is to "salt the oats"—giving them a thirst to learn more—not to dazzle them with your fancy biblical footwork.

S Safe environment. Success in all of the above demands that you create for them a safe environment where they can explore God's Word. Remember, their feelings are more important than your truth.

VI. The "Training" Process.

This process equips people to know, do and be what you know, can do and are! Quality training is a key to a ministry movement. You START training when you....

S Show them how to do it. You can't pass on what you don't possess. Model it first!

T Tell them how to do it. Give enough explanation to help them understand the task/skill.

A Allow them to do it while you watch.

R Review the results in an encouraging yet instructive way. Repeat the A and R steps until they have the task/skill down.

T Turn them loose with mentoring. Release them to do the task with ongoing mentoring and periodic on-the-job assessment.

VII. The "Enabling" Process.

This process enables national leadership to lead and own the ministry. No true movement can be built that is dependent on expatriate or outside "experts" to sustain it. Indigenous leadership must be trained and enabled to take over the ministry. This can be very threatening, since it is difficult to pass on a ministry for which we have sacrificed much. But we must move beyond our own personal longing for significance and dare to do the New Testament thing of enabling others to succeed. In so doing, we will truly succeed in God's eyes. The VITALS of this process are:

V **Value** them, what you can learn from them and how God will use them to build the movement. Only with such core convictions going in will we dare to enable others.

I **Involve** them in the ministry with you from the very beginning. Your rule should be: don't do for them what they themselves can do. Find something for them to do.

T **Train** them how to do what you do and to be what you are (remember START). Be continually working yourself out of a job. With training, a national will be able to do the work of ministry in his own culture far better than you ever will.

A **Applaud** them. Be their biggest fan, their cheerleader. Make sure they get credit for success. Resist the urge to make yourself look good. Put them into the limelight instead.

L **Let go** and get out of the way. Practice "benign neglect" when appropriate. At first they may be unwilling to carry the ministry load, especially as long as you are around. Once you feel they are able to do so, engineer another "obligation" that takes you off the scene. With you gone they will flourish and see God use them. The bottom line in enabling: work toward the ultimate goal of transferring total ownership of the ministry to them.

S **Serve** them in the background. You must never abandon them. You will have, if you have enabled properly, ongoing spiritual and relational authority with them. But they must have the line authority. Your role is one of watch-care— like that of the first-century apostles—a role of being a trusted servant resource who prays for them, encourages them, mentors them and visits periodically, but is generally off the scene so they can run with the ministry that is now theirs.

EXPLANATION: FOUNDATIONS
Our "Direction Finder" that Guides Us to Where and How We Should Fish

I. **Goal:** The ministry goal of each CoMission team was to develop Neighborhood Christian Education Classes (NCECs) that are multiplying and under indigenous national leadership.

- *In these Neighborhood Christian Education Classes,* small groups of people meet together to study the Bible and grow in their commitments to and walks with Christ.

- *How many?* To saturate an area, 100 NCECs (on average) needed to be started by the end of the three years that CoMission teams were in that area. Key to achieving this goal: the multiplication of new NCECs by existing ones.

- *National leaders.* Essential to such multiplication was the development and enabling of indigenous leadership. These leaders must own the vision for multiplication.

II. **Strategy with Developmental Stages:** Every goal must have a strategy for attaining it. The CoMission strategy provided a framework for accomplishing the CoMission goal and gave a template for developmental stages along the way. These three stages (see the Rocket Diagram) were guidelines, not rigid steps which must be followed.

III. **Attitudes and Perspectives:** A person's attitude toward ministry and the nationals was extremely important. One could master the processes and tools, but if attitudes or perspectives were wrong, the ministry and team would be hindered.

IV. **Values and Philosophy of Ministry:** Behind every ministry were certain values which drove it and a philosophy which guided it. What God hopefully imparted during the training were the unique CoMission ministry values and philosophy that drove us.

EXPLANATION: TOOLS
Knowing How to Use the Five Types of Tools in Your "Tackle Box"

I. **Bible Only:** the Scriptures themselves and tools that enable contextual Bible study

- *New Testament*

- *Bible*, both Old and New Testaments

- *Children's Bible*—a pictorial Bible for children

- *Bible Reading Club*—a pamphlet to help people start reading their Bibles

- *Genesis Course*—designed to help people study the book of Genesis

- *Romans Course*—designed to help people study the book of Romans

II. **Bible-based Printed Materials:** biblical topic study materials

- *Foundations for Christian Ethics*—course materials for use in both primary and secondary school classrooms

- *Parenting course*—biblical perspectives and practices of parenting children

- *Investigative Bible Studies*—topical Bible studies that investigate the claims of Christ

- *CrossWalk*—Follow-up materials that ground people in the relational aspects of the Christian life

III. Video Only: videos that were self-contained ministry tools

- *The JESUS film*—a dramatized film based on the Gospel of Luke that communicates the person and work of Jesus Christ

- *International Video Bible Curriculum*—various video messages from Walk Thru the Bible on practical topics relevant to living the Christian life

- *James Dobson films* on marriage and family

IV. Video-based Materials: video courses with accompanying printed helps

- *7 Laws of the Learner.* A Walk Thru the Bible course on teaching more effectively. A good tool for developing school teachers professionally as well as spiritually.

- *Teaching with Style.* A Walk Thru the Bible course on improving communication and teaching style.

V. Audio and Other: cassette tapes and miscellaneous tools

- *Praise music tapes* for use in teaching worship through music

- *ESL Materials* for teaching English as a second language. May be helpful in making contacts and building bridges.

The Training Cycles

Cycle 1 – October 1992

Cycle 2 – January 1993

Cycle 3 – July 1993

Cycle 4 – January 1994

Cycle 5 – July 1994

Cycle 6 – January 1995

Cycle 7 – July 1995

Cycle 8 – January 1996

Cycle 9 – July 1996

Cycle 10 – January 1997

Cycle 11 – July 1997